FORSTER VS. PICO

The Struggle for the
Rancho Santa Margarita

Pío Pico in his old age,
much as he was seen by the
jurors in his trial against
John Forster.
*Courtesy, California Historical
Society, Ticor Collection, University
of Southern California Libraries.*

John Forster about 1876.
Beyond the passage of time,
his struggle with the Picos,
financial worries, and the
deaths of his closest friends
had taken a heavy toll.
*Courtesy, Thomas Anthony "Tony"
Forster Private Collection,
San Juan Capistrano*

FORSTER VS. PICO

The Struggle for the
Rancho Santa Margarita

by
Paul Bryan Gray

UNIVERSITY OF OKLAHOMA PRESS

NORMAN

LIBRARY OF CONGRESS CATALOG CARD NUMBER 97-39049

Gray, Paul Bryan.
    Forster vs. Pico: the struggle for Rancho Santa Margarita/
by Paul Bryan Gray.
    p. 256 cm.
    Includes bibliographical references and index.

    ISBN 978-0-8061-9097-6 (paper)
    1. Rancho Santa Margarita (Calif.)—History. 2. Land titles—History—19th century. 3. Pico, Pio, 1801-1894—Trials, litigation, etc. 4. Forster, John, 1814-1882—Trials, litigations, etc. 5. Mexicans—Land tenure—California, Southern—History—19th century. 6. California—History—1850-1950. 7. California—Ethnic relations.
    I. Title.

    F868.S34G73   1998

    978.4'78—dc21

To my mother, my wife Feli,
Chris, Mark, Elsa, Robert, and now, little Erik

Contents

Illustrations

Preface

The late Terry E. Stephenson was one of the first to appreciate the incredibly rich source of historic material contained in the 1873 lawsuit between John Forster and Pío Pico. Over sixty years ago, he published an article entitled "Forster v. Pico, A Forgotten California Cause Celebre," in the *Historical Society of Southern California Quarterly* (June 1936). Stephenson, described by the great Robert Glass Cleland as a "lover and student of California History," was chiefly a newspaper editor. He alternated his professional duties on the *Santa Ana Register* with a passion for historical writing. I have attempted to explore the case of *Forster v. Pico* more deeply than was done in Stephenson's article but in the same spirit and in tribute to him.

This book would never have been published without the advice and assistance of Dr. Doyce B. Nunis Jr. He read the first draft of the manuscript and made corrections of obvious errors without the least motive for such kindness. As a long-time university professor, editor of the prestigious *Southern California Quarterly* since 1962, and author and editor of innumerable works on California history, Dr. Nunis is regarded by many as the greatest living authority in the field. He has my gratitude and respect.

I have also been fortunate to have criticism and advice from the noted legal historian Dr. Gordon Morris Bakken. As an author, lawyer, and history professor, his support has been invaluable.

Other persons who read the manuscript and made signifi-
cant contributions include John Robinson, Charles A.
Goldsmid, Michael Nunn, Lyn Sherwood, Mel Gilman,
Kathy Saylor, Evelyn DeRousse, Mark Gilman, Midge
Sherwood, Monte Mansir, Dr. Gary Hopper, Judge Richard
Van Dusen, Dr. Robert Herman, and my brothers, Stephen
H. Gray and Dr. Thomas C. Gray.

Several people at institutions where I did research proved
to be exceptionally helpful. At the Huntington Library,
William Frank made important criticisms of the manuscript.
Sally West of the San Diego Historical Society Archives was
an excellent resource. Bonnie Clemens of the Honnold
Library at the Claremont Colleges and Suzanne Dewberry
of the Federal Records Center at Laguna Niguel have facili-
tated my studies.

No one has more of my esteem than Tom Owen of the Los
Angeles Public Library. He is a treasury of historic information who often sent me items that he knew would be useful
and which were invariably cited in the manuscript. I will
always have the greatest appreciation for his interest and
expertise.

Bill Johnson, chief of the Los Angeles Superior Court
Archives, has been unfailingly patient in locating ancient
lawsuits from the old "round files" under his care. It has been
a privilege to know him.

I am indebted to Bradley Williams, director of the Ninth
Judicial Circuit Historical Society who confirmed my belief
that legal cases are a valuable source of historical research
material. He was indirectly responsible for my undertaking
this book in the first place.

Robert A. Clark of The Arthur H. Clark Company has
always been accessible by telephone. He has gone out of his
way to assist me in preparing for the publication of this book.

I would like to thank Thomas Anthony "Tony" Forster of San Juan Capistrano for unselfishly donating his family's records to the Huntington Library and for his constant encouragement in writing this book. Tony is a wonderful friend and a boon companion.

Albert Pico invited me to his home and graciously allowed me the use of several original letters of his great-uncle, Pío Pico. He also told me some of the stories that have circulated around his family for generations concerning the struggle with John Forster.

Finally, Patricia Kirkpatrick has been the person responsible for preparation of the typewritten draft of the manuscript. She has assisted me from the beginning. Without countless hours of effort on her part, this project would never have been completed.

.

Introduction

The American conquest of California and the subjugation of its Hispanic peoples were not complete until land ownership was transferred to the conquerors. This took place fairly rapidly, but it was not achieved by confiscation at the point of a bayonet. To the contrary, the Americans guaranteed Mexican landowners the continuance of their rights and the protection of the laws. However, not long after the Americans were established in California, it became clear that the new order would inevitably destroy Mexican patterns of land tenure.

The Americans had a fundamentally different view of land ownership than the Mexicans. To those from the United States, land was a capital asset that should produce income. A reflection of this attitude was the imposition of a general property tax on land shortly after the Americans took over.[1] It was assumed that farms and ranches would be worked, made productive, and their commodities shipped to market to profit the owner. Since land brought wealth, the Americans felt it was fair to impose the tax. Such land taxes were universal throughout the United States.

The Mexican view of land ownership did not necessarily involve its use as a means to project saleable commodities to an outside market. Instead, land was used for self-sufficient estates, much like medieval manors. Those fortunate enough to obtain land grants from Mexican authorities by virtue of political or social connections set themselves up as masters

---

[1]Robert Glass Cleland, *Cattle On a Thousand Hills*, 117.

over their Indian laborers and lived without regard for any larger forces at work in their lives such as a market economy. Except for occasionally bartering hides for manufactured goods and luxury items from Boston trading ships, the Mexican ranchers of California lived in an almost entirely closed world.[2] There was little need for money. Mexican ranchers were not entrepreneurs. They were members of an aristocratic elite whose land ownership in a distant province of Mexico gave them great independence and the highest possible status in a pastoral society.

There was no charge on land ownership in California before the American conquest. The previous Mexican provincial government sustained itself by port charges and import duties.[3] The direct taxation of land imposed by the Americans was a novel and distressing concept to Mexican *rancheros*. The state tax rate in 1853 was 60¢ on each $100.[4] County tax rates were another $1.00 to $1.25 per $100 beyond that, for a total of roughly $1.60 to $1.85 in taxes imposed on each $100 of assessed land value.[5] It cost rancheros, depending on their holdings, a few dollars to several hundred dollars each year for the privilege of holding land. Although taxes were not great enough to bankrupt them immediately, they relentlessly increased until a lien for back taxes could result in a sheriff's sale and the loss of one's property.

Although taxes were a nuisance — even a potentially dangerous one — the greatest threat came from an act of the U.S. government. Congress passed the Land Act of 1851 which required landowners in California to prove that titles originating with the Mexican regime had been validly issued

---

[2]Ibid., 30.
[3]Ibid., 117.
[4]Hubert Howe Bancroft, *History of California*, 6: 613.
[5]Cleland, *Cattle On a Thousand Hills*, 118.

under Mexican law. To confirm the authenticity of their Mexican claims, California landowners had to go to San Francisco to appear before a three-man commission.[6]

The process was expensive because unreasonably long appeals could be taken by either the owner or the government through the federal court system. American lawyers made a great deal of money confirming land titles, sometimes fraudulently.[7] Most titles were confirmed as valid under Mexican law, but the cost of doing so was catastrophic.[8] The effect of American taxes and legal threats was to force the *Californios* to use their land in ways to generate income. For the first time, they began to have a great need for money.

During the first decade of American rule, it became increasingly difficult for native Californians to change from subsistence ranching to profit-making enterprises. The accrual of taxes and demands for legal costs were relentless. Worse, the Californios had a tendency toward self-destructive spending. Whatever money came into their hands was soon wasted or gambled away. This prompted many Americans to offer them loans at fantastic interest rates, which were invariably secured by a mortgage on the land they owned.

Predictably, loans were made which were impossible to repay. Most Mexican ranches throughout California were lost to foreclosure because of excessive borrowing at outrageous rates of interest. One of many examples which illustrates the phenomenon is the case of Rancho San Rafael. On January 2, 1861, its owner, Julio Verdugo, borrowed $3,445.37 for numerous expenses, including the payment of taxes. Typically, although incredibly by modern standards, the loan's interest rate was 3 percent per month, payable quarterly. The result was inevitable:

---

[6]Ibid.
[7]Leonard Pitt, *Decline of the Californios*, 91.
[8]W. W. Robinson, *Land in California*, 106.

At ten o'clock on March 8th of 1869, Sheriff Burns offered at public auction the property that had been mortgaged to Jacob Elias. Eight years of mounting debt, built up by interest rates that were customary but ruinous, had brought the $3,445.37 up to $58,750 and with it foreclosure and ruin to the son of the retired corporal of the Royal Presidio of San Diego.[9]

Rancho San Rafael encompassed 36,403 acres, about fifty-seven square miles. It was soon subdivided and sold by American developers. The city of Glendale occupies the center site today.

Such unhappy stories gave rise to modern Southern California. By 1870 only a few Californios were still in possession of their ranches. An analysis of the U.S. censuses of 1850, 1860, and 1870 confirms a sweeping change of ownership from Mexican to American hands.[10] Only a tiny number of Californio ranches had owners who successfully resisted American foreclosure. One of the most notable was Rancho Camulos in Ventura County, precariously held by Ignacio del Valle until his death in 1892. Luckily, his son Reginaldo was able to sell the ranch to a Swiss oilman in 1924 for the spectacular sum of three million.[11] Nevertheless, history was against the Mexican ranchers of California. An aggressive American culture, taxes, the Land Act of 1851, and the propensity of improvident Californios to borrow money from Americans at unconscionable interest rates all helped to insure the destruction of their holdings.

Some historians have taken a sympathetic view of the plight of the Mexican ranchers in the loss of their land. They attribute the fall of the Californio ranchers more to racism, fraud, violence, and unjust treatment than a lack of personal financial prudence. One example is Leonard Pitt, who wrote:

---

[9]W. W. Robinson, *Ranchos Become Cities*, 42.

[10]Walter C. McKain Jr. and Sara Miles, "Santa Barbara County Between Two Social Orders," 316.

[11]Richard Griswold del Castillo, "The del Valle Family and the Fantasy Heritage," 10.

The gringo behaved more violently, maliciously, and immorally than he thought: it was he who first guaranteed the Californians full citizenship, he who agreed to treat them as equals and not as a conquered people; he who broke his word by declaring open season on the rancheros.[12]

Other historians assign no guilt to the Americans for the dispossession of the native rancheros from their soil. They blame the Californios themselves for their losses by gambling and generally living beyond their means.

Without consideration for the Californios' own ancient Hispanic civilization, some writers have criticized them for not immediately conforming to the newly imposed, alien American culture. The traditional easygoing, pastoral lifestyle of the Mexicans was hard to change. Thrift and industry did not figure prominently in their values. Paul W. Gates, a harsh critic of the Mexican failure to adapt to American thinking, expresses an ethnocentric view in his treatment of the reasons for the loss of Mexican land ownership in California. He defends the arbitrary Land Act of 1851 by which the rancheros were forced to prove the validity of their land titles at a ruinous cost by claiming that they could have done so but for their extravagance and lack of foresight:

It should be remembered that California was not the first state in which private land claims dating from earlier foreign governments had to be tested. In the testing process the United States had developed a procedure that was fair, and its courts leaned over backwards to confirm claims where equity was on the side of the claimant. Also, it should be said that it was no more the cost of litigation than the extravagance of the old families, their neglect to pay taxes, their dependence on loans carrying high interest rates, their failure to realize that the day of the sparsely grazed ranchos had gone and that their lands called for a heavy investment of capital to make them productive and able to bear taxation, that broke up the large estates.[13]

[12]Pitt, *Decline of the Californios*, 283-84.
[13]Paul W. Gates, *California Ranchos and Farms*, 10

A stridently individualistic and expansionist American people cared little about the welfare of a relative handful of Californios whose roots were in Mexico. Coupled with a basic incompatibility of the two cultures, one increasingly industrial and the other traditional and pastoral, was a profound sense of the Anglo-Saxons that all other people were inferior. The Mexicans in California suffered both subtle and blatant manifestations of American racism. They were, in fact, frequently the victims of American violence, fraud, and injustice.

It is also true, however, that most Californios did not protect themselves from the American threat. They must bear some responsibility for the loss of their land. Instead of being cautious about the demonic qualities of compound interest, even after bitter experience, many continued to borrow money recklessly and spent it on gambling and other pleasures with abandon. Those writers who blame the Americans for the downfall of the Californios and those who blame the Mexicans themselves are both partly right.

To the themes of American greed and Mexican improvidence must be added natural disasters such as the drought which occurred from 1861 to 1864. Mexican ranchers lost huge parts of their herds during the devastating drought which was an economic *coup de grace* to the already suffering Californios. Burdened by staggering debts from the loans of prior years, their mortgage foreclosures soared since they had no cattle to sell to raise money. J. M. Guinn, a contemporary observer, wrote of the impact the drought had on the Californio ranch owners:

> Their doom came quickly, nearly all the great ranchos were mortgaged. With no means to restock them, without income to pay interest or principal, the [mortgagees] foreclosed and took possession of the desolated cattle ranches. Within five years after the famine nearly all the great ranchos had changed owners.[14]

---

[14]J. M. Guinn, "The Passing of the Cattle Barons of California," 59.

The transition from a Mexican province to an American state is one of the most crucial periods in California's history. The loss of land by Mexicans to American newcomers was a process that involved many complex factors, all of which are clearly evident in the lawsuit between John Forster and Pío Pico. Although the contestants for the Rancho Santa Margarita were a Mexicanized English pioneer and a Californio, their struggle involved the major historic patterns of the era and eventually resulted in a large portion of Southern California falling into American hands.

Unlike the vast majority of Mexican land in California, title to the Rancho Santa Margarita was not changed to American ownership by virtue of a foreclosure. Instead, there were the intervening features of a contract between Pío Pico and John Forster to avoid creditors and a bitterly contested allegation of fraud. Nevertheless, the basic causes of Mexican land loss are interwoven in their story. A new culture imposed by military conquest, taxation, outrageous interest on loans, proceedings before the Land Commission, Mexican improvidence, and a devastating drought all prominently figure in their struggle and the ultimate fate of the Rancho Santa Margarita. Consequently, the case of *Forster v. Pico* deserves attention for reasons beyond the fascinating characters and events that gave rise to a famous jury trial.

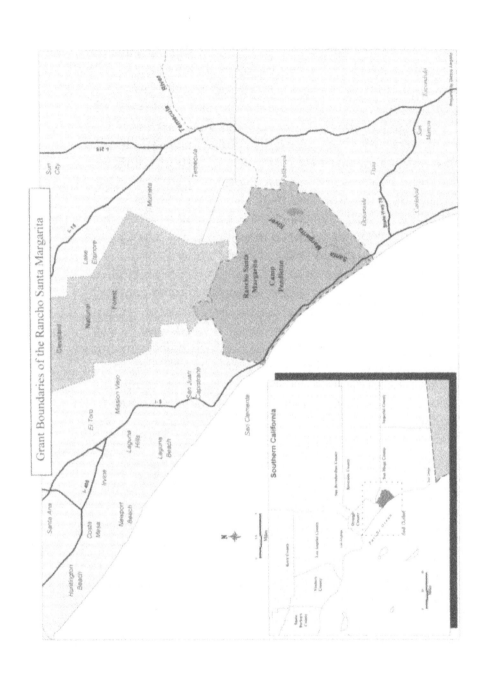

Grant Boundaries of the Rancho Santa Margarita

CHAPTER ONE

The Men and The Land

During 1873 a jury trial took place in San Diego to decide whether Pío Pico, the last Mexican governor of California, had been the victim of a fraud by his brother-in-law, John Forster. The voluminous records of the case now lie in the Archives of the San Diego Historical Society, entirely extant, a rare example of a complete nineteenth-century jury trial.[1]

The allegations of fraud were simple. In 1864 Pico was the owner of the Rancho Santa Margarita y Las Flores in San Diego County. At that time, he owed a large debt to a firm of money lenders in San Francisco, Pioche and Bayerque, which was secured by a mortgage on the ranch. Because he could not pay off the debt and was threatened with foreclosure, Pico offered title to one half of the ranch to Forster if he would assume what was owed on the outstanding mortgage.

Forster accepted Pico's offer and brought him a deed in English, which Pico thought conveyed only one-half of the ranch. Since he had known and trusted Forster for decades, Pico blindly signed the deed at once. Pico could not have read it anyway; he was totally ignorant of English, a fact well known to Forster. Four years later, in 1868, Pico accidentally discovered that Forster had given him a deed to sign which transferred the entire ranch. Pico charged that Forster had

---

[1]Forster v. Pico, Case No. 898A, in Collection No. R3.38, Box No. 53, in the Archives of the San Diego Historical Society.

purposely tricked him. According to Pico, he unwittingly divested himself of half the property by Forster's deceit.

It is reasonable to assume that each man could have clearly presented his version of the transaction in open court. As it turned out, however, several weeks of trial only resulted in a pitiful, fumbling attempt by Pico's lawyers to state their case and a series of blustering denials and evasions by Forster. The truth of what happened between Pío Pico and John Forster has long remained uncertain.

The prize they sought in court was the ownership, in full or part, of the Rancho Santa Margarita. The enormity of the ranch can still be appreciated, because in 1942 the federal government purchased the property and converted it into the Camp Pendleton United States Marine Corps Base.[2] At that time it was still being used for raising cattle under the Santa Margarita brand. But for this fortuitous action by the federal government, no doubt the ranch would long ago have been destroyed by residential and commercial development. As it is, Camp Pendleton conforms to the original lines of the Rancho Santa Margarita, encompassing the same open land. It is a roughly rectangular area of approximately 208 square miles, about 5 percent of San Diego County. For decades it was the largest military installation owned by the U.S. government.

Camp Pendleton is confined on the north by Orange and Riverside counties. The western boundary is the ocean, as the coastline extends southward for a distance of seventeen miles from San Clemente to the city limits of Oceanside. A coastal freeway runs the entire length of Camp Pendleton between these cities. By federal mandate, this highway has no business development, not even roadside services. The coast is a marine terrace, a series of cliffs fifty to seventy feet above pristine beaches unspoiled by urbanization.

---

[2]Jeanne Skinner Van Nostrand, "The American Occupations of Rancho Santa Margarita y Las Flores," 176.

A range of hills runs south of the Orange County line parallel to the sea at a distance of only a few hundred yards from the water's edge. The highest of them is Mount San Onofre, rising to 1,725 feet. Further along the hills veer east and diminish until they flatten into lowlands that occupy the southern section of Camp Pendleton. Near Oceanside the bluffs of the coastal terrace begin to decline, making the start of a system of wetlands.

From the ocean, Camp Pendleton spreads in a general northeasterly direction, forming a series of valleys and hills that gradually increase in height. Approximately twelve miles inland, it terminates in a mountainous area, part of the California coastal range. The highest point of this region is Mount Santa Margarita, attaining 3,189 feet.

Several water courses descend from the mountains in a southwesterly direction toward the sea through canyons deepened by eons of run-off. Some notable examples are San Mateo, San Onofre, and Las Flores creeks. The largest source of water coming from the mountains is the Santa Margarita River, regarded as the last unobstructed natural river in Southern California and a haven for many endangered animal species. The river's flow is seasonal and irregular, sometimes ceasing entirely.

Although the Santa Margarita River supports a tenacious riparian plant and wildlife community, most of Camp Pendleton is arid. From the ocean to the one-thousand foot elevation level, the land is in the coastal sage scrub zone, characterized by sagebrush and laurel sumac. Above it is the chaparral zone, preferred by the ubiquitous plant family that can withstand long periods without water. During much of the year coastal scrub and chaparral appear dead as they await the uncertain rainy season. Their rugged, unyielding appearance results from the dry environment to which they have superbly adapted.

Endless rolling hills dominate the country. Most present a starkly barren aspect, covered by short brown grass occasionally mingled with inhospitable sagebrush. Except for sycamore trees that trace the course of bottom land creeks, only a few isolated oaks soften the harsh landscape. It appears much the same as it was when John Forster and Pío Pico knew it. Even the original adobe ranch house built by the Pico family and improved by Forster is used as quarters for the commanding general at the Marine base.

Today, the great Rancho Santa Margarita, now in the guise of Camp Pendleton, can still be seen. As a federally protected area, it prevents much of Orange and San Diego counties from being linked by a solid mass of coastal development. With the end of the Cold War and reduction of military bases, it is impossible to say how long it will remain a buffer between urbanization from north and south. At least for now it remains a living tableau of how old Southern California once was. This nearly empty area still offers beautiful vistas and the pungent scent of mesquite and chaparral borne by ocean winds.

What follows is an account of how the magnificent Rancho Santa Margarita was lost by Pío Pico and fell into the sole dominion of John Forster. Since the contestants were wealthy and famous men who met in a court of law, their struggle is preserved in great detail within several massive court files containing hundreds of pages of testimony and a formidable collection of supporting documents. To a large extent, we can know more than the details of how an important part of Southern California slipped away from Mexican ownership. The court files also reveal much about the world in which they lived.

The Pico family was eventually crushed by the economic forces of the last century. However, Pío Pico resisted financial collapse for an astonishingly long time. He was finally made bankrupt when he was in his late eighties, but only by the acknowledged perjury of a bribed witness in another lawsuit concerning his land holdings. For all the irregularity in his life and business affairs, he was a cunning, even astute survivor.

In comparison to Pico, many Anglo-Saxon ranchers in Los Angeles County fared no better or even worse. In 1859 the rancher Lemuel Carpenter committed suicide because of the loss of his property through foreclosure.[3] Pico was a guarantor of the loan and the courts forced him to pay it.[4] Nevertheless, he survived the loss with aplomb.

Abel Stearns was once the richest man in Los Angeles and its greatest landowner. During the 1860s he became insolvent and was rescued only through the sale of his land by a trust which was created and controlled by other people.[5] In contrast, Pico endured the same depression era and continued relatively unaffected and independent for another twenty years. The Englishman Henry Dalton, owner of the Rancho Azusa, was seasoned in the commercial practices of both Mexico and the United States, but he too fell into bankruptcy by 1881.[6] Pico at that time was struggling, but still hanging on.

For most of his life, Pío Pico enjoyed the company and support of his brother Andrés. During the Mexican regime, Pío was more famous and powerful than his younger brother. After the American conquest, Andrés became a public figure whose celebrity eclipsed that of Pío. Despite moments of discord, they usually remained closely united, presenting a common front against their enemies and creditors. Many find the political attainments of Andrés Pico under the American regime surprising. During the 1850s and 1860s he held vari-

---

[3]Cleland, *Cattle On a Thousand Hills*, 113.
[4]*McFarland v. Pico*, 8 California Reports 626 (Oct. 1857).
[5]Cleland, *Cattle On a Thousand Hills*, 203-6.
[6]Sheldon G. Jackson, *A British Ranchero in Old California*, 232.

ous positions of authority and power: assemblyman, presidential elector, receiver of public money, state senator, and brigadier general in the California State Militia. Sometimes his politics were wrong-headed and unprincipled, but he was an influential and esteemed figure most of his life among both Americans and Californios.

There is a tendency for historians to ignore the lives of the Picos after the American conquest except to mention that they were among those who lost their wealth in the new order. In reality, the brothers remained financially afloat and extremely active for decades after the American takeover. Both left an abundant and fascinating record of their lives.

John Forster formed close bonds with the Pico brothers during his early sojourn in California, but the dispute over the Rancho Santa Margarita separated them forever. Apart from his conflict with the Pico family, Forster had few unpleasant encounters of a legal or personal nature. Despite a lack of formal education, his correspondence shows that he was surprisingly literate, a shrewd man of great intelligence. Today, numerous descendants of Forster live in Southern California. Some are the direct beneficiaries of wealth he accumulated in his lifetime.

When the Pico brothers and Forster entered the courtroom at San Diego in 1873, they came to present a lawsuit based on a transaction that arose out of a long series of events extending over many years. To understand the case, it is necessary to know something about their background. The story of the Picos and Forster in old California is worth telling. It will help us to appreciate the historical richness of the trial and the profoundly interesting nature of the famous characters who sat at the counsel table and in the witness box. Although a full treatment of the colorful lives of these men is not possible, enough can be told to give a sense of the time and place in which they lived and the forces that acted upon them. In this way, we will see the roots of a bitter struggle between them that culminated in the best-preserved court-room drama of old Southern California.

CHAPTER TWO

The Background: Early California

The Pico family arrived in California from Mexico with the overland expedition of Lieutenant Colonel Juan Bautista de la Anza during 1775–1776. He was charged by the Spanish viceroy, Antonio María Bucareli, to escort some two-hundred immigrants to California as part of an attempt to populate the barren, remote province of Alta California.[1] Anza recruited the immigrants from the northwest provinces of Sonora and Sinaloa who, he reported to Bucareli, had been found "submerged in the direst poverty and misery . . ."[2] The adult males were enlisted in the Spanish army. The families were fed and dressed from head to foot at the crown's expense, replacing the rags the wretched people were accustomed to wearing. Anza refused to include any cash among the inducements for immigration lest the recruits immediately gamble it away.[3] They were the dregs of Spanish colonial society. From the point of view of these people the strongest argument for going to California was the army cook pot.

Among the immigrants was Santiago de la Cruz Pico, about forty-four years old, born in 1732 at San Javier de Cabazan, Sinaloa.[4] He was accompanied by his wife, María

---

[1]Zoeth Skinner Eldredge, *The Beginnings of San Francisco*, 1: 301-2; Helen Tyler, "The Family of Pico," 221-27.

[2]Herbert Eugene Bolton, *Anza's California Expeditions*, 1: 206.

[3]Ibid., 207.

[4]Marie E. Northrop, *Spanish-Mexican Families of Early California: 1769-1850*, 2: 205; Eldredge, *Beginnings of San Francisco*, 1: 301, states that he was born at San Miguel de Horcasitas, Sonora, in 1733.

Jacinta Bastida, and their five children. Like many of the immigrants, Santiago de la Cruz Pico was a mixture of races, This was a severe disadvantage in Spanish colonial society, which had a caste system that officially classified everyone by race and discriminated against all people other than white Europeans.[5] His wife displayed marked African characteristics which resulted in her being listed as a *mulata*—a one-half black woman—in the Spanish census of 1790 in California.[6] In colonial Mexico, Santiago was probably employed as a menial laborer.

Once in California, the recruits from the Anza expedition were assigned to duty in presidios where they resided with their families. For many years food rations were forwarded from Mexico together with other necessities. The military colonists supplemented their rations with gardening and hunting.[7] Over the years, male children were incorporated into the army, becoming soldiers in the absence of any other opportunity. José María Pico, one of the sons of Santiago de la Cruz Pico, had been about eleven years old during the Anza expedition. He also became a soldier and served at various posts including guard duty at the missions of San Luis

---

[5]A description of the Spanish caste system in California is found in Gloria Miranda, "Racial and Cultural Dimensions of *Gente de Razon* Status in Spanish and Mexican California," 265-78.

[6]William M. Mason, "The Garrisons of San Diego Presidio: 1770-1794," 419. This article contains a description of the Pico family in the census of 1790. The entire article is an excellent treatment of the racial origins of the first California settlers. Contrary to a persistent myth, few of California's Hispanic pioneers were Spanish. Instead, they were largely an admixture of Indian and African elements with only a small minority having any significant Spanish ancestry. See Jack D. Forbes, "Hispano-Mexican Pioneers of the San Francisco Bay Region: An Analysis of Racial Origins," 175-89. The important contribution of blacks and those of part-African ancestry in the Hispanic settlement of California was an outgrowth of a substantial black presence in northwest Mexico during the colonial period. See Jack D. Forbes, "Black Pioneers: The Spanish-Speaking Afroamericans of the Southwest," 233-46. The large numbers of African slaves brought to Mexico were gradually absorbed into the general population. They left a deep imprint on the Mexican gene pool. See Gonzalo Aguirre Beltran, *La Poblacion Negra de Mexico*.

[7]Mason, "Garrisons of San Diego Presidio," 408 .

Rey and San Gabriel. Curiously, the census of 1790 cited José María Pico's race as Spanish, but his brothers at Santa Barbara and Los Angeles were put down by the census taker as *mulatos*.[8] In 1789 he married María Eustaquia Gutierrez, who, like her husband had arrived with the Anza expedition. They had twelve children during their life in California, among them Pío and Andrés Pico.[9]

Pío was born at the Mission San Gabriel in 1801 while his father was a corporal of the guard. His brother Andrés was born about ten years later in 1810 at the Presidio of San Diego. José María Pico died at the Mission San Gabriel in 1819, at about the age of fifty-four, leaving his widow and children with little except a few entitlements from his lifetime of military service.

Pío and Andrés lived in San Diego after their father's death, drawing on the presidio for rations and supporting their mother and family however they could. Both young men were remarkably energetic and intelligent. Pío set up a little shop where he bilked customers by selling liquor out of a container made of horn with a false bottom. He also made profit as a *falluquero*—an itinerant peddler—carrying goods by mule back on a series of picaresque adventures which he enjoyed recounting in his old age.[10] In 1824 the Pico brothers built their mother a house at the foot of Presidio Hill, joining a few other families in abandoning communal life within the walls of the presidio.[11] Laid out around a central plaza, these adobes became the nucleus of the pueblo of San Diego, now known as Old Town.

The soldiers who guarded the missions, including members of the Pico family, eventually began to retire from the

---

[8]Ibid.; 419.

[9]Northrup, *Spanish-Mexican Families of Early California*, 2: 214.

[10]Pío Pico, *Historical Narrative*, 25-30.

[11]William E. Smythe, *History of San Diego*, 1: 132-33.

military, and in line with ancient Spanish tradition requested
land grants as a reward for their long service. The first grant
to a retired soldier was as early as 1784.[12] In 1802 even the
aged Santiago de la Cruz Pico was given a portion of the Rancho Simi in the jurisdiction of Los Angeles. These grants
were used as cattle ranches, a natural thing to do for immigrants from northern Mexico where ranching had been one of
the chief occupations since the Spanish conquest.[13] The first
ranches provided sustenance to the owners and even a crudely
pleasant lifestyle. The number of grants made to retired soldiers were quite limited. Care was taken to insure that no land
was awarded that impinged on the missions.

In 1822 William Gale, representing Bryant and Sturgis of
Boston, arrived on the coast of California in a ship laden with
merchandise to trade for cattle hides, tallow, and other ranch
products. Gale was the first person to attempt to establish
direct trade between Boston and California.[14] At about the
same time, William Hartnell and Hugh McCulloch, representing the English firm of John Begg and Company at
Lima, Peru, met with various missionary fathers and made
contracts for the purchase of mission hides and tallow, payment to be in money or goods, whichever was desired.[15] They
inaugurated a famous and profitable commerce between
Mexican California and the east coast of the United States.

The missions controlled gargantuan areas of land on
which they ran hundreds of thousands of cattle. They were
the main source of ranch products that maritime trading
companies such as Bryant and Sturgis wanted. Of necessity,

---

[12]Cleland, *Cattle On a Thousand Hills*, 7-18.

[13]Richard J. Morrisey, "The Northward Expansion of Cattle Ranching In New Spain,
1550–1600," 115-21; Donald D. Brand, "The Early History of the Range Cattle Industry
in Northern Mexico," 132-39; Charles Julian Bishko, "The Peninsular Background of
Latin American Cattle Ranching," 491-515.

[14]Bancroft, *History of California*, 2: 475.

[15]Ibid.; see Susanna Bryant Dakin, *The Lives of William Hartnell*, chapt. 2.

commerce with the Boston ships in California was first carried out by Spanish missionaries. The scope of the trade is shown by the fact that Alfred Robinson, an agent for Bryant and Sturgis, allowed between $200,000 to $300,000 in goods to be taken on credit by the padres during 1831 in exchange for their promise to provide hides in payment.[16] The missions honored their debts faithfully, becoming administered almost like businesses. The impact of this trade on the missions has been well summed up:

> Some of the produce of the lands held in trust for the Indians was now transformed into commodities. Whereas initially production was only for subsistence, now some was for gain. California previously had a barter economy, but because of the increasing volume of trade with foreigners, money was now becoming the medium of exchange. The missions were clearly the economic mainstay of Alta California. They supported the military and the townspeople, the trade of their surpluses brought in manufactured goods, and it was they who were the earnest and vital producers.[17]

This situation was intolerable for those men like Pío Pico who desired to enrich themselves. They were the sons of presidial soldiers who realized that the source of social status and economic power was in land ownership. Their ardent desire was to strip the mission system of the wealth it controlled and place themselves on its lands. Theoretically, the government supported their position. The missions were always intended to be temporary. It was thought that perhaps only ten years would be required for them to convert the Indians to good Christian subjects of Spain. As early as 1813, the Spanish Cortés passed a law secularizing the missions so that their lands would return to the public domain, but it was never enforced.[18] The California missionaries successfully

---

[16]Adele Ogden, "Boston Hide Droghers Along California Shores," 362.
[17]Douglas Monroy, *Thrown Among Strangers*, 74-75.
[18]C. Alan Hutchinson, *Frontier Settlement in Mexican California*, 85.

argued that they needed more time to work with the Indians since they had not adapted to "civilized" norms as soon as anticipated.

After the independence of Mexico from Spain in 1821, a recurrent theme in its policy toward California was secularization of the missions to make their enormous lands available for public distribution and development. A noted historian described the conflict between the missions and the presidial class to which the Pico brothers belonged:

> Obviously California Indians were not ready for secularization and the management of their own affairs. The increasing white population, however, hungry for land and jealous of the organization that held the most and the best land, made secularization a hot and inevitable issue. Tremendous pressure was brought on the government.[19]

Finally, on August 17, 1833, the Mexican Congress passed a bill secularizing the missions. Vice President Gómez Farías signed it the next day.[20] This action was taken because of a longstanding belief by Mexican liberals that the missions prejudiced the welfare of the Indians and retarded further development of the underpopulated province.[21] Although passage of the Law of Secularization was not a direct response to agitation by Californians, it was what the presidial elite in the province fervently desired.[22]

After the decision to secularize the missions, tangible evidence of the great Spanish thrust to the northwest began to disappear. Their missions and presidios began to collapse during the 1830s. A melancholy abandonment of the great Franciscan establishments by the priests ensued. Govern-

---

[19]Robinson, *Land in California*, 29.

[20]Hutchinson, *Frontier Settlement in Mexican California*, 164.

[21]Ibid., 161-62.

[22]Charles E. Chapman, *A History of California: The Spanish Period*, 468; John Walton Caughey, *California*, 193; Manuel P. Servín, "The Secularization of the California Missions: A Reappraisal," 133-49.

ment appointed administrators remained at the missions who deliberately looted them.[23] Politics in Mexico City were so tumultuous and divisive that little attention was given to the distant province of California. The crumbling presidios were without funds for maintenance from the central government. Only a few tattered soldiers made a pretense of garrison duty. By 1835 the Presidio of San Diego, where Pío Pico's father and grandfather served as soldiers, was deserted, left to the work of the elements so that eventually there was no trace of its existence.[24]

The ranchos, however, were thriving. Following secularization in 1833, until the American invasion, California governors "issued fully seven hundred" land grants to private claimants.[25] Expropriated mission lands were prime subjects of division by the governors. These sites had been carefully selected by the early missionaries and their productivity was already proven. Excellent lands were made subject to grants based on friendship and political expediency. The large estates given in these grants were well worth having. One scholar observed:

> From an economic and social standpoint, the great ranches of the period had much in common with the medieval English manor. Except for a few luxuries obtained from trading vessels on the coast, each estate was virtually self-sustaining. In return for simple but abundant food, primitive shelter, and a scant supply of clothing, scores of Indians recruited chiefly from the fast-decaying mission communities served as vaqueros ...
> The deference shown to a California ranchero by members of his own family, as well as by his retainers, was like the homage rendered by his vassals to a feudal lord.[26]

[23]Andrew Rolle, *California, A History,* 121-22.
[24]Bancroft, *History of California,* 3: 610.
[25]Cleland, *Cattle On a Thousand Hills,* 23.
[26]Ibid., 30.

Severe class distinctions in the tradition of the Spanish nobility arose between the rancheros and their Indian servants and Mexican workers.[27] Since there was a tendency to grant land to those formerly connected with presidial service and their descendants, many grantees with aristocratic airs were not far removed from the Sonora and Sinaloa peasants that Anza had encountered "submerged in the direst poverty and misery." Included in this group, of course, were Pío and Andrés Pico.

In 1831 Pío led a successful rebellion against a governor sent from Mexico, Manuel Victoria, because he opposed secularizing the missions.[28] This was Pío's first major intervention in politics. For the next fourteen years, until he became governor himself, Pío had a hand in nearly every political intrigue in California. The basic motive for turmoil in the period was to insure that California had governors disposed to favor the growing ranchero elite.

Many governors sent from Mexico City to rule California were not to the rancheros' liking and were ejected from the province by force. These uprisings sometimes involved minor skirmishes and an occasional fatality. For the most part, however, there was a comic-opera quality about these affairs where gasconades and fiery *pronunciamientos* were more common than actual violence. When opposing sides squared off there were usually many attempts to parley before opening fire. After all, the belligerents came from a population so small that many were related or had known each other for most of their lives.[29]

During the decade prior to the American invasion, the rancheros promoted one of their own number, Juan Bautista Alvarado, as governor. Alvarado was a northerner from

---

[27]A good synopsis of this phenomenon is found in Miranda, "Racial and Cultural Dimensions."

[28]Bancroft, *History of California*, 3: 200-08.

[29]See introduction to Northrup, *Spanish-Mexican Families*, 1: xi, written by William M. Mason.

Monterey. After his assumption of office, a political rivalry intensified between the northern and southern sections of the province. During 1845 Pío was able to get himself recognized as governor and set up Los Angeles as his capital instead of Monterey.[30] By then he had severed his connections with San Diego and was to live in Los Angeles for nearly the next fifty years.

Pío was assisted in his political campaigns by his brother Andrés, who was recognized as a military man, having obtained the rank of captain in a special militia organized by Governor Manuel Micheltorena in 1844.[31] When the United States Navy initiated the American invasion of California by seizing Monterey on July 7, 1846, Pío had been in office about seventeen months. Although threatened by a northern rival, General José Castro of Monterey, Pío had mostly achieved his political goals. In the process, he received numerous land grants for property extending from Santa Barbara to Baja California. He held the greatest of them all, the Rancho Santa Margarita y Las Flores, with his brother Andrés.[32]

As governor, Pío Pico was generous to his friends and relatives who requested land grants from him. One of the natural objects of his bounty was his brother-in-law John Forster. This singularly intelligent and enterprising young Englishman arrived at Guaymas, Mexico, in 1831. His uncle, James Johnson, was a trader in that city at the time. Johnson had written to his sister in England asking her to send one her seven sons to assist him. John Forster was chosen to join his uncle in Mexico when he was only fifteen years old. He was born in Liverpool on September 16, 1814.[33] His parents were

---

[30]Bancroft, *History of California*, 4: 519.

[31]Ibid., 407.

[32]Ibid., 621, n.2.

[33]John D. Tanner and Gloria R. Lothrop, "Don Juan Forster, Southern California Ranchero," 195-201. This article is an annotated and revised version of a statement given by John Forster to Thomas Savage that Bancroft called "Pioneer Data From 1832."

probably members of the British lower class.[34] The Forster family must have been in desperate circumstances to permit a lad of such tender years to embark, at his uncle's expense, on a trip to a place so distant and alien at the time. After an emotionally wrenching farewell, Forster abandoned England permanently. He did not return for another forty-nine years.

After two years in Guaymas, Forster accompanied his uncle to California on the brig *Facio* with a cargo of Chinese goods that were sold in San Diego and Los Angeles. His uncle James, known as "Don Santiago," remained in Los Angeles until his death in 1847. Forster returned to Guaymas as soon as the cargo was sold to close up the business.[35] By the summer of 1833, Forster was back in Los Angeles after having made a return trip overland from Guaymas. In his old age, he claimed to be the second English-speaking person to make the journey across the great Sonora Desert to California.[36]

At age twenty, then, Forster was in Los Angeles perma-

---

[34]John Forster's sister Margaret corresponded with him over the years from England. In 1865 she wrote Forster a letter which illuminates their family background. Her position in the humbler classes is revealed by advising Forster that she intended to obtain an apprenticeship for her eleven-year-old son who she said was "tall for his age." She expressed the hope that her son would not be a sailor like Forster's brothers because they had gone through hardship during their careers at sea which she did not want her son to share. Forster's brothers seem to have been ordinary seamen, not officers. Seeking an apprenticeship and going to sea "before the mast" are signs that the family was well down in the British social order. She also mentioned her desperate financial straits, writing: "The money my Aunt Jane left me, 140 pounds, all went to pay debts off and I did not feel the benefit of it, although, of course, it saved us from bankruptcy. We are now in the same position as when we started, viz., struggling for the necessities of life." Margaret Cliveby(?) to John Forster, Feb. 10, 1865, Forster Collection.

During his stay in England in 1873, Forster visited three of his nieces, whose situation reflected a position in the lower classes. He wrote to his wife about them in Spanish saying: "Since the family is poor, their prospects in England are not promising. It is a shame that their situation [in life] is so hopeless." John Forster to Isidora Forster, May 18, 1873, Forster Collection.

[35]James M. Jensen, "John Forster—A California Ranchero,"37-38.

[36]Tanner, "Don Juan Forster," 201.

nently. The Guaymas enterprise had ended but Forster did not return to his family. At that time, little opportunity awaited him in the rigid social system of England. Instead, he acted as a trader along the coast of lower and upper California. This alert young Englishman could see the developing aristocracy of the rancheros and wished to join it. In order to qualify to own land under Mexican law, he became a Roman Catholic and a naturalized citizen. Pío Pico stood as godfather during his baptism into the faith. Then as now, this ceremonial relationship bore great weight in rural Mexican culture. Both men had occasion in future years to refer to this binding tie between them when requesting special favors from each other.

Not long after his baptism in 1837, Forster married Pío's sister, Isidora Ygnacia Pico. She was some six years older then Forster. This was a most advantageous marriage since it firmly placed him in one of California's most powerful families. He moved his bride into an adobe house in Los Angeles near the present intersection of Broadway and Temple.[37] Forster was only twenty-three years old. His marriage was, to some degree, a rejection of his English upbringing. Isidora would be viewed as an inappropriate, if not scandalous, bride in England since she was only partly of European descent and quite visibly mixed with African and Indian elements. Forster did not care about her racial background. Throughout his life, as far as is known, he remained devoted to her. Unlike his brothers-in-law, Pío and Andrés, Forster seems not to have had any sexual peccadillos or illegitimate children during his marriage.

In 1840 Abel Stearns entered into a contract with Forster concerning the management of the Casa de San Pedro, a warehouse near the sea where rancheros brought their hides to trade for merchandise. It was a lucrative enterprise by

---

[37]Jensen, "John Forster," 38.

which Stearns made himself the wealthiest man in Los
Angeles. Forster ran the place in exchange for a salary of
four-hundred pesos annually and one-half the net profits.[38]
When their contract expired in 1844, Forster wrote a letter to
Stearns thanking him for the opportunities he had provided.[39] The operation was successfully conducted by Forster,
and the men parted harmoniously.

During these years Forster was aggressively seeking ownership of real property as a basis of wealth. His connection
with the Pico family provided a distinct advantage. On July
26, 1843, Governor Micheltorena, influenced by the Picos,
granted Forster the Rancho Nacional on the south shore of
San Diego Bay. This ranch later became the site of Chula
Vista and National City. In February 1845 Pío Pico became
governor and was instrumental in helping Forster to acquire
land in the vicinity of San Juan Capistrano. By April 1845
Pío had granted Forster an area known as Potreros de San
Juan Capistrano, a prime tract around the former mission. At
almost the same time, Pío also gave him the nearby Rancho
Trabuco, a princely estate of over six square leagues. Forster
astutely expanded these grants by purchasing the Ranch of
Misión Vieja and the Rancho Los Desechos in the same
vicinity. The ascent of Pío to the governorship was an enormous boon to Forster. In only ten months after Pío took
office, Forster found himself the owner of 105,460 acres of
ideal ranch land.[40] At thirty-two years of age, he already had
the nucleus of his fortune thanks to his godfather and brother-in-law, Pío Pico. It had come suddenly, providentially, and
mostly in the form of gifts.

[38]Contract between Abel Stearns and John Forster dated July 21, 1840, Stearns Collection.
[39]John Forster to Abel Stearns, Aug. 13, 1844, ibid.
[40]John Douglas Tanner Jr., Introduction to "Pioneer Data From 1832; The Reminiscences of Don Juan Forster, An Englishman in Mexican California," Masters Thesis,
Claremont Graduate School, 1967, 5.

The capstone of Forster's good fortune occurred on December 6, 1845, because of an earlier decision by Pío Pico to sell off five of the secularized missions. On that date, Forster purchased the Mission San Juan Capistrano, including its gardens, orchards, furniture, and fixtures for the absurdly low price of $710 in the form of cash, hides, and tallow.[41] Technically, James McKinley was also a purchaser, but Forster soon liquidated his interest. Pío's disregard for the value of the mission was a blessing to Forster. He decided to use it as the headquarters from which he could administer ranch work conducted on his newly acquired properties. Forster moved Isidora and their children from Los Angeles to San Juan Capistrano. They lived in the mission building itself, in the south part of the structure containing the Serra Chapel, which is now used as a gift shop.[42] Ornate furniture, carpets, and drapes were placed in the rooms they occupied, creating an inner sanctum that an outsider would not detect from observing the decay of the old stone buildings.

For the next twenty years the Forster family remained in the mission, comfortably attended by a large retinue of Indian servants. For the time and place they had a splendid, even baronial, lifestyle. A corps of Indian servants removed the drudgery that nearly everyone in the nineteenth century endured. One of Isidora's photographs depicts a pleasant lady looking placidly in the distance, holding a book in her lap. Her hands show little sign of the unceasing labor that characterized the time. In an age without electrical appliances, hot running water, or any conveniences whatever, she was exempt from work. The grinding round of scrubbing, cleaning, ironing, and cooking was only for Indian labor. The census of 1860 shows that there were five persons who were immediate members of the Forster family at the Mission San

[41]Zephyrin Engelhardt, *San Juan Capistrano Mission*, 157.
[42]Pamela Hallan-Gibson, *Two Hundred Years in San Juan Capistrano*, 45.

Juan Capistrano. They were Forster, his wife, and their three
sons: Marcos, age twenty; Francisco, invariably known as
"Chico," age nineteen; and Juan Fernando, usually called
"Juanón," who was sixteen years old. The entire household
consisted of twenty-one people, nearly all of them servants.
Isidora Forster used six adult Indians exclusively for domestic
chores.[43]

Harris Newmark wrote of a visit to the mission church in
1863, while the family was still there: "When I first saw the
Mission, near Don Juan Forster's home, there was in its open
doors, windows, and cutstone and stucco ruins, its vines and
wildflowers much of the picturesque."[44] In this romantic and
beautiful place, Forster held sway for many years. He became
so identified with the village that instead of being called
"Don Juan," he was often referred to humorously as "Don
San Juan."[45] He created an indelible impression on the community. As late as the 1920s, resident storytellers still told
tales in which Don Juan's family played a part.[46] The memories of his prominence were gradually transmuted to legend.

Only seven months after Forster took title to the mission,
Pío Pico's tenure as governor came to an abrupt end through
a naval attack on California by the United States. The reaction to this invasion by Forster and his brothers-in-law
speaks of the differences between them. Pío Pico tried to
reach Mexico in a vain search for military aid. For several

---

[43]The U.S. Census of 1860 shows twenty-one persons in the Forster household at the
Mission San Juan Capistrano. They included Forster, his wife, and their three sons, a
nuclear family of five. There were also three guests present. Besides these eight persons,
there was a clerk, a cook, five vaqueros, and six general domestic servants, all employed by
Forster. Forster's family of five persons had thirteen servants, almost three for each family
member. Census of 1860, Schedule 1, San Juan Township, Los Angeles County, Federal
Archives, Laguna Niguel. (It should be noted that in 1860 Orange County had not yet been
formed and San Juan Capistrano was in Los Angeles County.)

[44]Harris Newmark, *Sixty Years in Southern California*, 326.

[45]Ibid., 173.

[46]Charles Francis Saunders and Father St. John O'Sullivan, *Capistrano Nights*, 15-16,
76.

weeks he was forced to hide on the Rancho Santa Margarita. At this time, he wrote a strange document disposing of the Rancho Santa Margarita which became part of the legal contest between Forster and the Pico family twenty-seven years later. With Forster's help, Pío avoided capture, and he finally slipped into Baja California on September 7, 1846.[47] He did not return to Los Angeles until the middle of the 1848, after hostilities were concluded. Pío sat out much of the war playing cards in Guaymas, getting only as far into Mexico as Hermosillo, the capital of Sonora.[48] His constant letters to Mexico City did not result in any material assistance for California.[49]

Pío lacked a certain martial spirit which Andrés possessed in abundance. Even so, when the American fleet arrived in San Pedro on August 6, 1846, Andrés did nothing. Resistance to the foreign invasion seemed useless. The American commander, Commodore Robert Stockton, occupied Los Angeles peacefully until September 2, 1846, when he returned his ships to Monterey under the impression that California had been quietly secured for the United States.[50] On departing, Stockton left a Marine officer, Captain Archibald Gillespie, with a small force to garrison Los Angeles. Gillespie proved to be a bad choice for the assignment. He was an oppressive officer who antagonized the town by senselessly imposing a curfew and forbidding ordinary activities of daily life. A popular uprising exposed Gillespie and his men to a jeering, violent mob. After a short siege of Gillespie's little command, he was permitted to withdraw his men from Los Angeles without bloodshed. Many of the Mexicans in Los Angeles now regretted their submission to

---

[47]Bancroft, *History of California*, 5: 279.

[48]Pico, *Historical Narrative*, 138-44.

[49]George Tays, "Pio Pico's Correspondence With The Mexican Government, 1846–1848," 99-149.

[50]Bancroft, *History of California*, 5: 286-87.

the Americans and resolved to give fight to the invaders. An extremely able and charismatic leader, José María Flores, was chosen to act as commander of the aroused Mexican resistance. Andrés Pico was named as a sub-commander under the orders of Flores.[51]

Commodore Stockton left Monterey when he heard of the rebellion in Los Angeles and proceeded to San Diego where he planned to supply and regroup his forces in order to march northward from that point and retake Los Angeles. Flores kept the Americans in San Diego under constant observation, intending to block any attempt to forage the countryside for supplies. On December 3, 1846, his spies noticed the departure of a small band of men under the hated Captain Gillespie proceeding toward the east. Andrés Pico was ordered to cut off Gillespie's return.[52] Flores and Pico were unaware that Gillespie's orders were to rendezvous with a United States Army column headed by Brigadier General Stephen W. Kearney, which was moving toward San Diego from New Mexico. Kearney's presence in Southern California had been announced to Stockton via messenger on the day Gillespie set out.

During the cold, rainy pre-dawn hours of December 6, 1846, part of Kearney's force, consisting of about eighty soldiers, discovered and attacked an encampment of the men led by Andrés Pico. This conflict occurred at San Pascual, an Indian village a few miles east of the modern city of Escondido. The Californios were taken by surprise since they were unaware that any U.S. Army units had arrived in California overland.[53] Pico's men were superbly mounted but armed with little except lances.

The decision to attack the Mexicans at that time was inex-

---

[51]Ibid., 309-10.

[52]Arthur Woodward, "Lances at San Pasqual," 25.

[53]Andrés Pico may have been told by an Indian that there were American troops in the area, but he refused to credit the story. Ibid., 29-30.

plicable. Kearney's men were exhausted, stiff from cold, and could not possibly fire their rifles or cannon because their gunpowder was wet. Besides, many of them were mounted on spent mules and half-broken horses commandeered on their arrival in California. Because they could not fire their weapons and were not properly mounted, the result of the American attack was tragic:

> Many of the Americans lost control of their half-broken, half crazed mounts and fell easy victims to the stabbing lances. Carbines were clubbed, but clubs and Ames sabers were poor weapons to put against lanzas wielded by men accustomed to feats of horsemanship and the dextrous manipulation of the long-shafted lances against bulls and the more ferocious grizzly bears. So the Americans died.[54]

Pico's men killed eighteen of the Americans in the brutal melee. Twenty more were wounded or missing. Three of the wounded died later. Kearney himself was lanced twice but managed to survive his injuries. The Californios suffered few, if any, casualties.

Ironically, Kit Carson, the famous scout and frontiersman, accompanied Kearney and had told him before San Pascual that based on his prior experience in California, the local Mexicans would cut and run at the first show of American force.[55] The Californios under Andrés Pico were therefore surprisingly formidable and courageous opponents. Kearney's men were driven to a hilltop where they remained under siege by Pico's forces. From their beleaguered position, the Americans dried their powder and prepared to employ their cannon against a Mexican assault up the hill. Pico was naturally reluctant to order such an attack by his horsemen armed only with lances. The stalemate was ended before American reinforcements arrived from Stockton's command in San

---

[54]Ibid., 37.
[55]Bancroft, *History of California*, 5: 341.

Diego. The Californios withdrew to Los Angeles, leaving the American army to bury its dead and tend the dying and wounded. The jubilant Mexicans dragged a captured cannon behind them, a trophy of their victory.

The Mexican success at San Pascual was a major triumph for Andrés Pico. There was little resentment toward him by the American military command for his wartime feat. The Americans greatly admired his military skills and leadership. For many years afterward, Andrés was a famous and highly regarded figure among both the Mexican and American elements in California because of his reputed valor at San Pascual.

Kearney's shattered column was led from San Pascual by Stockton's men to San Diego. On December 29, 1846, the combined commands of Stockton and Kearney set out to occupy Los Angeles by force. During this advance on Los Angeles, John Forster provided aid and supplies to the Americans. Forster had given twenty-eight yoke of oxen to help move Kearney's forces after they were disabled at San Pascual, and he supplied them with good horses at San Diego.[56] For most of the journey to Los Angeles, Forster accompanied the Americans, rendering valuable advice and information concerning local conditions. On the approach to Los Angeles, Forster alerted the Americans to an ambush planned by the Mexicans in the dense foliage of a southern crossing of the San Gabriel River which could have decimated their entire force. Accordingly, Stockton and Kearney altered their line of march to avoid it.[57] But Forster had also helped Pío escape to Mexico and provided assistance to Andrés after the incident at San Pascual. Despite appearances, Forster's position was not ambivalent. His aim was to preserve himself, his family, and his property. He clearly

[56]John Douglas Tanner Jr., "Campaign for Los Angeles," 225.
[57]Ibid., 229.

foresaw the inevitability of the American conquest of California and a future where he would want to be on good terms with both sides.

On January 8, 1847, the Californios made their last stand at the Paso de Bartolo, a northern ford of the San Gabriel River about fifteen miles southeast of Los Angeles. There about six hundred of them opposed an approximately equal number of Americans. José María Flores was in command of the entire Mexican force, and Andrés Pico led a squadron on the right flank. The Americans advanced in a tight, disciplined formation supported by highly effective artillery fire. One observer said that the Mexicans seemed to "rather give way."[58] The Californios had homemade gunpowder which could not equal the powerful cannonades of the invaders. All Mexican resistance soon dissolved into a dispirited retreat. John Forster observed the conflict from the American side. It is not known if he was able to distinguish his brother-in-law Andrés on the enemy side of the river.

The next day a skirmish occurred just outside Los Angeles at a place called La Mesa, with similar results. On January 10, 1847, the Americans entered the town. Forster had returned the day before to his home at San Juan Capistrano. Andrés Pico formally succeeded José María Flores as commander of the resistance since Flores decided to abandon California for Mexico. Stockton had refused to treat with Flores and threatened to execute him if he was captured. With no other options available, Andrés made a peace treaty with Lieutenant Colonel John Frémont, who was approaching Los Angeles from the north. This arrangement, called the Capitulation of Cahuenga, was grandiosely signed on January 13, 1847, by Andrés as "Squadron Commander and Chief of the National Forces in California."[59] At the time he

---

[58]Benjamin Davis Wilson quoted by Tanner, ibid., 231.
[59]Bancroft, *History of California*, 5: 405.

only had about twenty remaining followers. Frémont made the formal peace agreement in writing with Andrés, although he had no authority to do so, something Andrés suspected. The supreme American military authorities in California, Commodore Stockton and Brigadier General Kearney, were nearby in Los Angeles at the time, unaware of Frémont's activities. The peace was ratified by them, nonetheless. The war had ended.

These cataclysmic events had a profound impact on the Picos and their brother-in-law John Forster. Each had dealt with the American invasion in his own way. Pío escaped to northern Mexico where he dispatched a series of supplicating letters to a remote, disorganized Mexican government. Andrés put himself in the line of fire by opposing the Americans and thereby became one of the most famous men in California. Don Juan Forster adopted a conciliatory posture with both sides, keeping an eye toward preservation of his personal interests. In such fashion, each man began a new life in a world which was now dominated by an alien people from the other side of the continent.

CHAPTER THREE

The Adaptation to the New American Order

The greatest challenge to the Picos was not the physical presence of Anglo-Saxon invaders. Both men had long since become accustomed to a growing number of foreigners arriving from the United States and England. Soon after direct commerce was established with the Boston hide and tallow ships, Yankee traders began to take up permanent residence in California. Men like William A. Gale, Henry Delano Fitch, Abel Stearns, and John Temple all settled in Los Angeles or San Diego before 1830. These worldly Americans had a great deal of knowledge which was both instructive and entertaining for isolated young Mexican provincials like Pío and Andrés. The Picos knew these foreigners and not only accepted their presence, but formed close bonds of friendship with some of them, even going out of their way to render special favors. For example, during his early years in San Diego, Pío, along with his mother, took responsibility for the upbringing of Anita Gale, the daughter of William A. Gale by a California woman who died in childbirth.[1] In 1829, Pío helped the sea captain Henry Delano Fitch elope from San Diego with Pío's cousin, Josefa Carrillo.[2]

---

[1] Helen Tyler, "The Family of Pico," 235.
[2] Bancroft, *History of California*, 3: 141.

About 1831 Jonathan Trumbull Warner arrived in San Diego. He was much esteemed by Pío, who gave away his adopted daughter, Anita Gale, in marriage to Warner in 1837.[3] Warner was a literate, sophisticated man who became a newspaper editor, state senator, and a political force under the American regime. He adopted the Spanish name Juan José when he was baptized as a Catholic under the sponsorship of Pío. He insisted on being known as J. J. Warner the rest of his life. His friendship with Pío was so strong that more than half a century later, when both were old men, he gave Pío refuge in his home after the loss of Pío's fortune.[4]

Between 1830 and 1845, numerous other English-speaking foreigners settled in and around Los Angeles. Nearly all of them converted to Catholicism, became naturalized citizens, and took Mexican wives. The majority of foreign immigrants became wealthy and respected by adoption into the ranchero elite. Among them were William Wolfskill, Hugo Reid, Benjamin Davis Wilson, William Workman, John Rowland, Alexander Bell, and Henry Dalton. Pío was on intimate terms with most of them and even organized the newcomers into a special military company for use during his struggle to overthrow the Mexican governor, Manuel Micheltorena, during February 1845.[5] As long as California belonged to Mexico, these early arrivals were no threat to the province. On the contrary, they adapted quite well to local conditions by learning Spanish and adhering to Mexican customs and usage to such a point that they became regarded as equivalent to *hijos del país*—sons of the country.

Some Americans were content with life in Mexican California. Ten years after the conquest, Thomas O. Larkin, one such American immigrant, wrote nostalgically to Abel Stearns:

---

[3]Tyler, "Family of Pico," 236.
[4]Henry D. Barrows, "Pío Pico," 55.
[5]Bancroft, *History of California*, 4: 504-07.

I begin to yearn after the times prior to July 1846 and all their honest pleasures and the fleshpots of those days. Halcyon days they were. We shall not enjoy their like again.[6]

There was little alien about men who enjoyed life in Mexican California and conformed to its attitudes and living patterns. The truly alien and destructive force that acted on the Picos as well as all of California was the imposition by military conquest of a new dominant culture. The legal, economic, and social manifestations of the new American order inexorably destroyed the elite ranchero class to which the Picos belonged. After the conquest, much of their lives were spent in an attempt to adjust to it.

The peace Andrés made with Frémont in the Capitulation of Cahuenga stated that the Californios "shall be guaranteed protection of life and property . . ."[7] During January 1847, Andrés met with the actual American commander, Commodore Robert Stockton, at the Avila Adobe which still stands on Olvera Street in Los Angeles. Andrés was told that the agreement he signed would be honored even though Frémont had no authority to make it, as Andrés had suspected. The anticipation of this first contact with Stockton was a harrowing experience for Andrés, who was mindful of Stockton's earlier threats to execute his predecessor, José María Flores. Andrés was considerably relieved by Stockton's assurances.[8] He attended a holiday ball on July 4, 1847, given by the U.S. Army in Los Angeles, where his presence was noted in the journal of a young officer.[9]

The American military government soon determined to make use of the prowess shown by Andrés at San Pascual. On

---

[6]Thomas O. Larkin to Abel Stearns, April 24, 1856, Stearns Collection.

[7]Word of the surrender flashed through the American forces. The *California Star*, a newspaper begun by Americans in San Francisco (then known as Yerba Buena), printed the only copy of the Articles of Capitulation at hand, one in Spanish, on Feb. 27, 1847.

[8]Narrative of Benjamin Davis Wilson, Dec. 6, 1877, Wilson Collection.

[9]"Journal of John McHenry Hollingsworth," 239.

February 14, 1848, he was dispatched a letter requesting him to organize a force of Californios to protect Southern California from marauding Indians.[10] Although his authority was later revoked, Andrés was prepared to do it. His willingness to cooperate with American authorities would be typical of his conduct in years to come.

Pío returned to San Diego from Mexico on July 6, 1848. He was apparently under the impression that the Treaty of Guadalupe Hidalgo ending the Mexican-American War had restored him to the governorship of California.[11] When this opinion was expressed to the American authorities, he was detained briefly and only granted his freedom by the intervention of his old friend, the Scotsman Hugo Reid, who mollified the concerns of the military government about Pío's pretentions to office.[12] Pío, upon his release, immediately went to San Fernando for a reunion with Andrés.

The homecoming of Pío nearly coincided with word of the discovery of gold in Northern California. Within a few weeks the Picos concocted a plan to take a group of Mexican *peones* to the mine fields. They contracted with about thirty men from Sonora to outfit them and pay all their expenses, possibly in exchange for a share of what was found.[13] Ignacio

---

[10]Colonel Jonathan D. Stevenson to Andrés Pico, Feb. 14, 1848, California Historical Documents Collection.

[11]Bancroft, *History of California,* 5: 588.

[12]Susanna Bryant Dakin, *A Scotch Paisano in Old Los Angeles,* 143-44.

[13]There are numerous documents in Spanish relating to this venture, all dated during the first half of 1849. Most of them are statements of account in which the Mexican peones acknowledged receipt of clothing, equipment, cash, and the like from Andrés Pico. It appears that these men were recruited in Los Angeles, Santa Barbara, and other points on the way to the gold fields. They were to repay their indebtedness with gold procured from their labor in the placers. Most were unable to sign their names. It is not clear from the documents how the amount of their debts was fixed or how they were to share any gold discovered. These documents are in the Del Valle Collection, Seaver Center for Western History Research, Los Angeles Museum of Natural History.

Antonio Coronel, a contemporary of Andrés Pico, who was also in the gold fields stated: "Don Andrés had brought a party of Sonorans to Stanislaus from Los Angeles and fully equipped them, on condition they pay him back in gold at the going rate." Apparently, he

del Valle recruited the men and kept the records of account. The scheme was consistent with the view the Picos had of themselves. As leaders of the ranchero elite, their high status would not permit them to grub in the dry diggings or wade in cold streams and rivers. A crew of lesser men would actually do the work, just as labor was performed on their extensive land holdings.

Andrés was in charge of the whole operation. Pío remained in Los Angeles but was an investor in the scheme. By September 26, 1848, Andrés had the company of men digging about thirty miles south of Sutter's Fort. At this time, Andrés had a pound of gold delivered to his Santa Barbara friend, Pablo de la Guerra, for safekeeping.[14] During the same month, the Belgian-Mexican, Agustín Janssens, found John Forster and Hugo Reid abandoning a dry dig in the placers. He wrote, "There I was promised better results, because those men were leaving and they gave me all their equipment."[15]

Andrés did not give up prospecting for gold until well into 1849. It is possible that he found his band of Sonorans and himself under hostile pressure from the influx of eager Americans to retire from the gold country. Bayard Taylor, a reporter at the scene for the *New York Tribune*, wrote in 1849:

> The first colony of gold-hunters attempted to drive out all foreigners without distinction, as well as native Californians. Don Andrés Pico, who was located on the same river, had some difficulty with them until they could be made to understand that his right as a citizen was equal to theirs.[16]

On the other hand, the same author also wrote:

---

meant that prices in the gold fields would be much higher than where the equipment was procured and thereby Andrés Pico would make a profit. See Antonio Coronel, *Tales of Mexican California*, 56.

[14]Cesáreo Lataillade to Pablo de la Guerra, Sept. 26, 1848, De la Guerra Collection.

[15]Agustín Janssens, *The Life and Adventures in California of Don Agustín Janssens*, 137-8.

[16]Bayard Taylor, *Eldorado*, 1: 87.

We had a visit one day from Don Andrés Pico, commander of the Californian forces during the war. He had a company of men digging at the Middle Bar, about a mile above.
He is an urbane, intelligent man of medium stature, and of a
natural gentility of character which made him quite popular
among the immigrants.[17]

Antonio Coronel of Los Angeles, a friend of Andrés, was
also in the gold fields and was driven out by racist Yankees.
Much later he wrote about the abuse he suffered in bitter
terms.[18] The reason for the final withdrawal of Andrés is not
clear. It is likely that he had the same experience as his friend,
Don Antonio. On April 22, 1849, Hugo Reid wrote to Abel
Stearns in Los Angeles, "No one must think of making
money by taking persons to work on shares or wages; it will
not hold good, Andrés Pico's case being a solitary exception,
only half carried out as yet."[19] Reid implies that Andrés met
with a measure of success before he left the mines, but how
much gold he took remains unknown.

The gold rush caused a tremendous imbalance in the distribution of California's population. Without gold or abundant
water, Southern California was unattractive to immigrants. As
a result, the Southland lay dormant for more than two decades
after statehood in 1850. By that year, the entire population of
Los Angeles County totaled about 3,530 people, the vast
majority of them Mexicans. In contrast, the rest of the state,
mainly the northern counties, contained approximately
92,597 inhabitants, most of them Americans, with thousands
more goldseekers arriving each month. Even twenty years
later, in 1870, Los Angeles County had only some 15,309 people, compared to the total population, overwhelmingly found
in the north, of 560,247 persons.[20]

---

[17]Ibid., 1: 92.

[18]Coronel, *Tales of Mexican California*, 60-67.

[19]Hugo Reid to Abel Stearns, April 22, 1849, Stearns Collection.

[20]U.S. Interior Department, Ninth Census, Vol. 1, Population and Social Statistics,
Population By State and Counties, 1790–1870, Tables I and II.

Despite its lack of natural resources, the Southern California region contained thousands of Spanish cattle, a commodity desperately needed in the north. In 1849 it occurred to Abel Stearns, the largest landowner in Los Angeles, that beef cattle could be sold to a huge market being created by the exploding population in the north. Hugo Reid wrote a letter to Stearns from Monterey on April 22, 1849, which contained an observation that fired Stearns's imagination: "People will have to go south for stock very soon, the consumption being far ahead of the increase."[21] During the next month, Reid proposed that Stearns send dried beef north by chartered ship. Instead, Stearns sent a herd northward on the hoof. The movement of cattle from Los Angeles to the Bay Area proved a great success. The demand for beef was such that fabulous prices were readily paid for the long-horned, thin Spanish cattle.

All the Southern California rancheros, including the Pico brothers and John Forster, soon began driving their herds to the new market. They became rich almost overnight. The land grants, used for running cattle by the presidio veterans and their descendants, became sources of enormous wealth. Steers which before the gold rush were worth only about two dollars for their hides, were actually sold for as much as fifty to seventy-five dollars a head during the early 1850s on the San Francisco market.[22] The pueblo of Los Angeles was suddenly transformed by an incredible flow of cash from the north. One historian observed:

> With its new prosperity, El Pueblo went mad. Californians knew how to spend money. They bought fancy clothes, added second stories to their townhouses on the Plaza, built large ranch homes, put on better horse races, and were heavy patrons of the gambling houses. They imported carriages, thousand-dollar shawls, and lace curtained, four-poster bed-

---

[21]Hugo Reid to Abel Stearns, April 22, 1848, Stearns Collection.
[22]Cleland, *Cattle On a Thousand Hills*, 106.

steads. Don Jose Sepulveda and Don Vicente Lugo wore thousand-dollar suits, and their horses were equally resplendent. The money Californios spent did things to the shopkeepers, to the craftsmen in leather and silver, to the gamblers, to all the unsavory characters who came in for a share, and to the town itself.[23]

The Picos readily accepted their new wealth as if it were their due. Pío, who had an adobe townhouse on the Los Angeles plaza, expanded his living accommodations by purchasing the Rancho Paso de Bartolo piecemeal from the heirs of Juan Crispin Pérez from 1850 to 1852. He gave this eight-thousand acre ranch the affectionate name of the "Ranchito" and built a large, rambling adobe mansion on it near the east bank of the San Gabriel River.[24] Thereafter, he divided his time between the Ranchito and his adobe townhouse in Los Angeles, about fifteen miles distant. A portion of Pío's original home at the Ranchito still exits, preserved as a state park in the town of Whittier, at the southwest corner of the intersection of the 605 Freeway and Whittier Boulevard.

Surrounded by a large retinue of Indian and Mexican servants, Pío lived like a kind of old Spanish grandee. An American contemporary passing by the Ranchito on his way from Los Angeles to Santiago Canyon with a hunting party on November 15, 1859, commented:

> We came by way of the Ranchito, on the east side of the San Gabriel River, then the home of Ex-Governor Pío Pico. He lived at that time in all the state of a feudal lord . . . The smaller dwellings of the working people and other dependencies of the ranch comprised quite a village of themselves, there being perhaps one hundred people employed in various capacities. Don Pío owned at that time thousands of acres of as fertile land as could be found in Southern California, some

---

[23]W. W. Robinson, *Los Angeles From the Days of the Pueblo*, 64.

[24]Marion Parks, "In Pursuit of Vanished Days: Visits to the Extant Historic Houses of Los Angeles County," 159-70.

The north side of Pío Pico's ranch house in Whittier about 1891. Standing on the balcony, Pico is about to serve a lady visitor from a decanter.
Courtesy, The Huntington Library.

A view from the west of Pío Pico's ranch house in Whittier during 1900.
*Courtesy, California Historical Society, Ticor Collection,
University of Southern California Libraries.*

The patio and entrance to Pío Pico's ranch house
in Whittier from the east about 1920.
*Courtesy, California Historical Society, Ticor Collection,
University of Southern California Libraries.*

of which was tilled and irrigated, but the greater part, of
course, served as a pasture for his vast herds of cattle and
horses, stock raising being the principal industry of the country.[25]

When not at the Ranchito, Pío found entertainment in
the social life of Los Angeles. In addition to such American
diversions as balls, banquets, and horse races, he enjoyed the
Mexican amusements of bullfights, fandangos, and cock-
fights.[26] Social affairs hosted by Pío at his Los Angeles townhouse were always newsworthy events.[27]

[25] J. E. Pleasants, "A Visit to Santiago Canyon," 141-42.
[26] Henry Winfred Splitter, "Los Angeles Recreation, 1846-1900," 40.
[27] *El Clamor Público*, Oct. 2, 1855.

Pío Pico and his wife, María Ignacia Alvarado, about 1852.
A few years earlier, a U.S. Army officer described Pico as
"corpulent, very dark, with strongly marked African features."
Courtesy, Seaver Center for Western History Research, Los Angeles County Museum.

Pío's domestic arrangements were extremely irregular. Although he had a widely attended wedding at the Plaza Church in Los Angeles when he married María Ignacia Alvarado in 1834, he had no children by her.[28] Pío proved a fickle husband; he entertained little sense of fidelity toward his wife up to her death on February 21, 1854, in Santa Barbara.[29] Throughout his marriage he had a series of illicit relationships that produced several children. In 1838 Ascención Avila gave birth to Pío's illegitimate daughter, Griselda Pico. The same woman also presented him with another daughter,

---

[28]Northrup, *Spanish-Mexican Families*, 2: 214; Bancroft, *History of California*, 4: 779.

[29]*El Clamor Público*, Aug. 7, 1855. The funeral of Pío's wife waited for over a year, perhaps so she could be interred in an elaborate family tomb Pío built in Los Angeles.

Joaquina Pico. As late as March 19, 1871, he was the purported father of Alfredo Pico by Felecita Romero.[30] At this
latter birth, Pío was already seventy years old.[31] On August
29, 1883, a twenty-one-year-old man named Ranulfo Pico
was shot to death by a jealous young woman in a cornfield
near Los Nietos. Alfredo Pico identified the deceased,
claiming that Ranulfo was his brother.[32]

Good evidence exists to support Pío's paternity of all these
children. There were undoubtedly others whose connection
with Pío was never made known. Some living members of
the Pico family assert that their ancestors were adopted by
Pío, and therefore, no blood relationship exists with him.
This view, of course, spares Pío's memory from what some
may regard as a taint of licentiousness. The historical record,
however, supports Pío's paternity. His interest in women

---

[30]After Pío's death, the probate court in Los Angeles ruled that Griselda Pico, Joaquina
Pico, and Alfredo Pico were his natural children and rightful heirs. This ruling was made on
"good cause shown." *Estate of Pico*, Probate Case No. 1010, Los Angeles Superior Court
Archives.

During the U.S. Census of 1860, Griselda Pico was present in the San Juan Capistrano
household of John Forster. Schedule 1, San Juan Township, Los Angeles County, Federal
Archives, Laguna Niguel. She is listed as nineteen years of age. Her obituaries in the *Los
Angeles Times*, Dec 21, 1897, and the *San Francisco Chronicle*, Dec. 31, 1897, state that she
was Pío's natural daughter by Ascención Avila and confirm that she died at age 59 in Los
Angeles at 136 West 15th Street, where Pío also passed away. Accordingly, in 1860 the census correctly gave her age as nineteen, and supports her identity as Pío's daughter. She had a
connection to the Forster household through Isidora Forster, her aunt.

Shortly before her death, she joined with her sister Joaquina to assert legal claims to land
formerly owned by her mother. The local press gave their efforts extensive coverage, identifying the sisters as the natural children of Ascención Avila and Pío Pico. *Los Angeles Times*,
Sept. 5, 1895. It is significant that no challenge was ever made to the paternity of the sisters
by any family member or other interested party. Their status as natural children of Pío was
common knowledge. Griselda never married. Joaquina married Juan Moreno.

[31]The death certificate of Alfredo Pico states that his birth date was March 19, 1871.
Pío Pico is named as his father. His mother is listed as Felecita Romero. Death certificate,
Los Angeles Hall of Records. Griselda Pico and Joaquina Pico recognized him as their
brother. They assigned him their interest in Pio's estate as "the rightful heir." *Los Angeles
Times*, March 27, 1897.

[32]*Los Angeles Times*, Aug. 31, 1883.

seems to have extended from the daughters of elite Californio families to lowly Indian servants.[33]

Meanwhile, Andrés had situated himself in a manner similar to Pío during the early 1850s. He alternated between living at an adobe townhouse on the Los Angeles plaza and one of the most palatial residences in the entire state of California.[34] In 1844, Andrés leased the southern half of the San Fernando Valley from its owner, Eulogio de Celis, including the complex of buildings that made up the Mission San Fernando Rey de España. The largest building at the mission was not the church, but the Moorish style *convento*, originally intended as a seminary and residence for priests. This twenty-two-room building was used by Andrés as his home when he was not in Los Angeles. It was surrounded by fruit trees of every variety and well-watered gardens of dense greenery.[35] A Spanish fountain played at the entrance to the convento, further giving the estate the appearance of a luxurious oasis in the bleak landscape of the valley.[36] In 1854 Andrés was able to purchase the land and mission buildings, thereby taking title to almost sixty-thousand acres of ranch property and the spectacular convento.

Andrés had a lifestyle that was no less aristocratic than Pío's. At mealtimes he had Indian servants in attendance and musicians to play for his guests. A visitor at the San Fernando residence in 1856 wrote this interesting description:

---

[33]Ascensión Avila, born in 1820, was the daughter of Antonio Ignacio Avila, a member of the ranchero elite. Northrup, *Spanish-Mexican Families*, 1: 54. Felecita Romero seems to have been from the lesser ranks of California society, and was likely an Indian servant.

[34]Newmark, *Sixty Years*, 92.

[35]Henry Miller, *Account of a Tour of the California Missions and Towns, 1856*, 43-44. Shortly after the death of Andrés Pico, an excellent description was given of the San Fernando estate in Ludwig Louis Salvator, *Los Angeles in the Sunny Seventies*, 161-62. A romantic but fairly accurate description of the huge interior of Andrés' residence, including its reception rooms and wine cellar, is found in Benjamin C. Truman, *Semi-Tropical California*, 190.

[36]This fountain was restored in 1922. Newmark, *Sixty Years*, 92, n.2.

He lived in a luxurious style and had a large household of trained servants, chiefly Indians. Like the grandee that he was, he entertained lavishly. His silver and china table-service made a brilliant display. His household furnishings were plain but massive and luxurious. The plain old mission furniture was retained but many an expensive and more ornate piece had been added. His table afforded an ample style of living; the dinners consisted of five to six courses—all of the far-famed California-Spanish cookery, which no nation—not even the French, has ever excelled. Two young Indian boys served as waiters. They were clad in the simple tunic of the day. Before the meal, one of them stood by the host, Don Andrés, at the head of the table and said grace, and at the close of the meal, the other took his place and returned thanks. At the mid-day and evening meals, and on the veranda in the evening, we were delightfully entertained by native musicians who played on three stringed instruments then mostly in vogue—the harp, violin and guitar.[37]

Andrés was an open-handed host who enjoyed putting on balls, formal dinners, and barbecues for those he invited to spend several days at a time in the lush environs of his estate.[38] The convento building where Andrés lived for nearly thirty years still stands at the Mission San Fernando and contains a few pieces of furniture and paintings from the period when Andrés was its owner. The visitor wandering through the stately building today is impressed by its ample dimensions and rare beauty, evoking the splendor of life at the Mission San Fernando during Andrés' time.

The rough and tumble of ranching life appealed to Andrés. He was a superb horseman who enjoyed rodeos, riding contests, and had a special love for bullfights. For example, on July 9, 1847, an American soldier saw one of the many

---

[37]J. E. Pleasants, quoted in W. W. Robinson, "The Rancho Story of San Fernando Valley," 226-27.

[38]W. W. Robinson, *The Story of the San Fernando Valley*, 17. Frank M. Keffer, *History of San Fernando Valley*, 40.

corridas de toros in which Andrés participated both on foot and on horseback. The soldier reported:

> Expert Californians, mounted on spirited horses, fought the bulls with spears or lances. Several horses were killed and their riders saved by their comrades throwing blankets over the bulls' heads to blindfold them while the dismounted men escaped from the corral. Two men were considerably hurt . . . General Pico took an active part in these exercises, and the barbarous scenes were witnessed by several hundred people.[39]

Among his numerous ranch hands were tough veterans of his army days. On the least pretense, Andrés would round up an improvised force of his men to punish Indians or capture whatever outlaw group had incurred his displeasure. On such occasions, Andrés adopted a military air, commanding his men not only by virtue of his wealth and status, but also because he was a genuinely popular and charismatic leader. The role of Andrés as a peacekeeper in the 1850s endeared him to the Americans and earned him great prestige.[40]

The domestic life of Andrés was as chaotic as that of Pío, if not more so. For many years he had lived with Catalina Moreno and permitted her to be regarded as his wife, but never actually married her.[41] It appears that no children came from this informal union. Nevertheless, Andrés was almost certainly the father of Rómulo Pico, who was born about 1847, and whose mother was María Antonia Dominguez. At the time of Rómulo's birth, his mother was married to Vicente Moraga, making Rómulo the result of an adulterous relationship. This scandalous situation was brought to light by Rómulo himself after the death of Andrés.[42]

During the early 1850s, Forster was mainly involved with

---

[39]Daniel Tyler, *The Mormon Battalion in the Mexican American War, 1846–1848*, 297.

[40]See Chapter Four, *post.*

[41]*Estate of Pico*, Case No. 1159, Los Angeles Superior Court Archives, confirms that he was never married. Catalina Moreno did not qualify as a spouse and heir at his death.

[42]See Chapter Ten, *post.*

improving his position in the cattle market. He had suc-
cumbed to few of California's pleasures. Most of his time was
spent travelling to and from San Francisco by steamer in
order to make deals for the sale of his herds. Los Angeles was
a constant stopover on his trips where he visited the homes of
friends. One was Abel Stearns, who had the largest adobe in
Los Angeles, popularly called "El Palacio," which once stood
where the Hollywood Freeway now cuts through Main
Street. Forster made many contacts in San Francisco through
his knowledge of English and gained information which
placed him in a superior business position compared to the
less-informed, Spanish-speaking rancheros. He sent droves
of cattle northward with his own men at previously arranged
prices, seldom relying on brokers who would buy cattle in
Southern California for the least cash possible and take them
north on speculation. Forster was shrewd and prudent, characteristics not entirely shared by his brothers-in-law, Pío and
Andrés, or many others of the Los Angeles ranchero elite.

When the Picos spent time at their townhouses on the
plaza in Los Angeles, it was obvious that the American
takeover had not necessarily improved the quality of life.
Although the discovery of gold had created a huge demand
for Los Angeles beef and flooded the pueblo with money,
this prosperity had a price. The same mining country banished dangerous criminals and psychopaths from its midst
on pain of death, vigilante style. Most of these highly undesirable types drifted into Los Angeles to take advantage of
plentiful money and the proximity of Mexico in case of a
need to escape. During the 1850s their presence produced a
climate of violence unprecedented in the once tranquil
town.[43]

Saloons and gambling houses sprung up all around the

---

[43]Cleland, *Cattle On a Thousand Hills*, 90-101.

plaza, especially on a little street Californios called Calle de los Negros, just east of the plaza, which was dubbed "Nigger Alley" by the Americans. It became a jungle catering to the most depraved tastes of the newly arrived criminal element. Nights were made horrendous by raucous music, pistol shots, and screams. Each morning the area was littered with the bodies of men in a drunken stupor, even occasionally a corpse. Harris Newmark, an eyewitness to all this in 1853, wrote:

> Human life at this period was about the cheapest thing in Los Angeles, and killings were frequent. Nigger Alley was as tough a neighborhood, in fact, as could be found anywhere, and a large proportion of the twenty or thirty murders a month was committed there.[44]

This was a dangerous nuisance for the rancheros who kept townhouses on the plaza. At least the adobe walls were thick and the windows barred. Those living on the plaza must have ruefully considered the difference between the hard men drifting down from the north and the gentler Americans who had quietly and respectfully embraced the Mexican way of life before 1846.

Both Pío and Andrés attempted to participate in the new American order. In 1850 Los Angeles County was officially organized as a political unit of the state of California. In that year, Andrés Pico and Abel Stearns were elected to the state assembly to serve in its second session beginning in January 1851.[45] No political parties had yet been organized in the state, much less in Los Angeles County.

In the first legislature held between January and April 1850, a law was passed prohibiting any person of one-eighth Negro or Indian blood from testifying against a white man in

---

[44]Newmark, *Sixty Years*, 31.
[45]Bancroft, *History of California*, 6: 644.

a court of law.[46] This statue reflected the racial prejudice the Americans brought to California, which the Picos somehow had to confront.

It is reasonably certain that José María Pico was one-quarter black and therefore his sons, Pío and Andrés, were at least of one-eighth African descent. The first set of opinions issued by the California Supreme Court in 1850 contains an appendix on the Mexican *alcalde* system which reprints a letter stating that Pío Pico was "corpulent, very dark, with strongly marked African features."[47] Accordingly, members of the legislature, many of whom were lawyers, were aware that Andrés was partly black. The appearance of Andrés did not immediately confirm this, but he certainly did not appear "Anglo-Saxon." Ironically, since Andrés was at least of one-eighth African ancestry and had even more Indian blood, he theoretically could not have testified against a white man to enforce the laws he was elected to enact.

This absurdity was the basis of an actual incident during 1857 in San Francisco when Manuel Dominguez, a wealthy and distinguished Californio who had been a delegate to the state constitutional convention eight years before in Monterey, was not allowed to testify in court against a white man because of his "Indian" appearance.[48] Andrés appears to have ignored any racial bias against him. There is no evidence that

---

[46]This statute, like all such racist laws, was hard to enforce. In its edition of Feb. 2, 1851, the *Alta California*, a San Francisco newspaper, published the following:

In the cause before the Superior Court, yesterday, the proceedings were brought to a stand by the introduction of a Hindoo witness. Under the statutes of this State, persons having one-eighth part or more of negro blood, blacks and Indians, are excluded from being witnesses in cases where white men are parties, and it was contended that under this law the Hindoo should not be allowed to testify. The case was adjourned to this morning.

[47]*California Reports*, the official record of cases decided by the State Supreme Court (San Francisco: A.L Bancroft, 1850), 1: 579. This volume can be found in any California public law library. By legal custom and usage, it would be cited as 1 California Reports 579.

[48]Leonard Pitt, *Decline of the Californios*, 201-2.

he complained about his treatment in the legislature. His colleagues did not desire to address the implications of the racial laws they had passed. By unspoken consensus, Andrés was deemed to be, for legislative purposes, a "Spaniard."

The legislature met on January 6, 1851 in San Jose. Andrés was fortunate that the other assemblyman from Los Angeles was Abel Stearns. Stearns had resided in Mexico and California since 1828 and could provide quick Spanish translations as well as explain the mysteries of parliamentary procedure. Andrés was severely handicapped by his inability to understand English, a problem that he never fully overcame.

The great issue of the legislative session was the election of a U. S. senator. At that time, senators were chosen by the state legislatures, not by popular vote. John C. Frémont was the United States senator from California whose initial brief term had expired. He was a candidate to succeed himself and was in attendance at the legislature to campaign to retain his seat. The other senator from California, William M. Gwin, was still in Washington, D.C., since his term was not yet completed. The session had attracted great interest, filling San Jose's hotels with office-seekers and politicians of every variety. A reporter for the *Daily Alta California,* covering the first day of the session on January 6, 1851, wrote:

> The bar room of the Mansion House is not the most quiet place in the world, as you might well imagine. State Senators, log rollers, officials and politicians, "native and to the manor borne," are all engaged in the most earnest conversation, while the clinking of the glasses at the bar is proof positive that electioneering and legislating is rather dry work. In front of me a couple of billiard players are knocking the balls about at a great rate, as is dimly perceptible through clouds of tobacco smoke. The day has passed and the organization of the Legislature has been accomplished without any impediment, but the tug of war is yet to come.[49]

---

[49]*Alta California,* Jan. 7, 1851.

Scenes such as the one at the Mansion House were exactly
what Andrés had come to see. He had arrived at the heart of
the new American political system and was to profit by it.

Andrés voted with Stearns on nearly every question. They
split, however, "in the tug of war" for senator since Stearns
opposed Frémont. Both Pío and Andrés greatly esteemed
the man to whom Andrés surrendered at Cahuenga in 1847.
They were not alone in doing so among the Californios.
Andrés was joir.ed in the legislature by his old compadres
Pablo de la Guerra and José María Covarrubias, who had
been elected senator and assemblyman from Santa Barbara,
respectively. They too strongly favored Frémont. During the
senatorial election, the *Daily Alta California,* observed, "An
interesting fact presented by this vote is that the native Californian members of the Senate and Assembly voted for Frémont and stuck to him from the first to the last ballot."[50]

The attempt to elect a senator was unsuccessful, each vote
ending in a deadlock. There were 147 ballots taken before it
was decided to postpone the senatorial election until the next
term. After the nineteenth ballot even Pablo de la Guerra
and Andrés Pico began receiving a few scattered votes for the
office.[51] When the legislature adjourned on May 2, 1851, it
was criticized for having done little, but Andrés had learned a
great deal.

During the legislative session of 1851, both Andrés and
Pablo de la Guerra were constantly pressed to join either the
Whig or Democratic party. Southern California, although
lightly populated, was an area each political party wanted to
dominate. Andrés Pico in Los Angeles and Pablo de la Guerra in Santa Barbara controlled the Mexican vote in their
areas, which was the great majority of the population. On

---

[50]Ibid., Feb. 20, 1851.
[51]Ibid., Feb. 26, 1851; Bancroft, *History of California,* 6: 646 n.7.

May 1, 1851, they felt obliged to jointly publish an announcement in the *San Francisco Herald* where, referring to themselves in the third person, they said: "The political divisions of the American people are to them objects of the utmost attention and interest, but their acquaintance with them is not sufficiently intimate to warrant them in identifying themselves with them on one side or the other."

In September 1851 Andrés was again elected to the assembly. This time the other Los Angeles assemblyman was a close friend, Ignacio del Valle.[52] Meanwhile, during October, Pío was appointed by Benjamin Davis Wilson to the central committee of a convention in Santa Barbara demanding a division of California into northern and southern sections.[53] Pío still had considerable prestige. His name appeared at the head of a demand for division of the state published in the *San Francisco Herald.*[54]

The legislature of 1852 met at Vallejo on January 21. Andrés and Ignacio del Valle took rooms with their friends, Antonio María de la Guerra, who had replaced his brother Pablo as senator from Santa Barbara, and José María Covarrubias, an assemblyman from the same place.[55] The most important item initially before the legislature was a resump-

---

[52]*San Francisco Herald*, Sept. 25, 1851.

[53]Ibid., Oct. 28, 1851.

[54]Ibid., Sept. 25, 1851.

[55]Antonio María de la Guerra to Pablo de la Guerra, Jan. 29, 1852, De La Guerra Collection. During the legislative session of 1852, Antonio María de la Guerra sent a series of letters in Spanish to his brother Pablo de la Guerra, who was in Santa Barbara acting as a U.S. marshal. These letters describe the escapades and difficulties of himself, Andrés Pico, Jose Covarrubias, and Ignacio del Valle while rooming together during the legislative session. They are in the De la Guerra Collection, and all of them are entertaining. Antonio María writes of such things as their being driven out of bed in their underwear by a fire alarm which turned out to be false [Jan. 29, 1852]. Covarrubias was surprised in his room after midnight in a compromising position with a married woman he had picked up at a theater [Feb. 14, 1852]. When Andrés learned that a certain Mr. Cook of Santa Cruz had died, he immediately pronounced romantic intentions toward the widow [Feb. 19, 1852]. They had to change boarding houses because they were being eaten up by fleas [Feb. 24, 1852].

tion of the selection of a U.S. senator. Frémont had withdrawn his candidacy, leaving the field open to contestants
John B. Weller and David C. Broderick. Both men were
leading members of the California Democratic party, but
they represented entirely different factions of it.

The Democratic party in California was a reflection of the
party as it existed throughout the country, consisting of three
main divisions. The largest was the conservative element,
sometimes called the "Hunkers." They were mainly found in
the northern states and were basically indifferent to the issue
of slavery. The second division, also centered in the north,
was the radical Free Soil wing of the party. It consisted of
those Democrats opposed to slavery or its extension into the
territories. The opponents of the Free Soil wing, commonly
called the Chivalry, were based in the South and favored slavery and its extension. This was the third division. The conservative majority had little effective leadership and was
constantly shifting its support between the Free Soilers and
the Chivalry depending on the rewards to be gained.[56]

David C. Broderick, a product of New York ward politics,
was the leader of the California Free Soil Democrats. He was
a superb political strategist and a master at controlling meet-
ings. Broderick had unsuccessfully opposed the passage of a
tax on foreign miners enacted by the first legislature in 1850
when he was a member of the senate. It had been used
against native Californians even though they were not "foreigners." The Spanish-speaking population appreciated the
efforts of Broderick in condemning the discriminatory legis-
lation. A biographer of Broderick wrote:

> Broderick's opposition to the law reflected his own Irish
> immigrant background and his conviction that all groups in
> California's population were entitled to full participation and
> equal rights. He expressed his concern for the rights of the

---

[56]Roy Franklin Nichols, *The Democratic Machine, 1850–1854*, 17-18.

foreign-born repeatedly; and Californios, Mexicans, French, Negro, German, and Irish residents of California came to look upon him as a friend and ally.[57]

The Californio delegation gave Broderick its unqualified support throughout three days of balloting.[58] The election for senator was won by the Chivalry candidate, John B. Weller, on the tenth ballot.[59] Although Weller was placed in opposition to Broderick, he was not the leader of the Chivalry. The other U. S. senator, William M. Gwin, a native of Tennessee, was chief of the Chivalry faction and the true adversary of Broderick in the contest for political dominance in California.

Within a few days after Broderick's defeat, Andrés joined the Democratic party. On February 26, 1852, he attended a state Democratic convention in Sacramento held to elect delegates to the national convention in Baltimore.[60] Andrés was honored by an appointment as vice president to his first convention in gratitude for bringing the Los Angeles Mexican vote into the fold. His friend José María Covarrubias was stunned by his own election as one of the four delegates from California to the national convention. He tried to make a stammering acceptance speech in Spanish with the substance of his comments translated to the members. Since the convention was controlled by the Chivalry, the delegates to Baltimore were instructed to vote for nominees who were "neither Free Soilers nor Abolitionists." One Chivalry member advocated the introduction of slavery to California and disgustingly declared that he would never bring his wife to California "until it was a Nigger state." According to the *San*

---

[57]David A. Williams, *David C. Broderick: A Political Portrait*, 32-33.

[58]During a marathon series of ballots on January 29, 1852, which did not end until 3:00 A.M. the next day, Pico, De la Guerra, Del Valle, and Covarrubias held fast for Broderick. *San Francisco Herald*, Jan. 30, 1852.

[59]Ibid., Jan. 31, 1852.

[60]Ibid., Feb. 26, 1852.

Francisco Herald, "Immense cheering followed the annuncia-
tion".[61]

There was another Democratic convention in Benicia on
July 20, 1852, which the Free Soilers attended in force. Its
purpose was to choose presidential electors. Broderick nominated Andrés Pico for one of four electors. After several ballots, Andrés emerged in the group of winners.[62] Broderick
intended to favor Andrés as part of an effort to woo him into
the Free Soil faction. During the presidential campaign, the
names of the electors were printed on every ballot and in
every newspaper throughout the state. They were held out as
leading figures at political functions and rallies. It was a sig-
nal honor. Significantly, one of the alternate electors behind
Andrés was another Democrat from Los Angeles, a young
lawyer named Joseph Lancaster Brent.

Brent was an ardent promoter of the Chivalry. Born in
Maryland, he was a Roman Catholic of great personal mag-
netism who made a successful effort to learn fluent Spanish.
Because of his charm, Catholic religion, and willingness to
communicate with the natives on their own terms, he soon
had a thriving law practice. Shortly after arriving in Los
Angeles during 1851, he rented rooms for his office from
Ignacio del Valle, the old friend of Andrés, across from the
adobe "Palacio" of Abel Stearns on Main Street. Much later
in life, Brent wrote:

> I was in my twenty-third year when I opened my law office in
> Los Angeles. I was a perfect stranger in the town, and the
> tongue of nine-tenths of people was Spanish, which I could not
> speak. But in a very short time, owing to necessity and constant
> practice, aided by my acquaintance with French and especially
> Latin, I began to talk with Spanish clients and was, among other
> things, able to discuss the question of fees with precision.[63]

---

[61]Ibid., Feb. 27, 1852.

[62]Ibid., July 23, 1852.

[63]Joseph Lancaster Brent, *The Lugo Case, A Personal Experience*, 6.

One of his first advertisements appeared in the *Los Angeles Star* on August 23, 1851, in Spanish. It seems strange that Brent could have learned the language so quickly, but correspondence in his own handwriting confirms a surprising mastery of it.[64] Brent's account of a visit by some Californios vividly depicts the nature of his clients and the wealth brought by the northern cattle market to Los Angeles:

> It was interesting to see the superb and rich appearance of these opulent rancheros, as the owners of estates stocked with cattle were called. With saddles heavily plated with silver, rich jackets and trousers trimmed with silver bullets or buttons, mangas or riding cloaks fringed with heavy gold bullion, fine horses, as pretty as Arabians; and swords attached to the saddles and not to the person, they made a strange group as they rode up and stopped at my office door.[65]

Under the tutelage of Brent, during the latter part of 1852, Andrés spent much of his time campaigning for Franklin Pierce, the Democratic candidate he was pledged to vote for as a presidential elector. The Los Angeles correspondent of the *Alta California* advised:

> Politics has reached what might be properly termed a white heat ... Don Andreas [*sic*] Pico is devoting his energies to the Democratic ticket; and what with the great and little fry electioneers, there is no danger of any person coming unbidden to the great election feast of Nov. 2d, 1852.[66]

Pierce carried California by a good margin. The Chivalry had the two U. S. senators from California, Gwin and

---

[64]Brent wrote a letter from Baltimore after the Civil War to his Los Angeles compadre, Ignacio del Valle, in Spanish. Although he said that after so many years away from California "I find it difficult to express myself in Spanish," he nevertheless wrote a quite credible letter in the language. He even spoke of philosophical matters, a trip to Europe, and his deepening Catholic faith. Joseph Lancaster Brent to Ignacio del Valle, Feb. 27, 1868, Del Valle Collection.

[65]Brent, *The Lugo Case*, 10.

[66]*Alta California*, Nov. 1, 1852.

Weller, as their leaders. The Free Soiler, Broderick, had lost to Weller earlier in the year and his political career was floundering. Brent persuaded Andrés that his future lay with the Chivalry. A strong inducement offered to Andrés by Brent was the position of receiver of public money in the Los Angeles Federal Land Office.

On March 31, 1851, Congress passed a law which required landowners in California holding claims under Mexican grants to prove the validity of their titles before a three-man commission no later than March 31, 1856. There was concern by the federal government that some land grants had been issued illegally by Mexican authorities or that certain alleged owners had no title at all. The law required proof that a land grant had been properly made under Mexican law. The U.S. Land Commission held the bulk of the hearings in San Francisco. If it was determined that a grant was valid under Mexican law, the United States government issued a document called a patent which confirmed the validity of the title. If not, the owner was stripped of the property which reverted to the public domain. The burden of proof was solely on the owner.

The Federal Land Office in Los Angeles was to sell Southern California land acquired by the government from those whose Mexican claims were rejected. Two positions were created to administer the land office: a register to dispose of the property and a receiver to safeguard funds taken in from its sale. Both positions were political plums controlled by the Chivalry leader, Senator Gwin, since President Pierce let his higher ranking elected supporters handle local patronage.[67] The appointment as receiver was a reward to Andrés for joining the Chivalry. Brent was close to Gwin and often spent time with the Gwin family when he was in San

---

[67]Nichols, *The Democratic Machine*, 190.

Francisco. The young lawyer had become the leading political force in Los Angeles which was full of southerners of the most rabid Chivalry persuasion.

Andrés accepted his appointment as receiver during the early part of May 1853. At about the same time, Pío was elected as a Los Angeles city councilman.[68] Both of the brothers had made substantial adaptations to the new society in which they found themselves. Of the two, Andrés was the most active, but he found himself in a ridiculous position. He had joined a faction of the Democratic party that relentlessly advocated the slavery of blacks, a people who significantly contributed to his own ancestry. Andrés could not have been unaware of his family background. He must have experienced occasional discomfort or even trauma in dealing with Americans who were hypersensitive to racial differences.

The register appointed to serve with Andrés resented his place in the Land Office on racial grounds. He was Hilliard P. Dorsey, an ill-tempered, thirty-one-year-old Chivalry member from Georgia, who wrote in a report to his superior in Washington, D.C., "I hope you will extend to me all the favor in your power; as you know I have a Spaniard with me and I cannot do as I otherwise would."[69] On September 7, 1858, Dorsey was shot to death in El Monte by his father-in-law, William Rubottom, over a dispute concerning Dorsey's cruel treatment of his wife. Rubottom, popularly known as "Uncle Billy," was a restaurateur and innkeeper for many years near Rancho Cucamonga and later at Spadra. He was not charged with the killing of Dorsey on the ground that it was justifiable homicide.[70] Dorsey had been a founding

---

[68] *Los Angeles Star*, May 7, 1853.

[69] Hilliard P. Dorsey to Commissioner John Wilson, General Land Office, Washington, D. C., July 10, 1853, Records Group 49, Bureau of Land Management Records, Los Angeles District Office, Records of the Register, National Archives, Laguna Niguel.

[70] *Los Angeles Star*, Sept. 11, 1858.

member of the local Masonic Lodge and his portrait still hangs in Lodge Number 1 on Main Street in Los Angeles today.

During the four-year term of President Pierce, Andrés retained his position at the Land Office, drawing pay and doing virtually nothing. He was a delegate to most of the county and state Democratic conventions, always as a member of the Chivalry in support of Brent. The estate of Andrés at San Fernando was the scene of many social events with political overtones. Brent was a frequent visitor who enjoyed the revelry of a good Mexican fiesta. However, Pío did not hold with the Chivalry position of his brother and Brent. Pío seems to have rejected Brent's company, as well as his politics. In matters of legal business, Pío used Brent sparingly. He usually retained other lawyers even though Andrés had several cases pending before the Land Commission which were handled by Brent.

During the presidential campaign of 1856, Pío supported John C. Frémont as a Free Soil candidate on the Republican ticket.[71] Several editions of *El Clamor Público* that year contained a message from Pío, who urged the election of Frémont. Pío's announcement had a list of other Republican sympathizers who joined him in supporting Frémont, including John Forster. At about this time, Pío and Abel Stearns took part in a Republican convention in Los Angeles which nominated John Forster as a candidate for assembly. Pío himself was nominated for the office of county supervisor.[72] Forster and Pío collaborated in an easy way at this time on political matters.

Candidates supported by the Democratic Chivalry won the elections for national office during November 1856 in Los Angeles. Nevertheless, the Republicans made a good

[71] *El Clamor Público*, Oct. 4, 1856.
[72] Ibid., Oct. 25, 1856.

showing for Frémont, largely because of Pío's efforts. The Democratic presidential nominee, James Buchanan, got 722 votes and Frémont took 522 votes for the Republicans.[73] As usual, the Chivalry swept the elections for local offices. Although his time as the receiver for the Land Office had ended, Andrés chose not to be a candidate for any political position. The Pico brothers were then leading members of opposing political parties. Of the two brothers, Pío was in the most comfortable position. As an opponent of the Chivalry slavery party, Pío's beliefs were in accord with his own nature and personal background. Any discomfort Andrés may have experienced from his bizarre selection of political company was not shared by his brother.

---

[73]Ibid., Nov. 9, 1856.

CHAPTER FOUR

Debts, Bandits, and Decline

The year 1856 foreshadowed major problems for rancheros in Southern California, which especially affected the Picos. The cattle market in San Francisco declined to the point where prices dropped to sixteen dollars a head. Competition from new ranches in Northern California and Nevada began to undercut the Southern California "cow counties." Even ranchers from as far away as the Missouri frontier and Texas contributed to a glut of the San Francisco market.[1] This was not predicted by the Californio rancheros, who naively assumed that the fabulous prices caused by the mining boom would last indefinitely. Most of them, including the Picos, lived beyond their means even during times when money was plentiful.

Apart from operating their properties at the Ranchito and San Fernando in a profligate, semifeudal style, the Pico brothers enjoyed all forms of gambling, particularly horse races. On October 20, 1852, Andrés took time out from his duties campaigning for the Democratic presidential nominee, Franklin Pierce, to wager $15,000 in cash and cattle on a horse which lost by two yards.[2] A few weeks before he had lost another $1,000 on a similar race.[3] Roughly speaking, one dollar in 1852 had the same purchasing power as seventeen

[1]Cleland, *Cattle on a Thousand Hills*, 109-10.
[2]*Los Angeles Star*, Oct. 23, 1852. *Alta California*, Nov. 1, 1852.
[3]*Los Angeles Star*, Sept. 18, 1852.

dollars in 1991.[4] Therefore, the $15,000 and $1,000 lost wagers made by Andrés would be somewhat equivalent in the 1990s to $255,000 and $17,000, respectively. This staggering waste of money was not unusual for the Pico brothers. In the same year, Pío raced his famous horse Sarco against Black Swan, owned by José Sepúlveda, and lost. Over $50,000 in money, land, and cattle was wagered by those who backed Pío's horse.[5] A substantial part of the losses were suffered by Pío. This $50,000 would approximate $850,000 in 1991 money.[6]

At this time, coffee was twenty-four cents a pound on the San Francisco market.[7] Hotels in Los Angeles charged nine dollars per week for room and board.[8] The cost for a drink of "high grade liquor" at the Montgomery House, the finest saloon in Los Angeles, was "invariably twenty-five cents."[9] Local wines could be had for fifteen cents a gallon![10] At these prices, the Picos were the equivalent of modern multi-millionaires, but their money was dissipated as soon as they received it.

Accordingly, at the first inevitable decline of cattle prices, the Picos were suddenly short of cash. Their response was to borrow money from more cautious persons, often Anglo-Saxons, like Abel Stearns or Benjamin Davis Wilson. As early as 1855, Pío empowered Andrés to take a loan for $25,000 from Píoche and Bayerque, money lenders in San Francisco, which was secured by a mortgage on the Rancho Santa Margarita. These loans, whether from "friends" or San

---

[4]John J. McCusker, "How Much Is That in Real Money? A Historical Price Index for Use as a Deflator of Money Values in the Economy of the United States," 328-32.

[5]Newmark, *Sixty Years*, 160-61. Cleland, *Cattle On a Thousand Hills*, 88.

[6]McCusker, "How Much Is That in Real Money?" 328.

[7]*Los Angeles Star*, Oct. 23, 1852.

[8]Ibid., Nov. 6, 1852. The Arkansas Hotel, a second-rate establishment, placed an advertisement for three meals a day and a room for nine dollars per week. Breakfast or lunch was fifty cents to the public. Dinner was seventy-five cents.

[9]Newmark, *Sixty Years*, 32.   [10]Ibid., 134.

Francisco lenders, had devastatingly high interest rates. Typically, it cost an incredible 3 percent interest a month, compounded monthly, to borrow money.[11] The Pico brothers began to implement their own destruction by borrowing large sums of money at interest rates so high that repayment was impossible. They made no attempt to reduce the grand scale on which they lived. Instead, they entered into a series of ever-increasing obligations that would haunt them the rest of their lives.

During 1857, the financial difficulties of the Picos were only beginning, and their debts were still relatively manageable. Financial concerns were overridden early in that year when an excitement arose which propelled Andrés into great popularity and gave him another fling at gringo politics. It began when a letter arrived in Los Angeles to Sheriff James R. Barton stating that some robbers headed by two outlaws named Juan Flores and Pancho Daniel had the village of San Juan Capistrano under siege. Barton set out with five men to investigate.

The next day, Sheriff Barton and his men were ambushed north of San Juan Capistrano, about where the San Diego

---

[11]Cleland, *Cattle On a Thousand Hills*, 111-16. The causes of such high interest rates in early California have never been adequately explained. Cleland, one of California's greatest historians, particularly of nineteenth-century economic affairs, found no apparent reason for lenders charging, and borrowers accepting, such outrageous rates of interest. He wrote:

> The extraordinarily high interest rates, which more than any other factor brought about the ruin of the landowners of the old regime, constitute an economic phenomenon difficult to understand. For twenty years loans of all kinds, irrespective of the security behind them, paid interest charges of the most fantastic character. Such rates were not limited to Southern California; borrowers everywhere, whether miners, merchants, shippers, or ranchers, paid substantially the same exorbitant charges and gave the same excessive hostages to fortune for the loans.

Cleland considered such possible causes as uncertain land titles, the absence of money, the lack of a banking system, and the instability of California in its formative period. But Cleland remained perplexed. He wrote, " . . . one still finds no rational explanation for a compound interest rate that frequently ran as high as ten percent a month and persisted for nearly twenty years."

Freeway and Laguna Freeway now meet. Barton and a pair of his men were killed in a running gun fight.[12] The surviving two members of the posse escaped to Los Angeles where news of the popular sheriff's death caused general hysteria in the American element. Harris Newmark said that when word of Barton's death reached Los Angeles, "the frenzy was indescribable."[13] This exaggerated response arose from fears generated by an incident during the previous summer when Deputy U.S. Marshal William Jenkins senselessly shot and killed a harmless Mexican named Antonio Ruiz. On that occasion, an armed force of Mexicans had attacked the plaza in Los Angeles with a view toward lynching Jenkins to avenge Ruiz. However, after an inconclusive nighttime foray into the plaza, the Mexicans retired into the surrounding hills where they remained a menacing presence for several days.[14]

Andrés Pico took the part of the Americans against the uprising in Los Angeles and scoured the countryside in search of its leaders. He managed to arrest Ferdinand Carriega, one of the organizers of the attack on the plaza.[15] The whole incident left the badly outnumbered Americans with fears of a general race war. For several months afterward, stories of hostile Mexican rebels operating just outside the pueblo circulated among the American residents. The *Los Angeles Star* reported many violent crimes allegedly committed by a mysterious group of Mexicans lurking somewhere nearby.[16] The nervous Americans in Los Angeles believed

---

[12]*Los Angeles Star*, Jan. 31, 1857.

[13]Newmark, *Sixty Years*, p. 207.

[14]*El Clamor Público*, July 26, 1856.

[15]Ibid., Aug. 2, 1856. Lawrence E. Guillow, "Pandemonium in the Plaza: The First Los Angeles Riot, July 22, 1856," 183-94.

[16]*Los Angeles Star*, Jan. 17, 1857. This edition, after several months of publishing news of accelerated incidents of crime by Mexicans, reported:

During the week we have had a repetition of crimes and outrages, which are sufficient to show that an organized band of ruffians are located in the neighborhood, and which, to be exterminated, must be acted against by a combination among the

that the bandits in San Juan Capistrano were part of an organized resumption of hostilities against them by a larger, more
determined force. Rumors flew of a veritable army of Mexicans approaching Los Angeles from the south to pillage and
kill.[17]

In the midst of utmost anxiety by the Americans in Los
Angeles, Andrés led nineteen Californios southward, all
armed with lances. At the Ranchito he met with Pío and got
some more men. After several other stops, he commanded a
company of fifty-one.[18] The willingness of Andrés to defend
the Americans from a hostile force of his own people calmed
the situation immeasurably. There was a great outpouring of
affection and gratitude toward him by the Americans,
accompanied by a lessening of racial tension.

Andrés, of course, was in his element. He was happiest at
the head of a column of armed men in the field. On their
arrival at San Juan Capistrano, the Californios found that the
outlaws had already fled. The residents told them there was
no army of Mexican rebels. The town had been looted by ten
young men and a teenage boy who killed a storekeeper
named George Pflugardt and ambushed Barton's posse. Don
Juan Forster and at least seven other men barricaded themselves in the mission until the arrival of Andrés guaranteed
their safety. Forster was ready to sally forth when the outlaws
were present, according to an account by one of the men
holed up with Forster, but "He heeded our wishes and most

citizens generally . . . This subject has been repeatedly pressed upon the attention of
our community—a great deal of talking has been done as one outrage after another
has been committed. But beyond that not a single step has been taken to protect the
community from those outrages which are almost of nightly occurrence—and from
their boldness, truly alarming.

On the same date, the Spanish language newspaper, *El Clamor Público*, agreed: "There
is no doubt that an organized band of evil-doers exists in this city. Our situation is truly
alarming . . ."

[17]Newmark, *Sixty Years*, 205.
[18]*Los Angeles Star*, Feb. 7, 1857.

particularly the supplications of his own wife and several other families that had rushed into his home for protection."[19]

The next day a company of Americans from El Monte arrived at San Juan and the two forces conferred. The suggestions of Andrés were accepted as a plan of action.[20] Indian scouts sent by Andrés located the outlaws in the Santa Ana Mountains northeast of San Juan where they were attacked by the joint force. The Americans captured Juan Flores and Pancho Daniel while the Californios made prisoners of Juan Silvas and a horse thief known as "El Ardillero." That night, Flores and Daniel escaped from a sleeping American guard. When Andrés learned of this the next morning, he became enraged and immediately hanged his two prisoners from a nearby sycamore.[21] It was alleged by some that Andrés cut the ears off the dead men to prove he had executed them.[22]

Flores was soon recaptured and taken to Los Angeles where he was hanged in an agonizing, horribly botched public execution.[23] It took eleven days for the Californio and American vigilantes to round up their quarry, most of whom were summarily dispatched by hanging in Los Angeles. Pancho Daniel was able to hide for almost a year before he too was arrested. He stayed in the Los Angeles jail nearly another year before a lynch mob became frustrated with the failure of the court to expedite his case. In the early morning hours of November 30, 1858, he was found strung up over the gate of the jail yard with a stool lying where it had been kicked out from under him.[24]

---

[19]Michael Kraszewski, quoted in Hallan-Gibson, *Two Hundred Years*, 49.

[20]*Los Angeles Star*, Feb. 7, 1857.   [21]*El Clamor Público*, Feb. 7, 1857.

[22]Ibid., March 21, 1857.

[23]*Los Angeles Star*, Feb. 21, 1857. Since the rope was too short, Flores did not fall far enough to break his neck. While slowly suffocating, the cords around his arms loosened, allowing him to grasp the noose. His hands were finally pried away, and he remained suspended in agony. The *Star* reported: "After a protracted struggle, very painful to behold, the limbs became quiet and finally stiff in death."

[24]Ibid., Dec. 4, 1858.

Andrés Pico, in full ranchero
regalia, at the height of his
political power, about 1858.
*Courtesy, Seaver Center for Western
History Research, Los Angeles County
Museum.*

Andrés returned to a relieved, exultant Los Angeles that
accorded him the honors of a conquering hero. The *Los
Angeles Star* gushed:

> Where all have been anxious to discharge their duty faith-
> fully and well, it would be invidious to mention names, but
> the exertions of the California company under Don Andrés
> Pico, are the theme of all tongues. Laboring under many dis-
> advantages, besides but hardly armed, they bravely set out on
> the arduous duty and well and nobly have they accomplished
> it. They have earned for themselves the respect and admira-
> tion of the whole community. It is pleasant to find that the
> only emulation among the Californian and American citi-
> zen, is who can act for, and defend, their common country.
> Thus may it ever be.[25]

The earlier American fears of a race war were assuaged not
only by the revelation of the true strength of the Flores band,
but also by the comfort of a Californio leader on their side.
True, a Spanish newspaper, *El Clamor Público*, groused that

---

[25]Ibid., Feb. 7, 1857.

"El Ardillero" did nothing wrong. He joined the gang only after it had already committed its crimes and therefore Andrés hanged an innocent man.[26] But few people cared about a known horse thief, not even *El Clamor Público*. The general mood was one of goodwill, forgiveness, and a desire to reward Andrés.

Six months after Juan Flores was hanged, the Democratic county convention, overwhelmingly Chivalry, met during August 1857 and nominated Andrés once again as an assemblyman to the state legislature.[27] Francisco P. Ramirez, the brilliant young Republican editor of *El Clamor Público*, approved of the candidacy in an editorial alluding to the capture of the outlaws:

> Don Andrés Pico, who so agreeably distinguished himself last winter, has taken the platform as a Democratic candidate for the Assembly. We have no doubt of the good intentions of Mr. Pico for his country and compatriots, and therefore we will make no more opposition to him than the public should do when it rewards him for services rendered to the people.[28]

In September, Andrés easily won election to the assembly. It was his third term in six years. The other assemblyman from Los Angeles was Henry Hancock.[29]

While Andrés was sitting as a member of the legislature during March 1858, Governor John B. Weller gave him a commission as brigadier general in the state militia.[30] From

---

[26]*El Clamor Público*, Feb. 21, 1857, reported that José Jesus Espinosa, a boy seventeen or eighteen years of age, was captured in San Buenaventura and hung for his part in the killing of Sheriff Barton as a member of the Flores gang. Before his execution, he confessed to a priest, Domingo Serrano, that El Ardillero was not present when Pflugardt, Sheriff Barton, or any of his deputies were shot. Espinosa said that in about a month the outlaws had managed to rob $120, steal ten horses, and kill five people. His confession was reduced to writing by the priest. In his final moments, the young man placed an "X" on the document, not knowing how to write his name.

[27]*Los Angeles Star*, Aug. 22, 1857.   [28]*El Clamor Público*, Aug. 22, 1857.

[29]*Los Angeles Star*, Sept. 5, 1857.   [30]Ibid., April 3, 1858.

that time forward, Andrés was seldom referred to in the press or in private without reference to his military rank. Henry Hamilton, editor of the *Los Angeles Star*, a diehard, Negro-hating Chivalry Democrat, constantly printed favorable comments about Andrés's role in the legislature, disregarding the racial background of his Chivalry colleague. For example, on January 27, 1858, the *Star*'s correspondent in Sacramento wrote some laudatory blurb, distorting historical fact:

> There is a peculiar pleasure in seeing the early sons of California in the halls of the Legislature of the state, more particularly those who fought so bold and bravely for the soil of their birth, who like Andrés Pico, never surrendered even to overpowering numbers.[31]

As long as Andrés remained loyal to the Chivalry, he would have good press in the *Los Angeles Star*. According to Henry Hamilton's correspondent from Sacramento, referring to Andrés on March 20, 1858, "he looks out sharp for the interests of his Spanish constituents and generally carries his point."[32]

Both Andrés and Hancock were elected again to serve in the 1859 legislative session. They were deeply involved in the most dominant issue of the session, a resolution for the separation of Southern California from the rest of the state at a point near San Luis Obispo. The new political entity was to be called "The Territory of Colorado."[33] It was the culmination of longstanding resentment toward the populous north, which dominated the legislature because it exempted northern mining interests from taxation but imposed onerous taxes on the agricultural south.[34]

Although Hancock created the resolution, Andrés was put

---

[31]Ibid., Jan. 27, 1858.
[32]Ibid., March 20, 1858.
[33]Ibid., Feb. 12, 1859.
[34]Cleland, *Cattle On a Thousand Hills*, 124.

forward as its proponent in the legislature. The resolution was easily passed by both houses. The vast majority of the population in the north cared nothing about losing the empty southern "cow counties." The resolution was later referred to a popular vote and was overwhelmingly approved. It was then forwarded to the U.S. Congress for acceptance. Congress received the petition to divide California with great distaste. It was the eve of the Civil War and certain states of the American South were seriously contending that they had a right to secede from the Union. The majority in Congress did not want to create a precedent for Southern arguments by splitting California into separate political units, one of which would be part of a state demoted to the status of a territory. Accordingly, the California resolution was ignored by a hostile national Congress.[35]

Drafting the resolution to divide California was well beyond the ability of Andrés. He barely had a broken command of English and was only semi-literate in Spanish. The complexities of the language in the resolution required that it be written by others, principally Henry Hancock. But Andrés was an effective advocate of its passage in the legislature. For example, Eugene Lies, an assemblyman from Santa Barbara, reported in a letter to Pablo de la Guerra that he had a drink with Andrés Pico and was persuaded to support his separation move.[36] It was even rumored that Andrés aspired to be the governor of the new territory. Several newspapers published a list of the names of those he intended to appoint to high office if he succeeded.[37]

During the 1859 legislative session, Andrés became reacquainted with his former enemy, Archibald Gillespie, who had provoked the rebellion of Los Angeles in 1846, and who

---

[35]Ibid., 125.

[36]Eugene Lies to Pablo de la Guerra, Jan. 27, 1859, De la Guerra Collection.

[37]*El Clamor Público*, Oct. 22, 1859.

was nearly killed at San Pascual. Gillespie sought employment as an assistant engrossing clerk and was unexpectedly helped by Andrés, who had forgiven him. It was reported in the San Francisco press that, "General Pico, who had put forward the name of Major Gillespie for the position, arose, and in his native tongue—which was translated to the House by Mr. Lies—made a brilliant and telling little speech in favor of his man."[38] As a result, Gillespie was chosen by a unanimous vote. Richard Henry Dana, author of the famous book, *Two Years Before the Mast*, was in Sacramento on a world tour at that time. During a visit to the legislature, he met Gillespie and reported their conversation in his journal:

> Met Major Gillespie who was in active work here in the war of 1846–47, commanding at Los Angeles. He was besieged there and capitulated, but with honors of war. He was present at the action of San Pascual, where Don Andrés Pico, with 70 men, defeated General Kearney with several hundreds, and at several other actions where Pico distinguished himself. He says Pico was as brave as a lion and the soul of honor.[39]

It is difficult to say how far Gillespie's assessment of Andrés and his exaggeration of the numbers of Americans he faced at San Pascual were influenced by gratitude.

When Andrés returned to Los Angeles during May 1859, "He was most cordially greeted by his many ardent friends in this city."[40] But he found a major problem was developing that would remove his political base in the Chivalry and cause him to shift his position toward that of his brother Pío and his brother-in-law John Forster, both staunch Republicans. Andrés discovered that Los Angeles was in revolt against the Chivalry controlled by Joseph Lancaster Brent. It

---

[38] *Los Angeles Star*, Feb. 26, 1859, reprinted from the *San Francisco National*, Feb. 16, 1859.

[39] *The Journal of Richard Henry Dana*, edited by Robert F. Lucid, 3: 921.

[40] *Southern Vineyard*, May 27, 1859.

began in earnest on June 8, 1859, during a Democratic county convention at the courthouse held to select delegates to the
state convention. A group led by John G. Downey claimed to
have twenty-three elected members whereas Brent's Chivalry group had only seventeen.[41] Downey headed the "Douglas
Democrats," who were opposed to the admission of Kansas
as a slave state under the Lecompton Constitution, despite
the support of President James Buchanan.

The entire United States divided over this issue, making it
the most hotly debated question of the day. On a national
level, the contest raged between President Buchanan and
Senator Stephen A. Douglas of Illinois. In California, Senator William M. Gwin, leader of the Chivalry, opposed Senator David C. Broderick, champion of the Free Soil
Democrats. The passionate controversy was carried out in
Los Angeles between spokesmen for the Chivalry such as E.
J. C. Kewen on one side and J. J. Warner on the other.[42] The
two disputing factions of the Democratic party in Los Angeles held separate county conventions and each elected their
own delegates to the state convention in Sacramento.[43] The
delegation sent by John G. Downey's group was accepted by
the Democratic convention. Brent's Chivalry delegation was
shut out completely.[44] Nevertheless, Andrés remained
attached to Brent and continued as a participant in the
Chivalry wing.

On September 7, 1859, Andrés was elected as a state sena-
tor for a two-year term representing Los Angeles, San
Bernardino, and San Diego counties.[45] One week later, on
September 13, 1859, Senator David C. Broderick was killed
in a duel near San Francisco by a Chivalry fanatic, David S.
Terry, at that time chief justice of the California Supreme

---

[41]*Los Angeles Star*, June 11, 1859.
[42]John Robinson, *Los Angeles in Civil War Days, 1860–65*, 31.
[43]*Los Angeles Star*, June 18, 1859.   [44]Ibid., July 9, 1859.
[45]Ibid., Sept. 10, 1859.

Court. The shattering news may have affected Andrés, but
he continued with the Chivalry. As late as August 1860, he
was chairman of a committee in Los Angeles to nominate
Chivalry Democrats to another state convention in Sacramento.[46]

Together with his old friend, Pablo de la Guerra, who was
also in the senate representing Santa Barbara, Andrés was
going through a political metamorphosis. The unified
national Democratic party was completely dead. The
Chivalry had nominated its own presidential candidate, John
C. Breckenridge of Kentucky, and the Free Soil Democrats
had nominated Stephen A. Douglas of Illinois.

Andrés observed that the legislature of 1860 contained a
majority of members opposed to the Chivalry. Newly elected
members were either Republicans or "Douglas Democrats"
adamantly in favor of the Union and opposed to slavery. In
the coming war between the states, most Californians were
lining up in favor of the North. While wandering through the
legislative chambers and saloons of Sacramento, Andrés
heard of little but the ascendancy of the Republican party and
the rewards to be had for joining it. Senator Gwin, chief of
the Chivalry, had no chance of re-election. The political
influence of Joseph Lancaster Brent, Andrés's Los Angeles
Chivalry mentor, was falling with the fortunes of Gwin.
Andrés, whose initial conversion to the Chivalry was based
on ambition, never embraced it because of heartfelt princi-
ples. In view of the Republican surge to power, it seemed
expedient to make a change.

Toward the end of 1860, Andrés abandoned the Chivalry
Democrats and made known his support for the Republican
presidential candidate, Abraham Lincoln. On November 12,
1860, Alfred Robinson, an old California pioneer who was
solidly Republican, wrote to his brother-in-law, Pablo de la

---

[46]Ibid., Aug. 25, 1860.

Guerra, concerning Lincoln's election. Demonstrating the widespread knowledge of Andrés's defection from the Chivalry, he wrote, "I see Don Andrés is finally on the right side of the fence."[47]

During the second year of his term as state senator in 1861, the onset of the Civil War and his change of politics altered the direction of Andrés's political career. Just a little less than two months before the beginning of the Civil War, he sent a letter from Sacramento to Enrique Avila in Los Angeles which expressed his new-found Republican sentiments. Written in his nearly illegible scrawl, it is difficult to decipher but seems to state the following when translated into English:

> From the Atlantic news it is clear that the Union is at risk of disintegrating, and if this happens we will have a civil war. It is important that we work for the Union. You and our friends in combination can prepare our Paisanos so that they will not be deceived [by the Secessionists]. You know I will make any sacrifice to help them. Tell them it is necessary to think of our country. Have them write to me, their letters are a consolation.[48]

After the outbreak of the Civil War at Fort Sumter, South Carolina, on April 12, 1861, the loyalties of those in California could not remain untested. Although the great majority in Northern California firmly supported the Union, the southern part of the state contained a large disaffected population of Confederate sympathizers. Los Angeles was rightfully considered a secessionist town by San Francisco's federal authorities. U.S. Army units were dispatched to Los Angeles to patrol the streets in case manifestations of Confederate support turned to armed insurrection. Many Chivalry members in Southern California eluded efforts to

[47] Alfred Robinson to Pablo de la Guerra, Nov. 12, 1860, De la Guerra Collection.

[48] Andrés Pico to Enrique Avila, Feb. 16, 1861, Del Valle Collection.

prevent them from leaving for Texas, where they enlisted in the Confederate army. A secret society known as the Knights of the Golden Circle was formed in Los Angeles and San Bernardino. It was composed of secessionists whose goal was to undermine Union authority and even strike a blow for the Confederacy if the opportunity arose. Many Southerners proposed that California break away from the Union to form a "Pacific Republic," which would remain aloof from the war between the states and which might even be later induced to support the South directly.[49]

In light of the pronounced Confederate sentiment in Los Angeles, it was deemed desirable for federal authorities to ascertain the extent of Union loyalty among the large Mexican element in the city. Union support by native Californios from Southern California would be a useful counterpoint to the secessionist immigrants from the American South. One federal official, Edward F. Beale, the U.S. surveyor general, undertook to verify the degree of Union loyalty held by the Pico brothers, two of the most prominent leaders of the Mexican population. Beale sent a letter to Andrés Pico on June 6, 1861, in which he effusively praised the role of Andrés as a political leader and concluded by saying, "I desire, then, to know if you are in favor of maintaining the present Federal Government of the United States at all hazards, or if you favor, under any circumstances a Pacific Republic, and the secession of this State."

Beale requested a response from both Pico brothers to his inquiry. An eloquent reply to Beale's letter was immediately sent by Andrés. Prepared in English by someone on his behalf, it contained a complete disavowal of the Chivalry and

---

[49]See generally, Robinson, *Los Angeles in Civil War Days*. The history of Los Angeles during the Civil War is superbly covered by Robinson in this book. It is one of the finest works ever written on a defined period of Los Angeles history. Unfortunately, it was issued in a limited edition of only three hundred copies and without an index or bibliography. This beautiful book deserves another printing and a proper publication.

a rebuke to the Confederacy: "Although my political opinions, as previously expressed, have differed from those of the
Republican Party, these considerations cease in the face of
the attack made against the Federal Government, and
unconditionally and at all hazards I am for the Constitution
and for the Union entire, to maintain which I would cheer-
fully offer, as a soldier, my sword, and as a citizen, my fortune."

Although the Republican allegiance of Pío Pico had long
been known throughout California, he nevertheless replied
to Beale, strongly reaffirming his pro-Union position: "My
acts, and vote placed in the ballot box, in favor of the worthy
President of the United States, are faithful testimonials to my
political opinions; to them I have now to add, that although I
lament the disturbances occasioned by the Southern states, I
approve the energetic measures adopted by the Government,
for the preservation, at all costs, of the Constitution and the
Union entire." Beale's letter to Andrés and the replies of the
Pico brothers were published in the San Francisco and Los
Angeles press.[50] After a decade of membership in radically
different political parties, the Pico brothers had at last reconciled their views. Both were now on the same side and dili-
gently working on behalf of the Republican party.

In October 1861 Joseph Lancaster Brent, accompanying
Senator Gwin, left California by ship from San Francisco.
Gwin eventually ended up in France at the court of Emperor
Louis Napoleon, advocating support for the Confederate
cause. He was afterwards in Mexico City promoting a min-
ing venture in Sonora. Brent made his way into Southern ter-
ritory and joined the Confederate Army. His parting from
Andrés is not recorded, but there was probably bitterness on
Brent's part over the apostasy of Andrés. John W. Shore, the
city clerk of Los Angeles, wrote a letter to Brent in 1865,

---

[50]*Alta California*, June 8, 1861; *Los Angeles Star*, June 15, 1861.

congratulating him on surviving the war and giving him an update on the fate of his old political enemies. Pío and Andrés were included on the list.[51] Brent rose to the rank of brigadier general with the Confederate army and later settled in Maryland and Louisiana. He never returned to California after the war. A little girl born on April 8, 1860, was adopted by Andrés and given the name of Catalina, in compliment to his common-law wife. There is some evidence that this girl, who later married Rómulo Pico, was the illegitimate daughter of Brent.[52]

In April 1862 the new Republican governor of California, Leland Stanford, replaced all general officers of the state militia appointed by his predecessors.[53] In this way, Andrés lost command of the First Military District, comprising almost all of Southern California. In a transparent attempt to place himself in the good graces of the Republicans, Andrés offered Stanford his personal services and a force of six hundred volunteers to suppress an Indian uprising in the Owens River Valley.[54] This tactic had always worked when Andrés wanted to ingratiate himself with the Americans, but Stanford rejected the offer. The state militia, in which Andrés no longer had a command, was sent instead. As a last minute convert from the odious Chivalry to the Republican party, Andrés joined too late to be trusted or rewarded.

The federal government was less squeamish about the uncertain politics of Andrés. Brigadier General George

---

[51]John W. Shore to Joseph Lancaster Brent, June 9, 1865, Brent Collection.

[52]Catalina Pico was raised by Andrés Pico. There is a photograph of her at the Seaver Center for Western History Research, Los Angeles County Museum of Natural History, depicting her as a twelve-year-old girl. On the back side is an old inscription which reads: "Catalina Pico, daughter of General Joseph Lancaster Brent." When she died, on January 29, 1925, her death certificate stated the name of her father as "Brent." Los Angeles County Bureau of Vital Statistics, Hall of Records. Her obituary identified her as "the daughter of Gen. Brent and was married to Rómulo Pico, son of Gen. Andrés Pico . . ." *Los Angeles Times*, Feb. 1, 1925.

[53]*Los Angeles Star*, April 12, 1862.

[54]*The Semi-Weekly Southern News*, April 25, 1862

Wright at the U. S. Army headquarters in San Francisco desired him as the commanding officer of a cavalry unit for use against the Confederates. On December 19, 1862, he wrote the War Department in Washington, D.C., "I request authority to raise four Companies of native cavalry in the Los Angeles District, to be commanded by a patriotic gentleman, Don Andreas [*sic*] Pico."[55] Andrés declined the command, probably because of illness.

In September 1863 Andrés ran for sheriff of Los Angeles County against his old friend and military subordinate Tomás Sanchez. It is likely that Andrés wanted the office because it was extremely well paid. At this point, his financial situation was critical. However, Andrés miscalculated the strength of Southern support in his home town. Los Angeles remained a Chivalry stronghold which would not forgive Andrés's treachery in abandoning the party. Sanchez remained a stalwart of the Chivalry throughout the Civil War. He beat Andrés by 1,007 to 665 votes.[56]

Slowly, the prospects of further public office faded. Andrés made various efforts to secure some kind of position from the Republican leadership but was always rebuffed. One ardent Chivalry member wrote on November 1, 1864, about the opposition of Andrés to the Chivalry and his search for an appointment with the Lincoln administration:

> The native vote seems united in our favor. I do not hear of but two men of standing going against us—Don Andrés Pico and Fernando Sepulveda. What a falling off in our friend Andrés—he hankers for the fleshpots of Abraham.[57]

---

[55]Brig. Gen. Richard H. Orton, *Records of California Men in the War of the Rebellion*, 304.

[56]*Los Angeles Star*, Sept. 12, 1863.

[57]John S. Griffin to Cave Couts, Nov. 1, 1864, Couts Collection.

CHAPTER FIVE

A Mysterious Transaction

The failure of Andrés to place himself within the Republican circle was not his greatest concern. After leaving the state senate following the 1861 session, financial problems were his main preoccupation. It has already been seen that the collapse of the San Francisco cattle market in 1856 did not diminish the spending of the Picos, and both had loans at such high rates of interest they could not pay them. Moreover, as generous, loyal friends of the ranchero elite, they had co-signed or guaranteed loans for other people.[1]

The first major attack by creditors occurred in early 1862. In that year, a writ of execution was used to seize all the cattle on the Rancho San Fernando owned by Andrés. As a result, he lost his status as a rancher. No more than ten head were left. These remaining few were not taken only because they were overlooked.[2] With the cattle gone, the next move of Andrés's creditors would be to seize his real property.

---

[1]Pío Pico guaranteed the loan of Lemuel Carpenter who lost his land through foreclosure and committed suicide. This is one instance of Pío standing good for the debts of his friends. He resisted a lawsuit against him by the creditors of Carpenter, even to the point of taking an appeal to the California Supreme Court, which he lost. See, *McFarland vs. Pico,* 8 California Reports 626 (Oct. 1857).

[2]Apparently no record exists of the lawsuit against Andrés Pico that gave rise to the seizure of his cattle. However, after his brother's death, Pío Pico filed suit against Rómulo Pico, the reputed son of Andrés, claiming the right to take three hundred head of cattle off the Rancho San Fernando which were the increase of the original ten head that escaped the judicial roundup. Gerónimo López, an adjacent landowner, testified that he witnessed the removal of Andrés's livestock in 1862 by court order. A sworn affidavit by Deputy U.S. Marshal William Jenkins was presented, which stated that he had been the officer responsible for taking the cattle away in obedience to the demands of judgment creditors. See *Pío Pico vs. Rómulo Pico,* Case No. 3292, filed Nov. 25, 1878, Los Angeles Superior Court Archives.

On May 21, 1862, in utmost desperation, Andrés conveyed all his land in California to his brother Pío. The transfer included everything, even Rancho San Fernando and
one-half of the great Rancho Santa Margarita.[3] It was
intended that Pío's ownership would at least temporarily
thwart Andrés's personal creditors.

It seems the brothers contemplated that Pío would return
legal ownership to Andrés when the threat of foreclosure was
past. Although circumstances never permitted this, Andrés
continued to operate his former holdings as if he were still
the owner. Pío later testified that he was merely a trustee for
his brother. Clearly, the men intended that someday their
accounts would be squared and their property put back on a
separate legal footing. In the meantime, Pío recognized
Andrés's entitlement, however informal, to share in the management and profits of the property they had consolidated
under Pío's ownership. This understanding is reflected in the
conduct of Andrés. He worked hard to promote Pío's interests without regard for his own lack of legal title. As we shall
see, both men frequently held themselves out as if they were
partners in a joint enterprise.

After taking the properties of his brother, Pío was forced
to add Andrés's obligations to his already crushing financial
burdens. At this time he was barely solvent. His precarious
financial condition was revealed in a letter written to John
Forster on June 27, 1861, when he was in San Francisco to
visit the moneylenders, Píoche and Bayerque. He went there
to seek an extension of time to pay the loan contracted in
1855 and to request additional sums to placate those to
whom he owed money. Apparently, Pío had represented to

---

[3]A copy of the deed from Andrés Pico to Pío Pico transferring the Rancho San Fernando and the rest of the properties of Andrés is found in *Andrés Pico vs. Arnot Durant*, Case
No. 985, filed Dec. 8, 1863, Los Angeles Superior Court Archives. In addition, copies of
documents showing the entire chain of title for Andrés's ownership of the Rancho San Fernando dating from 1844 are contained in this file.

various of his Los Angeles creditors that they would be paid on his return. Pío wrote:

> After a month's delay, waiting day to day for a favorable determination from the lending firm, not until yesterday was I able to have a conference with the gentlemen ... The result of the interview was that they would not receive cattle in payment of the mortgage, nor could they advance more money to raise the mortgage on the Ranchito.
>
> I do not know what road to take or how to present myself in Los Angeles. It looks like the time is approaching now for my last misfortune.[4]

The situation was so grave that Pío did not even have enough cash to pay his personal expenses in San Francisco. He mentioned a lucky encounter with Robert Ashcroft in a postscript to the same letter:

> Don Roberto paid me $360 on account of the cattle he bought. Had it not been for this, today I should be without a cent for my expenses for which I return thanks.

Being without money in San Francisco could have been a uniquely depressing experience for Pío. Not many men have been broke, even temporarily, in the greatest city of a land they once governed.

Pío returned to Los Angeles emptyhanded but was able to improvise a temporary solution to his immediate debt problems. Despite his narrowing prospects, somehow Pío juggled old creditors and new lenders adroitly enough to survive. The loan from Pioche and Bayerque was a constant problem, one he hoped Forster could solve. Pío wanted Forster to take the Rancho Santa Margarita in his own name and pay off the mortgage. The first evidence of this desire appears in another letter to Forster written by Pío from San Francisco on October 16, 1861:

---

[4]Pío Pico to John Forster, June 27, 1861, plaintiff's exhibit x-1. *Forster v. Pico.*

I believe it necessary that you should come here to secure to you the Santa Margarita. It appears that Messers Píoche & Bayerque have a purchaser and they wish to sell and they exact from me to state for how much the sale can be made . . . I believe that with your presence I may obtain another year's time and secure the interest at one percent [per month] which is the present rate upon the principal and your being here I will do whatever you tell me to do so that you will be secured.[5]

Forster did not respond to this letter by going to San Francisco. He was not inclined to rescue his brother-in-law just then. The comments of Pío to Forster manifested his inability to cope with his debts and stated what became a recurring proposition to Forster. After 1861 the Pico brothers continuously urged Forster to take the Rancho Santa Margarita and assume the mortgage.

During 1862 and 1863, Pío lived unhappily on the edge of bankruptcy. The liabilities of Andrés together with his own improvidence and outstanding debts were drowning him. The situation became even more intolerable through a calamity imposed by nature. During late 1861 and early 1862, a tremendous rain flooded Southern California which was followed by two years of the worst drought ever recorded. Practically no rain fell during the winter of 1863. In February of that year, a correspondent to Abel Stearns wrote:

> We have had no rain yet, there is no grass and the cattle are very poor; your Rancho men report a great many dying. Should we have no rain your cattle buyers will get nothing but hides and bones.[6]

The devastation of the drought continued unabated during 1864. A miserable spell of hot weather occurred unseasonably during the winter which aggravated the lack of rainfall. On January 23, 1864, the *Los Angeles Star* lamented, "The weather is now unusually warm, assuming in the day

---

[5]Pío Pico to John Forster, Oct. 16, 1861, plaintiff's exhibit x-21. *Forster v. Pico.*
[6]C. R. Johnson to Abel Stearns, Feb. 6, 1863, Stearns Collection.

time a temperature almost that of summer heat, withering every remnant of vegetation and leaving not a green spot on the whole plain." The same edition of the newspaper reported the horrible effects of the drought on the ranches:

> It is truly melancholy to learn of the great amount of cattle, that have died lately, on different ranches throughout the county. It is admitted, that on some, one-half the stock have perished from hunger and there is great apprehension that many more will yet be lost, if a favorable rain should not shortly come. In passing over the plains, it is sad to see the number of dead cattle, while those that survive, present an appearance, such as to produce sympathy for the suffering of the dumb animals. Many of them appear like skeletons, and seem unable to move far from the springs and water courses, from which they receive nearly all that prolongs life.[7]

It was impossible to drive the dying herds northward. The cattle trade ceased to exist along with the income that it produced. Southern California rancheros could not pay taxes or reduce the loans they owed. Gradually the local press began to publish ever-longer lists of those whose properties were being seized for delinquent taxes or sold through foreclosure.[8] The despair of those involved in the drought was compounded by an epidemic of smallpox that wiped out entire families. Guards were posted at some ranches to prevent the entry of strangers who might spread the disease. In Los Angeles the tolling of church bells was discontinued since deaths were so frequent that they would otherwise never stop ringing.[9] It was the blackest period of Southern Calfornia history, a nightmare of drought and death almost without relief.

In the midst of this crisis, just when the Picos were most vulnerable, Píoche and Bayerque began a campaign for payment of the 1855 loan owed by Pío and Andrés secured by a mortgage on the Rancho Santa Margarita. By early 1864,

---

[7] *Los Angeles Star*, Jan. 23, 1864.
[8] Cleland, *Cattle On a Thousand Hills*, 136.
[9] Ibid., 132.

even with a negotiated reduction of interest, the amount owing had soared from $25,000 to over $42,000. This was the largest indebtedness of the complicated mass of obligations that swamped the Picos. It was also the most dangerous. If the mortgage on the Rancho Santa Margarita were foreclosed, the land might be sold by Píoche and Bayerque for much less than the amount due. The balance still owed could be collected by selling other properties of the Picos, bringing them to utter ruin. This was the dreaded "deficiency judgment" of the last century, now seldom used in the foreclosure of California real property mortgages.[10]

For several years, Pío had done his best to get John Forster to take the Rancho Santa Margarita, but Forster steadfastly refused to give Pío the relief he requested. Despite the appeals of Andrés and Pío, Forster would not take on the huge burden the mortgage represented. Pío even paid persons who were friends of Forster to approach him with the proposition that he take over the mortgage. None were able to induce Forster to accept responsibility for the debt. Then, at the height of the drought, on February 25, 1864, Forster suddenly relented and agreed to do so.[11]

At some point during that day, Pío signed a deed transferring the entire Rancho Santa Margarita to Forster. Pío later said he intended to give Forster only one-half of the ranch even though his brother-in-law was to assume the whole mortgage. Pío believed the ranch was worth far more than what was owed to Píoche and Bayerque.

Andrés made all the arrangements with Forster. The con-

---

[10]In his testimony, Forster mentioned a possible deficiency judgment as one of the sources of the Picos' anxiety about the unpaid mortgage. The legal system at the time would have permitted it. See, B. E. Witkin, *Summary of California Law, Ninth Edition,* 3: 676. Gordon Morris Bakken, *The Development of Law in Frontier California,* 53.

[11]The account of the bargain between the Picos and Forster in this chapter is based on a synopsis of their testimony at trial. A more complete treatment of their testimony is set forth in Chapters 8 and 9, *post.*

tract, according to Andrés, was that the one-half he had given to Pío in 1862 would be transferred to Forster in exchange for paying off the mortgage. If the amount owed was more than one-half of the value of the ranch, Forster was secured by giving him 1,500 head of cattle and 150 horses as compensation for the difference. Andrés told Pío of the contract he had made so that Pío would be prepared to execute the required documents when Forster brought them.

According to the Picos, on February 25, 1864, Forster went to the Ranchito with a deed prepared under his direction by a notary public in Los Angeles named Ozias Morgan and had Pío sign it. At the same time, Pío also signed a bill of sale giving Forster 1,500 head of cattle and 150 horses from the brands owned by the Pico brothers on the Rancho Santa Margarita just as Andrés told him to do.

The three men had known each other for over thirty years. The Picos accepted Forster as a family member and reposed trust in him. Pío was Forster's godfather and had given him a fortune in land when he was governor. The men enjoyed strong personal ties and a confidential relationship. Therefore, the discovery that Pío had signed a deed for the whole ranch was cause for unspeakable anguish and rage. Forster knew very well that Pío was unable to read English and would rely entirely on Forster's judgment in signing the deed. Pío signed it without question, not even bothering to look at the English hieroglyphics it contained. When the deed was recorded by Forster, the fraud was complete.

Of course, Forster had a different perspective on the events of February 25, 1864. He asserted that his motives in taking ownership of the Rancho Santa Margarita were purely based on compassion. The Picos were aware that a foreclosure by Píoche and Bayerque on the ranch could lead to other properties being seized with a deficiency judgment. Moreover, the feared foreclosure was just about to happen. They urged

Forster for years to take the property and finally, "as an act of desperation," he took title to the property and accepted liability for the mortgage to help the Picos. The price Forster paid for the property was terrible. No one else would have paid it but him, and then only to rescue his brothers in-law.

Forster denied that the deed was signed at the Ranchito, as the Picos claimed. He said the deed was signed at Pío's townhouse on the plaza in Los Angeles on a sunny afternoon. Andrés obtained the services of the notary public, Ozias Morgan. Forster, Andrés, Pío, and Morgan all conferred on the proposed content of the deed at Pío's house. The substance of the deed was read to Pío, who approved it and signed in the presence of Morgan, who officially notarized it. Forster claimed that Morgan had a "most confidential relationship" with the Picos, and they instructed him in the matter. Thus, the stage was set for the conflict between Forster and the Picos.

A search for the truth of what happened between these men is confounded at the threshold by their odd behavior. A notable example is the fact that Forster resisted every attempt to persuade him to assume the debt owed to Pioche and Bayerque for several years, but inexplicably took the ranch and the debt at the worst possible moment during the dark economic abyss of the drought. For this reason, one historian wrote that Forster took the debt, "At great risk to his own solvency . . . "[12] If this were true, then it seems he was acting against his own interest in order to favor the Picos. This would provide Forster with a powerful argument against Pío's claims of fraud. Yet Forster never squarely confronted the accusations of the Picos despite numerous opportunities to do so. He spent years avoiding all attempts to elicit an explanation of why he had a deed to the whole ranch. Forster's conduct both before and during the trial did nothing to clarify the arrangement he made concerning the Rancho Santa Margarita. The

---

[12]Cleland, *Cattle On a Thousand Hills*, 113.

Picos were equally culpable of strange behavior. Neither of the Pico brothers was ever able to give a detailed, coherent explanation of their contract with Forster.

Contemporary public records relating to the Rancho Santa Margarita do not diminish the mystery of the transaction. For example, the Picos were required to prove the validity of their Mexican grant to the ranch before the U.S. Land Commission in San Francisco. The records of those proceedings show that their Mexican claim was confirmed on April 24, 1855. The decision was upheld by the U.S. District Court in 1864 and the U.S. Supreme Court in 1866. Since the proceedings originated long before 1864, there is no reference to John Forster as an owner of the Rancho Santa Margarita, much less an indication of how he took an interest in the land.[13]

Forster immediately moved his family to the old adobe ranch house on the Santa Margarita after taking the deed from Pío. He drove large numbers of cattle to the mountains where they had a better chance to survive the drought. By December 1864, a little over nine months after he moved onto the property, the drought broke. Forster began to bring his cattle down from the mountains in the area of Julian and Santa Ysabel. He wrote to Cave Couts:

> I fully appreciate our late glorious rain and the many times you drank my health last Sunday. The country generally is beginning to change its usual color...Ocampus says no snow had fallen when he left Santa Ysabel and there was one continuous string of cattle on the road returning home, but still I should like to be ahead of any amount of snow on the mountains in moving away.[14]

The relief brought by the rains of late 1864 and early 1865

---

[13]U.S. Land Commission, Case No. 388, "Rancho Santa Margarita," Spanish-Mexican Private Land Grants Records-California, National Archives, Laguna Niguel. The U.S. Supreme Court upheld the Land Commission decision in the case of *U.S. v. Pico*, (1866) 72 U.S. Supreme Court Reports 695.

[14]John Forster to Cave Couts, Dec. 2, 1864, Couts Collection.

A serene John Forster
about 1860, when he was a
prosperous rancher in San
Juan Capistrano.
*Courtesy, Thomas Anthony "Tony"
Forster Private Collection, San
Juan Capistrano.*

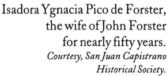

Isadora Ygnacia Pico de Forster,
the wife of John Forster
for nearly fifty years.
*Courtesy, San Juan Capistrano
Historical Society.*

was so great that the price of cattle increased to as much as twenty dollars a head and could be driven to market.[15] None of the cattle given to Forster by the Picos had died, so he could have sold the 1,500 head for as much as $30,000—a substantial credit to be applied to the mortgage.[16]

One of the adjustments made by Forster to his new surroundings on the Rancho Santa Margarita was that he

---

[15] John Forster to Cave Couts, March 31, 1865, Couts Collection.

[16] At trial, Forster admitted that none of the cattle he was given by the Pico brothers died during the drought.

formed a very close friendship with Cave Couts, the owner of the Rancho Guajome, who lived only seven miles away. The two men had known each other for several years and corresponded during Forster's residence at San Juan Capistrano. When Forster moved to the Rancho Santa Margarita, it was only natural that these two men would find much in common. Both were married to Californio women and operated their ranches in an isolated, Spanish-speaking world to which each had well adapted and even mastered.

Cave Couts was born on November 11, 1821, near Springfield, Tennessee.[17] His uncle, Cave Johnson, the postmaster general in the administration of President James K. Polk, arranged an appointment for Couts to West Point. In 1843 Couts graduated as a second lieutenant and began a military career which brought him to California in 1848. He wrote a journal during his trip to California which contained a number of original drawings that have been reproduced in many books and publications.[18] While still serving in the army, Couts married Ysidora Bandini of San Diego on April 5, 1851. She was the daughter of Juan Bandini, a famous and wealthy man of Mexican California. Couts resigned his army commission during October 1851, then served as a county judge in San Diego for two years.

Shortly after leaving the army, Couts was appointed to the California State Militia with the rank of colonel, a military title which he retained the rest of his life.[19] In 1852 his wife's brother-in-law, Abel Stearns, presented the Rancho Guajome to Ysidora Couts as a wedding present. Although the

[17]The data on Couts's life set out in this chapter is from Iris Wilson Engstrand and Thomas L. Sharf, "Rancho Guajome: A California Legacy Preserved," 1-14, and John Steven McGroarty, *Los Angeles From the Mountains to the Sea*, 3: 894-897.

[18]See one version of Couts's journal printed as *Hepah, California*.

[19]Couts's appointment as a colonel was part of Governor John Bigler's efforts to strengthen the state militia. At the same time, Andrés Pico and Jack Watson were also appointed to that rank. Judson A. Grenier, *California Legacy*, 74.

Cave Couts
*Courtesy, Security Pacific
Collection, Los Angeles Public
Library.*

ranch was small by the standards of the time, Cave Couts used the 2,219 acres to good advantage. He employed a force of three hundred Indians to build an immense twenty-room adobe house he designed himself. It was constructed in rectangular form with an inner courtyard in which were planted citrus trees and flowers. This house was owned by the Couts family until 1972, when it was transferred to San Diego County. It is now within a semi-rural county park in the city of Vista, a superb example of a Mexican-style adobe residence of the period.[20]

The ranch established by Couts at Guajome had barns, stables, corrals, and even a chapel where mass was said by a resident priest. Everything was planned and built by Couts. The whole enterprise was like a feudal manor. Couts, who was known as "Don Cuevas" by the Mexicans, kept a staff of cowboys, domestic servants, carpenters, blacksmiths, and

---

[20]The Rancho Guajome adobe is located at 2210 North Santa Fe Avenue, Vista, California.

general laborers who were mainly Indians. Eventually he consolidated about twenty thousand acres in and around the Rancho Guajome. It was an almost entirely self-sufficient estate. Judge Benjamin I. Hayes often visited the Rancho Guajome while travelling his judicial circuit and recorded his admiration of it in his diaries.[21] There was almost nothing that Couts did not grow, raise, or make for himself.

Perhaps because of his West Point training, Couts placed his correspondence and personal documents into orderly files which he retained throughout his lifetime. This mass of documents is now the Couts Collection at the Huntington Library, a rich source of information about daily life in Southern California at the time.[22] Among his records are his official acts as an Indian sub-agent and justice of the peace, positions which did not interfere with his residence at Rancho Guajome. He was an ardent partisan of the Chivalry, a political orientation consistent with his upbringing in Tennessee. As a result, much of the correspondence he kept alludes to political affairs in which he had an interest.

Couts had an unfortunate propensity to commit acts of violence that caused him great personal difficulties. This undesirable behavior may have been caused by excessive drinking, a problem that afflicted him most of his life and which could have contributed to his early death. In 1855 he was indicted by a San Diego grand jury twice for separate instances of whipping Indians to death. One victim was only

---

[21]On January 18, 1860, Hayes wrote in his diary, "This rancho [is] the abode of industry, elegance, and hospitality . . . Col. C. almost lives within himself." *Pioneer Notes From the Diaries of Judge Benjamin Hayes*, 202.

[22]Although Couts retained most of the voluminous correspondence Forster sent him over the years, there are few examples of letters from Couts to Forster. At the trial, Forster testified that he usually threw away letters he received, an unfortunate habit confirmed by the paucity of correspondence in Forster's personal documents preserved by his great-great-grandson Thomas Anthony "Tony" Forster of San Juan Capistrano. These documents were recently donated to the Huntington Library.

a boy, the other a male adult named Halbani.[23] Couts attained a dismissal of charges against him in both proceedings by improbable technical defenses. On February 6, 1865, Couts shot and killed a Mexican named Juan Mendoza in the Plaza at San Diego for having allegedly threatened Couts and his family.[24] The method employed was to wait in ambush. When the victim passed, Couts discharged a double-barrelled shotgun in his back. In 1870 Couts shot and critically wounded a young man named Waldemar Muller at Rancho Guajome.[25] Muller had been hired as a tutor for Couts's numerous children. Couts was not seriously prosecuted for his crimes against Mendoza or Muller and no conviction resulted in either case.

Despite the legal problems Couts created for himself through his drinking and violence, Forster became like a brother to him. The two men were continuously in communication. Forster settled into life on the Rancho Santa Margarita by expanding the ranch house and creating a courtyard somewhat similar, although on a smaller scale, to what Couts had designed for himself at Rancho Guajome.[26] The gardens and orchards on the Rancho Santa Margarita were improved and maintained to Forster's standards. New corrals and fencing were built. An extensive and costly system of roads was begun. At popular fiestas such as weddings and baptisms, Forster and Couts played at being lords of their manors. Forster once sent a note to Couts inviting his family to a baptism followed by a fiesta to be attended by his employees and ranch hands. An old Mexican custom, still observed, is for

[23]Richard F. Pourade, *The Silver Dons*, 211

[24]*Alta California*, Feb. 20, 1865.

[25]Susan Sullivan, "James McCoy: Lawman and Legislator," 46-47.

[26]Robert M. Witty, *Marines of the Margarita*, 46. Witty states: "The Rancho House was in such a dilapidated state when Forster moved his family there that he spent $30,000 in improvements. Still using adobe, he extended the L shape structure into a square with an inner patio and at least eighteen rooms."

the godparents at a baptism to toss money called the *bolo* to the celebrants, especially children. In those days, adult Indians and lesser ranch folk were not above joining in. For this reason, in the true aristocratic ranchero manner, Forster asked Couts to bring some extra coins "for the rabble."[27]

---

[27]John Forster to Cave Couts, Jan. 6, 1867, Couts Collection.

The Santa Margarita ranch house in 1882, from the southwest.
Courtesy, California Historical Society, Ticor Collection, University of Southern California Libraries.

The Santa Margarita ranch house from the east, in 1900.
Courtesy, San Juan Capistrano Historical Society.

CHAPTER SIX

The Pursuit of John Forster

Pío Pico's nephew José María Pico had been his *mayordomo* on the Santa Margarita before Forster acquired his interest. José María continued acting as such for years after Forster occupied the property. The presence of a mayordomo for Pío on the Santa Margarita would have been a singular fact if Forster had actually purchased the entire ranch. A mayordomo was appointed by the owner and held a position of great trust. At the trial, Pío Pico gave an accurate description of the office:

> My mayordomo is the person who represents my interests at the rancho and is subject only to the proprietor as owner of the ranch. His business is to take care of the cattle and do whatever is demanded, to deliver or sell cattle when he is commanded, and he arranges the labors.[1]

---

[1] *Forster v Pico*, WPA, 1: 39. This quote is taken from an unpublished typewritten transcription of the testimony of all witnesses who appeared in the trial. It was prepared in 1936 by the Works Progress Administration. A comparison of the actual court reporter's handwritten record of testimony in the file of *Forster v Pico* in the Archives of the San Diego Historical Society shows that the WPA version is accurate and infinitely more legible. The typewritten transcription is divided into four "volumes." They are contained in two separate book covers, each of which contains two "volumes." The outside book covers identify them as "Forster v Pico, Orange County Series." The interior covers state, "Works Progress Administration, Orange County Historical Project, #3105, Santa Ana, Calif. 1936." The complete set can be found at the Santa Ana Public Library, where they were copied by the author. Other copies are purportedly at the Anaheim Public Library and the University of California at Irvine. The smaller book, containing "volumes" three and four, is in the Honnold Library Special Collections, the Claremont Colleges. The transcription is extensively quoted in Chapters 8 and 9 of this book, where it is referred to as "WPA" with the appropriate volume and page number.

Forster had his own mayordomo, Blas Aguilar, as well as his sons to help him on the Rancho Santa Margarita. He never claimed that José María was his employee or mayordomo. The anomalous situation of José María remaining as Pío's mayordomo after a sale to Forster is difficult to explain. Moreover, Pío spent considerable sums of money to maintain the ranch the whole time his mayordomo was there. José María kept a running account of Pío's expenses.[2]

There seems to have been six to eight *vaqueros*—cowboys—in the service of Pío from the time of Forster's deed down to the time of the trial in 1873. They earned about $15 per month each, a total of $90 to $120, plus board. José María took another $30 as his wages so that monthly labor costs alone were about $120 to $150 at all times. The records show that supplying these men with rough country provisions—beans, corn meal, sugar, flour, coffee, potatoes, chiles, and the like, as well as a gallon or two of *aguardiente* and some tobacco thrown in—cost another $150 or so per month. José María also incurred costs for tools, nails, wood, and sundry hardware items that were used for improvements on the ranch. Pío seldom spent less than $400 a month for ranch expenses. In a typical year, say 1869, this would amount to roughly $4,000 in 1991 money.[3]

It could be said that Pío kept a mayordomo and a crew of vaqueros on the ranch simply to care for the cattle he left behind after the sale. If there was no evidence of involvement by Pío in the affairs of the Santa Margarita beyond raising cattle, we might conclude that Forster, as a friend and family member, allowed Pío the use of the ranch for that purpose, nothing more. However, there is abundant evidence that Pío retained his mayordomo and vaqueros on the place because he thought that he remained a one-half owner after signing

[2]Ledgers of José María Pico, defendant's exhibit PP 17. *Forster v. Pico*.
[3]McCusker, "How Much Is That in Real Money?" 328.

Forster's deed. For example, the correspondence of Pío to his mayordomo, José María, and others, demonstrates behavior one would expect of a man who believed he had not given up all his rights of ownership.

Two days short of the anniversary of his deed to Forster—well after the Forster family moved onto the ranch—Pío sent a letter to José María giving directions for the use of the land. At the time of the letter, which was dated February 23, 1865, Pío's brother-in-law José Joaquin Ortega was living on the Santa Margarita in the main ranch house. Ortega had been supervising the maintenance of an orchard and garden near the ranch house for a long time but intended to vacate the premises. Pío wrote to José María, saying:

> Tell my brother-in-law that if he goes away to give you the orchard so that you can take care of it. Also tell him that if it is convenient, to let you have the outside room when he vacates the house.[4]

Ortega saw the note addressed to José María. He wrote to Pío within a few days with some remarkable comments:

> I am ready to deliver to José María the room as you direct in your letter, but not the orchard. My compadre Don Juan Forster has taken possession of it, politely but in a silent manner, not having said a single word to me that he was going to take possession of it. I say that he has taken possession of it because he has pruned it, he is replacing vines, and has planted new trees and is plowing. I believed that he was doing all of this with your consent, but now that I have seen your note to José María, I believe I was mistaken.[5]

José María was also concerned about the fact that Forster had taken possession of the orchard. He sent Pío a request for instructions:

---

[4]Pío Pico to José María Pico, Feb. 23, 1865, defendant's exhibit PP 43. *Forster v. Pico.*

[5]José Joaquin Ortega to Pío Pico, Feb. 27, 1865, defendant's exhibit PP 15. *Forster v. Pico.*

I received your letter in which you say that my uncle
Joaquin is to deliver to me the orchard and the outside room.
As to the orchard, you already know that Don Juan has taken
possession of it and his servants have been working in it for
some time. Tell me what to do in this matter.[6]

Pío must have told his family members that he retained an
ownership interest in the ranch despite Forster's presence.
Clearly, they believed Pío had the power to make decisions
concerning the land itself, which in this case had been "in a
silent manner" frustrated by Forster.

There is no evidence that Pío protested the action of
Forster in taking over the orchard, but he continued to assert
control over the property. In response to a request by José
María to take some millstones off the ranch, Pío wrote him a
letter on July 12, 1865, in which he stated:

Whenever you wish, you can take the millstones,
whichever ones you choose. Notify whoever may be in the
house or Don Juan when you see him that you have taken the
millstones. If you wish, show him this letter.[7]

By acceding to his nephew's request, Pío showed a belief
that he had a right to deal with ranch property. In Pío's mind,
the ownership had been split with a separate delegation of
authority by each owner to his personal mayordomo. José
María did not represent Forster; otherwise, he would not
have had to ask Pico for the millstones and later notify
Forster of it.

There is no suggestion in the correspondence between Pío
and José María that the business they conducted on the Santa
Margarita was merely transitional or temporary. On February 12, 1866, José María sent Pío a letter in which he refused
to continue as mayordomo, even at an increased salary, unless
he was also "given annually, 100 calves and 10 colts at the

---

[6]José María Pico to Pío Pico, March 27, 1865, defendant's exhibit PP 14. *Forster v. Pico.*
[7]Pío Pico to José María Pico, July 12, 1865, defendant's exhibit PP 44. *Forster v. Pico.*

branding time."[8] As a young man, José María desired to build his own herd for the future. His proposal was based on an assumption that his uncle Pío had ownership rights in the Santa Margarita which could benefit him each year. Pío responded to Jose María's request on February 14, 1866:

> As soon as I see your uncle Andrés I shall tell him of your request about remaining on the Santa Margarita. There is here an American who wishes to buy 1,000 steers but I wish to know what number there is of steers from 2 to 3 years old and if it is possible for you to let me know, more or less, so that I may show him your letter on the subject. If you should get this in time send me an answer by the next stage.
>
> P.S. You may consult with Don Juan Forster about the cattle, as he may with better information let me know the value according to the kind of cattle there may be.[9]

This letter is one of many suggesting that Andrés was involved in business affairs with Pío much like a partner. However, its most important aspect was Pío's desire to know how many head of cattle he had available to sell on the Santa Margarita. The "American" at the Ranchito who "wishes to buy 1,000 steers" was actually an Englishman named Robert Ashcroft. He was a cattle broker and an intimate friend of Forster's who later testified at the trial. In his correspondence, Pío invariably referred to Ashcroft as "Don Roberto."

Pío's communication to José María assumes that there would be no objection by Forster to Pío's driving 1,000 head of cattle away. He suggested that José María discuss the matter with Forster, "as he may with better information let me know the value according to the kind of cattle there may be." Apparently, Pío felt that no consent by Forster was required. If he was only a half owner, Forster could not challenge Pío's

---

8 José María Pico to Pío Pico, Feb. 12, 1866, defendant's exhibit PP 32. *Forster v. Pico.*
9 Pío Pico to José María Pico, Feb. 14, 1866, defendant's exhibit PP 45. *Forster v. Pico.*

right to move about on the property and sell cattle of his own brand.

After adding the Santa Margarita to his other properties, Forster continued his frequent trips to San Francisco by steamer to contract for the sale of cattle. As usual, he kept Cave Couts constantly informed, especially about cattle prices. On February 22, 1865, he wrote to Couts, "Chico is at Las Flores with Ashcroft gathering yearlings for shipment per steamer . . . I expect they will bring $25 per head.[10] A week later, on March 2, 1865, he wrote Couts from Los Angeles saying that cattle from the Simi rancho was being driven overland to San Francisco at twenty-eight dollars a head.[11] The horror of the drought the year before when cattle were worth about two and a half dollars for their hides had ended. Raising cattle was becoming profitable again.

On November 2, 1866, Pío concluded his agreement with Ashcroft for the sale of cattle on the Santa Margarita. The number of cattle sold was increased from one thousand to two thousand at about eighteen to twenty dollars a head. On that date Pío wrote to José María:

> On the 31st of last October I sold the bearer of this, Don Roberto, two thousand (2,000) head of cattle of Santa Margarita which is under your care . . . In order to avoid any conflict with the purchasers, I send you this notice, hoping you will in all things act in accordance with my contract.[12]

As in most of his business dealings, it appears that Pío made the sale under great pressure from his creditors. He immediately left Los Angeles for San Francisco with the proceeds to pay them off. Forster approved of the sale. On November 11, 1866, he wrote to Couts:

> It appears that Ashcroft has paid $38,000 to Don Pío on

[10]John Forster to Cave Couts, Feb. 22, 1865, Couts Collection.
[11]John Forster to Cave Couts, March 2, 1865, Couts Collection.
[12]Pío Pico to José María Pico, Nov. 2, 1866, defendant's exhibit PP 49. *Forster v. Pico.*

account of 2,000 head of cattle. Don Pío has gone up to San Francisco with said funds to settle up. Bully for Ashcroft.[13]

Significantly, Forster did not make any objection or complaint in his letter to Couts about the transaction. None of Forster's correspondence questions the right of Pío to engage in business operations on the Santa Margarita. Certainly, if he had objections to any activities of Pío on the Santa Margarita, he would have stated them to his intimate compadre Couts.[14]

Pío made additional sales of livestock to Robert Ashcroft and others from the Santa Margarita. He ordered that rodeos be given on the ranch, a right exclusively reserved to the owner. On one such occasion, Pío wrote to José María from his plaza townhouse in Los Angeles:

Don Roberto has given me to understand that he desires to round up some calves for shipment to the market. According to the established custom, you will permit him to give a rodeo and take away the calves he desires.[15]

There could be no clearer statement that Pío still regarded himself as an owner of the Santa Margarita than that a rodeo be given by his order "according to the established custom . . ." By ancient tradition, passing directly to California from Spain and Mexico, no person except the owner of a ranch could order a rodeo. This rule and several other practical Mexican customs were adopted and adhered to by American ranchers as well.

In early California no fences divided ranches. Cattle from various owners would get mixed together on the same land. When a ranch owner called for a rodeo, he always invited his

---

[13]John Forster to Cave Couts, Nov. 11, 1865, Couts Collection.

[14]Forster often wrote to Couts about extremely personal matters. For example, in one letter, Forster assured Couts that his teenage daughter, Antonia Couts, was not pregnant after having run off with a vaquero. Antonia was subsequently banished to a Catholic girls' school in San Francisco for this scandalous escapade. John Forster to Cave Couts, April 7, 1868, Couts Collection. In light of Forster's willingness to commit such delicate subjects to writing, there is no reason to believe that Forster would have shrunk from complaints or criticism concerning the Picos in his letters to Couts if he thought he had good cause to do so.

[15]Pío Pico to José María Pico, March 7, 1867, defendant's exhibit PP 50. *Forster v. Pico.*

neighbors so their cattle could be sorted out and driven back home. An important incident of a rodeo was that the owner on whose ranch it was held was entitled to keep any cattle that could not be identified. These were usually weaned year-lings that wandered away from their mothers without a brand. Such cattle were known by their Spanish name, *ore-janos*. The right to claim orejanos was a benefit of land own-ership in early California. A major issue in the trial was whether Pío had claimed orejanos on the Rancho Santa Margarita after giving a deed to Forster. Nearly every witness was asked if Pío had taken orejanos. The question was not entirely settled, but certainly, Pío held rodeos and sold cattle for several years whenever he desired.

After Forster occupied the ranch, both he and Pío used the land for raising and selling cattle of their own brands. Each had a mayordomo and a crew of vaqueros, maintained at their own expense to care for their large herds and to conduct separate rodeos they ordered independently "according to the established custom." Neither man gave any sign of dissat-isfaction with the other. For a long time there was no hint of the bitter dispute to come.

Unfortunately, relations between Forster and Pío under-went a dramatic change in 1868. In that year, Alfred Beck Chapman, one of Pío's lawyers in Los Angeles with the firm of Glassell, Chapman and Smith, informed Pío that a deed recorded in San Diego showed that Forster was the sole owner of the Rancho Santa Margarita.[16] As a member of a firm representing Pío's legal interests, Chapman was no doubt disturbed by this discovery since it did not conform to his understanding of Pío's property ownership.

A few months later, Andrés Pico went to the San Diego

---

[16]Pío testified that Chapman advised him of Forster's deed to the entire ranch in 1868. Chapman did not testify at the trial so we do not know the degree of alarm he felt at the dis-covery. Since Chapman alerted Pío to Forster's claimed ownership at once, we may infer that Chapman felt some concern.

County Recorder's office with John Roberts, an attorney fluent in both Spanish and English, to investigate the deed. A copy was made out and read to Andrés in Spanish by Roberts. Andrés later said, "I was so astonished I went cold at what I had signed."[17] Although Pío had signed the deed and not Andrés, the emotion of Andrés was unmistakable. The deed clearly showed that John Forster, and no one else, was the owner of the entire Rancho Santa Margarita. Enraged, Andrés returned to Los Angeles to report this news to Pío.

Just at that time, Pío was negotiating with Isaac Lankershim for the sale of the Rancho San Fernando. As we know, Andrés owned the ranch prior to transferring it to Pío in 1862 to avoid foreclosing creditors. During July 1869 a sale of the property was made by Pío for $115,000. What part of this money, if any, was received by Andrés is unknown.

Pío's reaction to the discovery that Forster had not left him with a half interest in the Santa Margarita was to turn to Andrés to fix the problem. There was no time for Pío to deal with Forster at that moment. Although the sale of the former interest of Andrés in the Rancho San Fernando had brought Pío a cash bonanza, the San Francisco money lenders were in their usual advanced stage of collection procedures against him. He had to hurry north to pay off his most pressing debts. Some of the money realized from the sale of San Fernando was used to build the Pico House Hotel on the Plaza in Los Angeles. Pío laid plans for its construction while liquidating the San Fernando property, but this project was also left to Andrés.[18]

---

[17]This incident was related by Andrés in his testimony. He probably said in Spanish, "*Me quedé frío*"—roughly meaning, "I turned cold." It is one of the strongest expressions possible to convey astonishment in Mexican Spanish.

[18]During Pío's absence on his trip to New York, Andrés contracted for the construction of the Pico House at a total price of $32,585, payable in seven installments. He wrote a report to Pío which shows the nature of the progress payments and other contractual detail. See Andrés Pico to Pío Pico, Sept. 7, 1869, Del Valle Collection.

The magnificent twenty-two-room convento at Mission San Fernando,
the residence of Andrés Pico, about 1880.
Courtesy, California Historical Society, Ticor Collection, University of Southern California. Libraries.

After dealing with the press of creditors in San Francisco,
Pío did not return to Los Angeles. Instead, he unexpectedly
went to New York by the newly established transcontinental
railroad. Forster wryly commented on the situation to Couts
in a letter dated July 10, 1869, written while on one of his
constant cattle selling trips to San Francisco:

> Capt. Johnson and wife took a sudden notion and went to
> New York last Saturday. Your comadre and Don Pío went
> with them to Sacramento to see them off. She returned, not
> being in health for the trip but Don Pío was induced to go
> also to see the elephant at New York. Sudden impulses East-
> ward are now quite fashionable. Don Pío had only just com-
> pleted his sale of one-half San Fernando for $115,000
> receiving $65,000 first payment.[19]

---

[19]John Forster to Cave Couts, July 10, 1869, Couts Collection.

A few days later Forster wrote Couts, ". . . Don Pío telegraphed from Chicago and was pleased with his trip. Won't he be lionized at New York which will be pleasing to his vanity."[20]

On Forster's return from San Francisco, one hot afternoon during August 1869, Andrés met him on the veranda of the Lafayette Hotel in Los Angeles. Pío was still away on his trip to New York. Andrés approached Forster angrily, not recovered from the surprise contained in the deed to the Santa Margarita recorded in San Diego. At the trial later, Forster described this incident saying, "Don Andrés was hot, he wanted to fight." Both men agreed that "strong expression" and "hard words" were used between them.[21]

The confrontation must have been most unpleasant for Forster. Throughout his life he gave no signs of a capacity for violence. When threatened by some drunken U. S. Army deserters who invaded the home of a friend in Santa Ana, he fled for his life and hid in a nearby field.[22] On another occasion, in 1857, as we have seen, the bandit Juan Flores terrorized San Juan Capistrano with a small band of desperados while Forster barricaded himself in his home at the mission.

On the other hand, both as a military commander and private citizen, Andrés Pico was known to have a bellicose nature and hid from no one. As leader of the Mexican forces in the bloody melee at San Pasqual in 1846, he personally fought hand-to-hand in the defeat of General Kearney. It

---

[20]John Forster to Cave Couts, July 14, 1869, Couts Collection. Forster was probably wrong about Pío being "lionized at New York." No reference to Pío's visit can be found in the contemporary New York press.

[21]This incident marked a permanent rupture in good relations between Andrés and Forster. Their testimony nearly coincided on the details of the heated encounter, one of the few points on which they agreed during the trial.

[22]John Forster to Abel Stearns, dated only as "Friday 12 pm. Santa Ana. February 1852," Stearns Collection.

was Andrés who rescued Forster from the threat of Juan Flores in 1857 at the head of an improvised Mexican posse.

On an evening walk down Main Street near the Bella Union Hotel in Los Angeles with his friend Juan Sepúlveda in 1858, Andrés took offense at a young Mexican who he threw to the ground, struck repeatedly in the face with his fists, and savagely kicked in the head. The badly beaten young man's family was greatly distraught by the incident. Andrés was criticized for his conduct in the local Spanish press.[23] In 1866, when Andrés's authority to make decisions concerning the Rancho Santa Margarita was questioned by Cave Couts, Andrés rose up from a chair and seized Couts roughly by the lapels of his coat, almost coming to blows with him.[24] All of this was known by the more gentle Forster, who probably retreated from Andrés that day at the Lafayette Hotel.

We cannot know all of what was said between the men in the heat of the moment, but apparently Forster denied having purchased only one-half the Santa Margarita. He even claimed that he had not received the 1,500 head of cattle and 150 horses that Andrés considered part of their contract. On September 7, 1869, Andrés wrote to his nephew, José María, on the Santa Margarita from Los Angeles:

> The last time that Don Juan Forster was here, we had a difficulty and he told me that you had never delivered any cattle to him. If he denies this to me he will deny everything. I told him that if this cattle was credited to my account with him it was because you had given me his signed receipt for it and that perhaps you would not deceive me like him. I sincerely regret the unpleasantness with Don Juan but everyone will soon know the reasons for my conduct in the incident. I hope that you will not lose any writing or receipt that you

[23]*El Clamor Público*, Oct. 2, 1858.

[24]During the trial, several persons had knowledge of this incident. Robert Ashcroft testified he heard of it in Los Angeles, an indication of the wide comment it provoked.

may have [from Forster] because this case may get to a point where they will be needed.[25]

It is apparent from this letter that Andrés began collecting evidence of the agreement he made with Forster in 1864. He was already considering a lawsuit.

Following Pío's return to Los Angeles in late September 1869, Andrés attempted a negotiated settlement with Forster on the Santa Margarita question. According to his testimony in court, Andrés sought out and met Forster at San Juan Capistrano and later at the house of Abel Stearns in Los Angeles. Both times Forster avoided confronting him on one pretext or another. Frustrated in attempting to deal with the elusive Forster, on January 3, 1870, Andrés wrote him this letter:

> Dear Brother and Compadre: Desiring to have a definite understanding with you before taking another step, I want to know from you when I shall be able to have an interview with you in San Juan or in San Diego, whichever may be most convenient to you. I am impatient because my brother insists on something definite . . . Compadre and Brother, you may think it strange that I do not wish to go to your house to see you but nobody knows my character better than yourself. All will be resolved at our interview if the All Powerful concedes me this. Such is the desire of your compadre and brother.[26]

Andrés refused to go to Forster's home at the Santa Margarita to discuss the matter, perhaps not wishing to expose his sister to his conflict with her husband.

Since he received no reply to his letter, Andrés persuaded his old friend, Pablo de la Guerra, to attempt a settlement with Forster. The two men had a fruitless meeting on January

[25]Andrés Pico to José María Pico, Sept. 7, 1869, Pico Family File, San Diego Historical Society Archives. This letter is not among the exhibits filed in court and was therefore never considered at the trial. It is the most impressive document found in demonstrating the sincerity of Andrés' belief that Forster had betrayed him.

[26]Andrés Pico to John Forster, Jan. 3, 1870, defendant's exhibit PP 54. *Forster v. Pico.*

26, 1870. Forster resisted the intervention of De la Guerra even though he was one of the most influential men of his time. From an old Santa Barbara family, De la Guerra was an educated, refined man who spoke fluent English.[27] Among other distinctions, he had been a state senator from Santa Barbara and even president of the California State Senate during the administration of Governor John G. Downey.[28] At the time of his interview with Forster, he was the sole judge of the Seventeenth District Court in Los Angeles.[29]

The intransigence of Forster in the face of the distinguished Pablo de la Guerra caused Andrés to make one final effort to end the matter. On January 31 he wrote Forster a long letter which demanded an explanation of why Forster claimed the whole ranch:

> Dear Compadre: For reasons which you will not fail to know, I asked on the 26th inst., our mutual friend, Don Pablo de la Guerra, that he should see you in person in my name for the purpose of clearing up certain points relative to our contract of Santa Margarita, and I cannot do less than to manifest surprise to the reply that the said Mr. de la Guerra has given me, which was in substance as follows:
>
> 1st. That you never received my letter with reference to our transaction of Santa Margarita.
>
> 2d. That you treated with me for the whole of the Rancho Santa Margarita and not for the half of it.
>
> 3d. That you never received any cattle or horses of ours in payment of the part of the mortgage which corresponded to the one-half of said rancho.

---

[27]Newmark, *Sixty Years*, 48.

[28]Governor Downey was an active supporter of De la Guerra, who campaigned to elect Don Pablo to the presidency of the California Senate. John G. Downey to Pablo de la Guerra, Oct. 8, 1860, De la Guerra Collection.

[29]Although not a lawyer, De la Guerra replaced Benjamin Hayes in an election for district judge held on October 21, 1863. This bitter defeat sent Hayes to live in San Diego where he later became one of the attorneys for John Forster. For a discussion of De la Guerra and his campaign, see Pitt, *Decline of the Californios*, 234–39.

4th. That it is true that you owe us perhaps some cattle, but not on account of anything relative to the Rancho of Santa Margarita and that it is not so great a quantity as we say.

5th. That you never received from us any horses.

This obliges me to trouble your attention by asking some questions to clear up some of the points which your said reply contains, to which I hope you will please answer in writing for my ulterior purposes.

1st. Before you redeemed the mortgage of Santa Margarita, did you not know that they offered my brother Pío for said Rancho, the sum of $75,000?

2d. When, and by whom did you know that the house of San Francisco was pressing us for the money for the amount of the mortgage?

3d. If you never received any cattle on our part on account of Santa Margarita, then on whose account did you receive the cattle you say you owe us?

4th. If you have not received the quantity of cattle which we say, then tell me what the quantity is that you received, and what is it that you owe us?

I hope that excusing the trouble of these questions, you will please answer them as soon as may be possible.[30]

Although Andrés signed this letter, Pío collaborated in its preparation. Both were distrustful of Forster because he claimed that he had not received a prior letter about the Rancho Santa Margarita from Andrés. To insure that Forster could not deny the receipt of this one, it was sent by Pío to José María with a cover letter marked *Reservado*—Confidential. He wrote:

Your uncle Andrés says to acquaint yourself with the enclosed letter to Don Juan, then seal it and deliver it to him. If you can, do it before one or two witnesses and ask for a written answer. If he doesn't give you one, write down the

---

[30]Andrés Pico to Juan Forster, Jan. 31, 1870, defendant's exhibit PP 55. *Forster v. Pico.*

time and date of the delivery of the letter and do not speak to anyone about this matter.[31]

José María gave the letter to Forster as he was instructed. The suspicions of the Picos about Forster's intent respecting the Santa Margarita were fully justified by his response. On February 5, 1870, Forster sent an answer evading the questions in the letter and even contemptuously dismissing them. If Forster could justify his full ownership of the ranch as reflected in the deed recorded in San Diego, he should have set out the basis for it. His failure to do so invited an inference that he knew the transaction was intended to give him only half the ranch. Forster's reply was intended to put off Andrés and somehow avoid the question:

> My very esteemed Compadre and Brother:—On my return from Los Angeles, a few days past, I received your note of the 3d ultimo, which I did not answer, thinking it unnecessary, because already by Don Pablo de la Guerra, you will be informed that on the subject of a certain arrangement which he indicated (which arrangement Don Pablo explained to me, related to me) that you claim some right in this ranch of Santa Margarita. I suppose friend Don Pablo will have communicated to you my answer, and at the same time I would wish to use only words of the greatest courtesy so as not to offend your delicacy, I find myself in such a position that there remains no other course open to me, than to repeat, that I deny absolutely any right or pretention that you may set up. Furthermore, there has been delivered to me your note of the 31st last January, in which you make some interrogations, saying to me in conclusion that they were "For my ulterior purposes." This seems to me to be a threat, and in consequence, I have to tell you that I disregard any right of yours to catechize me in the manner you propose. Compadre and brother, it is very hard for me to express myself so decisively to a person with whom I have always had the best rela-

---

[31]Pío Pico to José María Pico, Jan. 31, 1870. The original document is in the private collection of Albert Pico. A copy is in the possession of the author through the kindness of Mr. Pico.

tions of friendship and esteem, and which I still retain. Nevertheless, being as you are a man of the world I rest assured that your friendship and common sense will excuse your affectionate brother and compadre.[32]

Since the confrontational efforts of Andrés failed to settle the matter, they were replaced by a softer approach from Pío. While Andrés was hard, Pío offered Forster other and sweeter inducements: appeals to friendship, family, and reconciliation. On December 5, 1870, Pío sent Albert Johnson to the Santa Margarita with a letter inviting Forster to a meeting in Los Angeles, strongly suggesting a desire to effect a complete reconciliation between them. Forster interpreted the letter to mean that Pío, wishing to restore family unity, had abandoned his claim to the Santa Margarita. Referring to this letter during his testimony at the trial, Forster said, "I was completely captured and acceded to his request to agree to an amicable arrangement and remain friends as in the former days."[33] Relieved and elated, Forster immediately responded to Pío's proposal to meet in Los Angeles in a letter of December 7, 1870:

> With great pleasure I have to acknowledge the receipt of your very welcome letter by favor of Mr. Albert Johnson, and I live thankful for the spirit of its contents to which I desire to correspond heartily and I confess that on your part you have omitted no means in order to arrange a dispute which unfortunately for us has arisen disturbing the family peace which has always existed between us. I can assure you I felt the same concern that you may have suffered from the same cause. Further, I can assure you that you are not mistaken in supposing that it will give me as much pleasure as it can you that in a

---

[32]John Forster to Andrés Pico, Feb. 5, 1870, defendant's exhibit PP 56. *Forster v. Pico.*

[33]Forster testified that Albert Johnson delivered him Pío's letter on December 7, 1870, and he immediately sat down and wrote an answer to send back with Johnson. Pio's letter had been written two days before, on December 5, 1870, a fact which Forster referred to in his written reply. The actual letter from Pío was lost or destroyed by Forster. As has been noted, he was very careless with his correspondence.

short time we may be able to give each other a sincere embrace of reconciliation.[34]

Soon after sending this letter, Forster arrived in Los Angeles for his visit with Pío. Whereas Andrés had offered to go to San Diego or San Juan Capistrano to meet Forster, the wily Pío suffered no such inconvenience. Now Forster came to Pío enticed by the hope of a surrender of the Santa Margarita and the emotional satisfaction of a family reconciliation.

Forster put up as a guest at the Ranchito, intending to stay several days. However, the true purpose of Pío's arranging the visit was driven home to Forster within hours. Pío did not speak of family unity. Instead, he forcefully demanded to know why Forster claimed the whole Rancho Santa Margarita. Forster recognized that he had mistaken Pío's intent in making the invitation. He had been lured to the Ranchito by Pío for interrogation, not reconciliation. Forster made some pretext for leaving to Albert Johnson during a momentary absence of Pío and bolted from the Ranchito. He did not spend a single night. Alarmed, Pío sent this desperate letter to follow Forster on his flight back to the Santa Margarita; he underlined a part to show his concern:

> My esteemed Godson: Although it caused me grief when I was informed that you had left from this place without taking leave, I quieted myself when Mr. Johnson informed me that you had charged him to make known to me that it was extremely necessary that you should absent yourself, *but that you would return* in a few days. So I consider it of the greatest importance that we take measures, Godson, to end this matter of Santa Margarita, but not on this account would I wish to cause you the trouble to come here repeatedly and it has occurred to me to send you these few lines to ask you if it would be agreeable to you that friend Mr. Antonio Cuyas who you already know would go and with him you would treat and arrange our business of Santa Margarita.[35]

---

[34]John Forster to Pío Pico, Dec. 7, 1870, defendant's exhibit PP 26. *Forster v. Pico.*
[35]Pío Pico to John Forster, Jan. 21, 1871, defendant's exhibit PP 25. *Forster v. Pico.*

Whether Forster met with Antonio Cuyas is unknown, although he sent a letter to Pío from the Santa Margarita on February 11, 1871, consenting to go to San Juan Capistrano to meet with Cuyas.[36] At this time Pío leased the Pico House Hotel in Los Angeles to Cuyas, a Spaniard. Pío apparently placed great confidence in Cuyas but nothing resulted from the efforts of his Spanish agent.

After fleeing the Ranchito in December 1870, Forster had no further direct contact with Pío. The two men were permanently estranged. Forster had successfully eluded Andrés and escaped from Pío. The pursuit of Forster had failed. Forster never explained why he had a deed to the entire Rancho Santa Margarita and not just one-half of it.

---

[36]John Forster to Pío Pico, Feb. 11, 1871, defendant's exhibit PP 27. *Forster v. Pico.*

The Temple Block in Los Angeles during 1875. The lead
attorneys for both sides in *Forster vs. Pico* had their offices
here. Note the sign of the merchant Adolph Portugal,
one of many agents used by Pío Pico.
Courtesy, the Huntington Library.

CHAPTER SEVEN

The Picos and Forster
Turn to the Law

Forster had more to deal with than the relentless claims of the Pico brothers. Between his constant trips to the San Francisco cattle market, he was observing a new phenomenon which could relieve him from the uncertainties of ranching and make him fabulously wealthy. He was closely watching the success of the Robinson Trust in subdividing ranch lands in Los Angeles and San Bernardino counties. The end of the Civil War brought a flood of immigration to Southern California by veterans from both sides who crossed the continent with their families in search of a new life. In 1868, to take advantage of a market created by the immigrants' demand for homesteads and small farms, a trust headed by Alfred Robinson acquired the right to dispose of the huge ranches of Abel Stearns by subdividing his lands into parcels of 20 to 160 acres.[1]

These parcels were sold on liberal terms with a percentage of the proceeds paid over to Stearns. The era of cattle raising was ending. There was enormous pressure to break up the remaining large Mexican ranchos to meet the needs of small farmers. During the course of the next two years the trust proved to be a smashing success.[2] Abel Stearns, the old

---

[1]Cleland, *Cattle On a Thousand Hills*, 203-7.

[2]One writer states that twenty thousand acres of Stearns's land was sold by 1871 at prices varying from eight to twenty dollars per acre. Glenn S. Dumke, *The Boom of the Eighties*, 7. Another writer believes that twenty thousand acres of land was sold by the trust as early as 1869 and that two million dollars had been made by 1871. Remi Nadeau, *City-Makers*, 18.

ranchero from Massachusetts, was rescued from bankruptcy. He died on August 23, 1871, just three years after commencing the trust, leaving his much younger Mexican wife, Arcadia, with the colossal amount of one million dollars.[3]

Forster wanted to emulate the success of the Robinson Trust on the Santa Margarita. He sent Max Strobel, who had been active in the founding of Anaheim, to recruit settlers from Europe.[4] The plan of Forster, long in the making, received notice in the *San Francisco Chronicle* on January 18, 1873. The item, which understated the size of the ranch, read:

Immigration to California

San Diego, January 17—Don Juan Forster, the owner of the Santa Margarita ranch, some 30 square miles, situated in this county has an agent in Europe sending out immigrants. Already 100 have been secured. Each immigrant is given 80 acres of land, for which he agrees to expend $1,000 in improvements the first year. A colony will be formed similar to that from which the town of Anaheim has sprung. Mr. Forster reserves each alternate section of 80 acres for himself.

At the same time, Strobel had interested European investors in the purchase of Santa Catalina Island, in which Forster had a part interest. The enormous amount of 200,000 British pounds was actually being offered by Lon-

---

[3]Hubert Howe Bancroft, *Literary Industries*, 487. This book contains an amusing account of a visit with the widow Arcadia Bandini de Stearns in Los Angeles during 1874. Bancroft wrote, "As it was, suitors were thick enough; there were plenty of men who would take her for a million dollars . . ." Among the suitors was the aging Alfred Robinson himself, who Bancroft described to as a "withered lover." The lucky man later chosen by Arcadia was Colonel Robert S. Baker.

[4]Max Strobel (sometimes spelled "Stroble") was an adventurous German who fought in the Revolution of 1848 in his native land and was later a member of William Walker's filibustering expedition to Nicaragua. In California he was a promoter, journalist, and politician who was the first mayor of Anaheim. He was involved in several unsuccessful projects such as oil boring on the Brea ranch and an attempted division of Los Angeles County to remove the southern portion, including the city of Anaheim, from its jurisdiction. See Newmark, *Sixty Years*, 406-7.

don investors.[5] Heady prospects danced before Don Juan Forster, the transplanted Englishman. His long sojourn in California and immersion into its early Mexican culture seemed at last about to make him exceedingly rich.

In the background, though, Forster was continually harassed by the Pico brothers. It was foreseeable that his feud with them over title to one-half the Santa Margarita would erupt into legal action at some point. His scheme for the subdivision of the ranch was well known throughout California. The Picos were aware that the value of the Santa Margarita had vastly increased under Forster's stewardship. The tax assessment on it, not even an index of its minimum value, skyrocketed from $7,000 in 1864 to $79,848 in 1872.[6] The actual value of the ranch was several times greater. Still, neither Pío nor Forster brought any lawsuit to adjust their differences. As is often the case in life, the event which finally precipitated decisive action came from a most unexpected quarter.

Toward the middle of 1872, Magdalena Pico made a stunning announcement. She claimed that her husband, José Antonio Pico, the older brother of Pío and Andrés, had been the owner of a one-quarter interest in the Santa Margarita since 1846. The basis for this assertion was a document executed by Pío Pico in that year which purported to grant ownership of the Santa Margarita in equal parts between Pío and his wife, María Ignacia Alvarado, and his brothers José Antonio Pico and Andrés Pico.[7]

Magdalena was the second wife and widow of José Antonio Pico, who died in 1871. She was the stepmother of José Antonio's adult children, including José María, Pío's mayor-

---

[5]Ibid., 407.

[6]Statements of John Forster, Lists of Property, Real and Personal, Subject to Taxation in the County of San Diego, 1864 and 1872, San Diego Historical Society Archives.

[7]Terry E. Stephenson, "Forster vs. Pico, a Forgotten California Cause Celebre," 50-54.

domo. The family had lived on the Santa Margarita for many years with the consent of both Pío and Don Juan. During his lifetime, José Antonio had requested both to grant him some legal title to a portion of the ranch, but each had refused. The paper produced by his widow and her demand for part ownership was therefore an astonishment.

Magdalena showed the document, written in Spanish, to an attorney from San Diego named Charles P. Taggart. He construed the instrument as a deed, noting that it had been recorded in San Diego County on August 18, 1853, some seven years after its execution. If he was right, José Antonio died with an undivided one-quarter interest in the Santa Margarita. Magdalena retained Taggart to file a lawsuit against Forster to quiet title to her husband's part ownership. Taggart was a good choice to file such a suit. He was deeply involved in San Diego real estate and shared title to some five miles of tidelands between San Diego and National City with Volney E. Howard. Because of this, he was active in promoting San Diego as a railroad terminus. Taggart was also prominent in Republican politics and was an editor of the *San Diego Union*.[8]

A Los Angeles lawyer, Anson Brunson, was chosen to assist Taggart with the representation of Magdalena Pico and her children. Brunson was born in Ohio in 1834 and graduated from the University of Michigan in 1857.[9] He settled in Los Angeles in December 1868 and was regarded as "an amiable, courteous man, quick to take advantage in a trial, and a better pleader than average."[10] During the 1870s he formed a partnership with James Eastman which proved catastrophic for both men. Although they were great friends, each was a bad influence on the other. They plunged into a

---

[8]Richard F. Pourade, *The Glory Years*, 70, 87-90, 105.
[9]William W. Clary, *History of the Law Firm of O'Melveny and Myers*, 1: 7.
[10]W. W. Robinson, *Lawyers of Los Angeles*, 50.

scandalous bout of alcoholism for several years. One historian observed: "The troubles and dissipations of these two partners were the talk of the town."[11] Taggart employed Brunson just prior to his association with Eastman and therefore would have found him more useful than after his unfortunate partnership.

The document Taggart construed as a deed does resemble one. Unfortunately, it was merely a copy since the original was lost years before. Further, it should have been dated 1846 and not the year 1845 shown on the copy. Translated, it read:

> I, the undersigned say that the property known as Santa Margarita y Las Flores and all other lands, houses and improvements thereto are by equal shares to my wife, Dona Maria Ygnacia Alvarado, and of my two brothers, Jose Antonio and Andres Pico, and myself, having acquired same by our mutual industry and work without any of them bettered to the prejudice of the others, for be it known to all persons that these presents may see, and in particular to all authorities that by virtue of their office may take cognizance of the same in equity, and in all cases that may occur, that these lands, improvements and other property belong in common to the persons aforesaid and to none others. In faith of which truth, and for the purposes that may be convenient I give this document that [it] may serve to secure the persons aforesaid to entire title to them, as if it were acknowledged before a competent judge signing the same of my own hand on common paper not having any stamp.

> Santa Margarita, October 6, 1845.

> Pío Pico [12]

Forster contended that the document was a will made by Pío in 1846 during the American conquest of California. In

---

[11]Ibid., 50. See J. A. Graves, *My Seventy Years in California*, 282-83. Graves, once a partner with Brunson and Eastman, reports Brunson's recovery from alcoholism, and unfortunately, Eastman's continued decline and miserable death as a virtual tramp. See also, Newmark, *Sixty Years*, 593.

[12]Stephenson, "Pico v. Forster," 52.

that year Pío decided to flee to Mexico rather than surrender himself and his governorship to the American military authorities. While hiding himself on the Santa Margarita, en route to Baja California, he hastily executed the document, the nature of which still remains a mystery.

If it was a will made in anticipation of Pío's capture and possible death, as Forster contended, it is odd that Pío made himself one of the beneficiaries. Moreover, not even the most careful scrutiny of the instrument shows the slightest use of testamentary language. The document purports to dispose of the whole property, but Andrés was a half owner and had been since Governor Juan Alvarado granted the ranch to the brothers in 1841.[13] It might be thought that Pío himself would be the best source of information about his intent when he wrote the document, but he was in a muddle about the affair. Pío never gave a coherent statement at trial of what the paper meant.

By May 1872, then, Forster had a lawsuit pending against him by Magdalena Pico for one-quarter of the Santa Margarita and was plagued by Pío Pico's claim to one-half of the same land. It appeared to Forster that the extended Pico family would only leave him with a one-quarter interest in the Santa Margarita if they had their way. Under these circumstances, Forster consulted with Volney E. Howard of Los Angeles, one of the best lawyers in Southern California. Howard's office was in the famous three-story brick building known as the Temple Block, just south of the Plaza on the west side of Main Street.[14] At this time he was about sixty-one years old, a corpulent man to whom a local wag, Matthew Keller, gave the nickname "Ponderosity" referring "more to his physical rather than his mental make-up."[15]

---

[13]Ibid., 22, and *Forster v. Pico*, 1 California Unreported Cases 841 (1874).

[14]*The First Los Angeles City and County Directory*, 6. In 1872 Howard's office was at Number 13, Temple's Block.

[15]John Steven McGroarty, *From the Mountains to the Sea*, 1: 345.

Howard was born in 1809 in Maine, but later moved to Mississippi where he became "southernized."[16] From the Deep South, he made an odyssey westward, practicing law in New Orleans and later Brownsville, Texas.[17] During his stay in Texas, he was elected to the U.S. Congress where in 1849 he voted against the admission of California as a state because its new constitution prohibited slavery.[18]

In 1853 the ex-congressman was in San Francisco as a law agent for the United States Land Commission.[19] During the vigilante movement there in 1856, Governor J. Neely Johnson commissioned him as a major general in the California State Militia and ordered him to suppress the mob rule occurring at that time. Howard failed to accomplish this mission and was even forced to flee the city.[20] Although he never exercised any further military functions, he was addressed as "General."[21] It was a custom of the period to refer to former military officers by their erstwhile ranks, especially lawyers, even when the source of their commission was somewhat dubious.[22] General Howard came to live in Los Angeles during August 1861.[23] He soon succeeded Joseph Lancaster Brent, who had left to join the Confederate Army, as the chief power broker of the Democratic party and obtained "the greater portion of the legal business of the county."[24]

With Forster's permission, Howard assembled a team of attorneys to defeat the Pico pretentions to the Santa Mar-

---

[16]Bancroft, *History of California*, 6: 374-75, n.5.

[17]Grenier, *California Legacy*, 38, 40-41, and 45-46.

[18]Bancroft, *History of California*, 6: 694, n.19.

[19]Ibid., 542, n.12.

[20]Samuel Lanner Kreider, "Volney Erskine Howard: California Pioneer," 124.

[21]Forster almost always referred to Howard as "the General" in his correspondence. Even thirty-three years after receiving his commission, the press still referred to him as "Gen. Howard." See Howard's obituary in the *Los Angeles Times*, May 15, 1889.

[22]This custom is noted by Robinson in *Lawyers*, 57.

[23]*Los Angeles Star*, Aug. 24, 1861.

[24]John W. Shore to Joseph Lancaster Brent, July 9, 1865, Brent Collection.

garita, one attorney from Los Angeles and two from San
Diego. The Los Angeles attorney he associated in the case
was Frank Ganahl, a Georgia-born newcomer who had
opened an office in the Downey Block, a large building a few
steps north of Howard's office, just across old Spring
Street.[25] He had come to Los Angeles in 1870 from Arizona
where he had been engaged in mining.[26] By 1872, Ganahl
was not yet fully settled in Los Angeles; he still rented rooms
in the Pico House.[27] Like General Howard, Ganahl held
strong beliefs of the Southern variety. Although once
described as "caustic," Ganahl was a very social person.[28] He
had a reputation as a wit and bon vivant.[29] In the tradition of
the period, Jackson A. Graves described him as "Major
Frank Ganahl" without stating a reason for the military
title.[30] Another writer reported that Matthew Keller called
him "Punchinello," like the comedian in an Italian puppet
show.[31] Ganahl made a good companion. Apart from his personal charm, Ganahl was "among the thoroughly able men at
the bar."[32]

The attorneys associated in San Diego by Howard were
William J. Gatewood and Benjamin I. Hayes. Hot-tem-
pered, Gatewood was a gentleman of Kentucky, a product of
the antebellum South where honor was sacred and duels were
frequent. He shot a certain Dr. P. Goodwyn to death during a
formal southern-style duel in 1859 in San Andreas, a gold
town in Calaveras County.[33] Such "affairs of honor" were
often tolerated by law enforcement officials of the time,
many of whom were of Southern origin. Gatewood was not
punished. By 1868 he had set up his residence in San Diego.
Not long after his arrival, he began printing a newspaper, the

[25]*Los Angeles City and County Directory*, ix.
[26]Newmark, *Sixty Years*, 416.
[27]*Los Angeles City and County Directory*, 5.
[28]Robinson, *Lawyers*, 52.
[29]McGroarty, *From the Mountains*, 1: 348-49.
[30]Graves, *My Seventy Years*, 14.
[31]McGroarty, *From the Mountains*, 1: 345, 348.
[32]Ibid., 348.
[33]*Los Angeles Star*, Sept. 24, 1859.

San Diego Union. He sold it to Charles P. Taggart, who later became Magdalena Pico's attorney. When Gatewood joined Howard in the case against the Picos, he was the editor of the *San Diego Bulletin* and practicing law. He also dabbled in land speculation and Democratic politics.[34] Known to the locals as Colonel Gatewood, he was an ideal point man for Howard in San Diego.

Benjamin I. Hayes was living in San Diego's Old Town in 1872, right on the northwest corner of the Plaza in a rented adobe.[35] Hayes had been a state district judge headquartered in Los Angeles from 1852 until he lost an election for the office to Pablo de la Guerra in 1863. Originally from Maryland, he practiced law for a time in Missouri before coming to California overland in 1850.[36] His life and travels are extremely well documented in a series of diaries and scrapbooks which have made him famous among California historians.[37] A sensitive and gentle person, he suffered from periodic alcohol abuse. While a judge, "on account of his love for strong drink, court on more than one occasion had to be adjourned."[38] A correspondent to Cave Couts wrote in 1867 from Los Angeles, "Hayes has been and is now drunk as a beast."[39]

---

[34]Pourade, *Glory Years*, 32, 40, 101.

[35]Hayes advertised his location in the local press along with that of his nineteen-year-old son, J. Chauncey Hayes, an aspiring real estate agent. *The San Diego Union*, Feb. 6, 1873, announced:

> Benjamin Hayes Attorney and Counselor at Law
> Residence Northwest corner of the Plaza, Old Town.
> All land matters attended to.
>
> ---
>
> J. C. Hayes & Co.

[36]Robinson, *Lawyers*, 29-57, contains a superb account of Hayes' career.

[37]Hayes sold most of his diaries and scrapbooks to Hubert Howe Bancroft. They are now a major historical resource at the Bancroft Library on the University of California, Berkeley campus. See Chapter 10, *post.*

[38]Newmark, *Sixty Years*, 46-47.

[39]Charles Robinson Johnson to Cave Couts, Oct. 4, 1867, Couts Collection.

Hayes had few, if any, instincts for business. During the year 1872, his tax returns show that his entire net worth was only about $200.[40] He occupied himself quietly with the law, his diaries, and a near obsession for collecting historical data for his scrapbooks. It is likely that Howard used Hayes to explore the historical context of the strange document that Magdalena Pico claimed had granted her deceased husband one-quarter of the Santa Margarita. The presence of Hayes also gave Forster's team of attorneys a certain degree of prestige. Hard-drinking was more easily forgiven in the last century and it did not greatly affect the wide respect the former judge enjoyed in Southern California.

Howard counseled Forster to press an attack and hazard everything in court against all the Picos by filing an action to quiet title. The trial would have to be in San Diego, the seat of the county where the land was located. On May 10, 1872, Forster advised Pío that he was one of the defendants in his quiet title suit. Not wishing to goad his brother-in-law unnecessarily, Forster couched the letter in exceedingly gentle terms:

> My esteemed godfather. In consequence of a claim which my comadre, Dona Magdalena, makes to a part of Santa Margarita, she and her children and I have had a considerable falling out, and in the answer to a suit which she had instituted against me, claiming besides the rancho a very considerable sum of money, I have been obliged to sue her and all the heirs of the late Don Jose Antonio, my compadre, and in instituting my suit, I have been made to understand that it is necessary to include you in the same suit, with the object in view of clearing up the question of their pretentions. The title they pretend is the identical Testamentary Statement that you made at Santa Margarita in my presence when you retreated from that point and the country for Mex-

---

[40]Statement of Benjamin I. Hayes, Lists of Property, Real and Personal, Subject to Taxation in the County of San Diego, 1872, San Diego Historical Society Archives.

ico when you were pursued by the invading forces. Said document was annulled by you on your return. Both documents are recorded in the county of San Diego. In taking this step, at first sight it would appear to be against you—perhaps it will be only a legal formality, nevertheless it has caused me considerable feelings to do it, because I never thought that what is called a formality would have created the necessity of placing myself in an attitude of antagonism with a person who I have honored so much for so long a time with friendship and esteem. Under these circumstances I hope you will excuse my action in the matter, and will not attribute to me motives but of the utmost necessity which I pray will not give place to anything but a continuance of friendly relations.[41]

Pío did not respond to the letter in the manner that Forster desired. Instead, he visited his attorney, Andrew Glassell, a neighbor of Howard in the Temple Block. Born in Virginia in 1827, Glassell was about forty-five years old in 1872. His father, a cotton planter, moved the family to Alabama where Glassell was apparently raised in genteel circumstances. He graduated from the University of Alabama with a law degree in 1848. Shortly thereafter, he took employment in San Francisco with the United States Land Office and eventually set up a private practice devoted to real estate law. At the outbreak of the Civil War he refused to subscribe to the loyalty oath demanded by Union authorities. Unlike many Southern attorneys, he did not slip away to fight for the Confederacy. He quietly withdrew to Santa Cruz where he engaged in gentlemanly farming and the lumber business throughout the war. Glassell resumed the practice of law in Los Angeles in 1865, probably at the urging of his boyhood friend, A. B. Chapman, with whom he formed a partnership.[42]

During 1868 they were joined by George H. Smith.

---

[41]John Forster to Pío Pico, May 10, 1872, defendant's exhibit PP 28. *Forster v. Pico.*

[42]Glassell's biography is set forth in McGroarty, *From the Mountains*, 3: 730-33. See also Newmark, *Sixty Years*, 350-51; and the *Los Angeles Times*, Jan. 29, 1901.

Andrew Glassell
*Courtesy, California
Historical Society, Ticor
Collection, University of
Southern California
Libraries.*

Smith had been a colonel in the Confederate Army, an experience which was a hallmark of his life. Although Smith was
born on February 5, 1834, in Philadelphia, he was from an
old Virginia family centered in Alexandria noted for producing lawyers and preachers. His father was an Episcopal min-
ister whose circumstances permitted him to enroll Smith in
the Virginia Military Institute, from which he graduated in
1853. At the outbreak of the Civil War, Smith was practicing
law in Alexandria. By July 1861, he was a volunteer captain in
the Confederate Army. Almost immediately thereafter,
Smith spent seven months as a paroled prisoner of war following his capture by Union forces at Beverly, Virginia, on
July 13, 1861. On February 20, 1862, he managed to obtain
his release and return to service.

Smith was promoted to full colonel on May 1, 1862. A
week later he was shot in the thigh during an engagement at
McDowell, Virginia. Later, at the second Battle of Bull Run
on August 29, 1862, he was severely wounded in the arm.

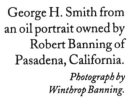

George H. Smith from
an oil portrait owned by
Robert Banning of
Pasadena, California.
Photograph by
Winthrop Banning.

Upon recovering, he was assigned command of the 25th Virginia Infantry Regiment. His most important duty occurred after May 19, 1863, when he was ordered to take charge of the 62nd Virginia Mounted Infantry Regiment, one of the units under the orders of Brigadier General John D. Imboden.[43]

It is no exaggeration to say that Smith's survival of the war was miraculous. His participation in the Battle of New Market on May 15, 1864, is a case in point. This engagement took place in the upper Shenandoah Valley of Virginia against the Union forces of Major General Franz Sigel. During a Confederate advance, a Union battery of cannon on elevated ground was inflicting heavy casualties on exposed Southern infantry. Major General John C. Breckinridge

---

[43]Smith's early life and military record are found in Civil War sources. See Richard L. Armstrong, *25th Virginia Infantry and 9th Battalion Virginia Infantry*, 235; Clement A. Evans, ed., *Confederate Military History*, 13: 233-36; Roger U. Delauter, *62nd Virginia Infantry*, 25-49, 106.

ordered Smith's 62nd Regiment and elements of the Virginia
Military Institute Cadet Corps to silence the battery. After
crossing a gulch, it was necessary to charge across three hundred yards of completely exposed terrain into the battery's
continuous fire of canister shot. Brigadier General Imboden
later wrote:

> Colonel Smith went into action with about 550 men of
> the 62d. Seven of his ten captains fell between the gulch and
> the battery, four of whom were instantly killed and three
> crippled for life. He reported the next day the total casualties
> of his regiment at 241 officers and men killed and wounded;
> and nearly all these fell in passing over that deadly three hun-
> dred yards up "to the cannon's mouth." My recollection is
> distinct that the losses in killed and wounded of the 62d. and
> the Cadet Corps constituted over one half of the casualties of
> the day in the whole of our little army of about 4,500 men.[44]

This episode is only one instance of Smith's survival being a
matter of pure chance. Brigadier General Imboden said that
Smith was "The bravest man I have ever seen."[45] It is a won-
der, in view of Smith's constant exposure to enemy fire up and
down the Shenandoah Valley for several years, that his military honors were not posthumous.

After all his efforts and sacrifice, Smith did not easily
accept the defeat of the Confederacy. With some like-mind-
ed comrades he drifted into Mexico where he tried to start a
cotton plantation near Tepic, a little town south of Mazatlan
on the Pacific coast.[46] These veteran officers, physically and
psychologically damaged by their war experiences, did not
prosper.

In 1868 Smith arrived in San Francisco, alone and broke.
He was soon drawn to Los Angeles by an arrangement to
work for the law firm of Andrew Glassell "at a salary of one

---

[44]John D. Imboden, "The Battle of New Market, Va., May 15th, 1864," 480-86.

[45]Delauter, *62nd Virginia Infantry*, 106.

[46]Robert H. Patton, *The Pattons*, 67.

hundred dollars a month with the privilege of studying California law."[47] Glassell's younger sister, Sue, who Smith had known as a youth in Virginia, was living in Los Angeles at that time. She was the widow of George S. Patton, a first cousin of Smith. Patton and Smith had been best friends when they attended the Virginia Military Institute and were rivals for Sue's affections. Smith withdrew as a suitor, leaving the way clear for his cousin to marry Sue Glassell in 1855. Patton was mortally wounded at Winchester, Virginia, on September 19, 1864. Like Smith, he had been a Confederate colonel and regimental commander. The distress of the South and the death of her husband caused Sue to seek the assistance of her brother, Andrew, in California.[48]

Smith's amorous feelings toward Sue were revived in Los Angeles. They were married in 1870. He became a doting stepfather of her four children and was adored by them. Sue's son, George William Patton, changed his name to George Smith Patton, reflecting his affection for his mother's second husband.[49] This same young man later joined Smith's law firm and became the father of the fabled World War II leader, General George S. Patton Jr. By 1871 Smith was well established in Los Angeles. It would be his residence for the next forty-four years.

It is difficult to understand why Pío would have chosen a rigid, aristocratic Southerner like Glassell as his attorney. Pío's mixed racial heritage was obvious to the race-conscious Americans. Perhaps Glassell had a degree of tolerance, warmth, or similar positive characteristics that the recorded observations of others and his background do not suggest. In any event, Pío remained loyal to Glassell for many years, even to the point of excusing a default judgment taken against him

[47]Midge Sherwood, *Days of Vintage, Years of Vision*, 2: 165.
[48]Patton, *The Pattons*, 26-30, 58-59, 63-64.
[49]Ibid., 67.

in 1869 through the neglect of Glassell's firm which resulted in a serious loss to Pico.[50]

Glassell did not establish his law practice in Los Angeles until 1865. He could not have advised Pío on how to make the transaction with Forster for the transfer of the Rancho Santa Margarita. During the course of his representation of Pío, he must have learned that Pío regarded his deed to Forster as having been for only one-half of the ranch. Otherwise, Glassell's partner, A. B. Chapman, would not have felt that there was anything out of the ordinary when he learned of a deed to the Rancho Santa Margarita showing that Forster was the sole owner.

The deed given to Forster had to be attacked on the ground that it was fraudulent. After signing before a notary public, Pío could only void the deed by proving that he was induced to sign it through some deliberate misrepresentation of fact. Glassell had no choice but to allege that Forster had presented a deed in English for Pío to sign with full knowledge that Pío could not read it and believed that it conveyed only one half of the ranch.

Glassell filed a cross-complaint against Forster based on fraud in the court of the Eighteenth Judicial District in San Diego during May 1872. There was little time to get ready for trial. As early as August 1872, it was necessary to ask for a continuance. To prepare for trial, Glassell should have spent much time with the Pico brothers probing the nature of their agreement with Forster and planning their testimony. He

---

[50]Glassell began his representation of Pío Pico not long after arriving in Los Angeles. He argued the case of *Pico v. Colimas*, 32 California Reports 578, before the state supreme court as early as July 1867. This case, which he won, involved the right to control water flow in an irrigation ditch which crossed Pío's land on the Ranchito. Counsel for the opposition was Volney E. Howard. Other lawsuits followed with Glassell representing Pío, and Howard acting for the other side. For example, see *Pío Pico v. Coleman*, 47 California Reports 65 (Oct. 1873); and *Henry Hancock v. Pío Pico*, 40 California Reports 153 (Oct. 1870). In the last case, Glassell failed to file a timely answer and lost by default in 1869. This unhappy result was upheld by the supreme court.

Volney E. Howard
*Courtesy, Security Pacific
Collection, Los Angeles
Public Library.*

needed to collect statements from persons who could establish that Pío believed he was still a one-half owner with Forster by doing such acts as ordering rodeos, claiming orejanos, and arranging the use of the land.

José María Pico would be invaluable for this, as would a host of adjacent landowners, friends, and business associates. There were witnesses who claimed to have heard damaging admissions by Forster in which he acknowledged that he was only a half owner. These friendly witnesses would have to withstand the hostile cross-examination that Volney E. Howard and Frank Ganahl would put them through. Conversely, it was necessary to identify those persons who would be witnesses for Forster and lay plans to discredit their testimony.

A crucial aspect of the Pico case were the letters sent to José María Pico. These documents demonstrate behavior of Pío consistent with the belief that he remained an owner of the Santa Margarita after delivery of the deed to Forster. Such conduct negated an intent to give Forster the whole ranch. It should have been apparent that this evidence was vital to the case. The legal basis for the admission of these let-

ters had to be carefully planned in advance with well reasoned arguments to meet the objections the opposition was
sure to make.

The scope of the preparation could have been wide if
Glassell had done his work properly. A key witness was the
notary public, Ozias Morgan, who had moved to New York.
His testimony, if believed, could have been decisive. Forster
claimed that Morgan was instructed by the Picos when he
drew up the deed transferring the whole ranch. The Picos
regarded him as an agent of Forster and a co-conspirator in a
fraud. Amazingly, Pío testified at the trial that he had met
Morgan in New York City during his railroad trip in 1869.
By then Pío knew from Glassell's partner, A. B. Chapman,
that Forster had a deed to the whole ranch which Morgan
had drafted. It would be interesting to know what the two
men talked about in New York, but Pío was not asked to
relate the conversation in court, and he volunteered nothing.
Glassell made a last-minute attempt to find Morgan as the
trial was starting, even asking for a continuance for that purpose, which was denied. Soon after grasping Morgan's role in
this affair, Glassell could have sent someone to New York, a
trip of seven days by railway, to look for him. If Pío encountered him in 1869, a determined investigator could find him
if he was still alive in 1872.

Forster's interest in finding Morgan was so slight that he
ignored an opportunity to search for him just one week prior
to the jury trial. At that time his son Chico was actually in
New York City on his way to Washington, D.C. Chico had
been sent on a trip to the capital by Forster to interview federal officials concerning Santa Catalina Island. On his arrival
in New York City on January 20, 1873, Chico sent his father
a letter in Spanish written on stationery of the Metropolitan
Hotel. He had traveled via the Union Pacific Railway and
planned to lay over in New York for three days. Chico merely

wrote about a nocturnal pickpocket on the train, his personal observations of New York City, and the weather. He made no comment about the impending trial or any reference to Morgan.[51]

The trial was set for the January 1873 term in San Diego, only eight months from the time Forster filed his complaint to quiet title. By that year, San Diego was no longer a cluster of adobes surrounding the original Mexican plaza that the Americans called Old Town. The transformation of San Diego began a few years before in 1867 when Alonso Horton arrived from San Francisco. Horton was a merchant born in Wisconsin who came to San Diego at the age of fifty-four already obsessed with the idea that the natural harbor there would give rise to a great city. He bought large tracts of barren municipal land adjacent to the waterfront from city officials in Old Town. Having suffered for years from severe economic depression, and with no faith in the future, the city virtually made Horton a gift of the land for a price of about twenty-seven cents an acre. The lots he purchased became known as Horton's Addition. With apparently unjustified confidence, Horton set out to promote San Diego real estate all over California.[52]

Shortly after the creation of Horton's Addition, Phineas Banning once gave fifty cents to an acquaintance who was going to San Diego and said, "Here, take this and buy Horton's Addition for me. You can keep the change."[53] Such cynicism was caused in part by the knowledge that William Heath Davis had lost a fortune trying to develop San Diego some years before. Providentially, Horton's promotional activities coincided with the great westward migration from

---

[51]Francisco Forster to John Forster, Jan. 20, 1873, Forster Collection.
[52]Elizabeth C. MacPhail, *The Story of New San Diego and of Its Founder Alonzo E. Horton*, 11-24.
[53]Ibid., 25.

the eastern and southern states following the Civil War. Largely because of this, Horton's efforts to develop San Diego had spectacular, almost miraculous results. By 1870 Old Town was nearly abandoned.

The center of San Diego shifted to Horton's Addition on the waterfront. On October 17, 1870, Horton opened a hotel which symbolized the growing status of New San Diego. It was called the Horton House, an elegant brick building two hundred feet long and two and a half stories high topped by an observatory overlooking the bay. It provided a vista that the *San Diego Union*, called "the most magnificent view in Christendom." The hotel cost over $150,000 to build. Its lavishly furnished rooms were heated and had hot and cold running water, a luxury for those times. There was a reading room and a bar and billiard parlor with a dais encircling it for observers. Every square foot of the hotel was covered with thick carpeting. Marble-topped furniture was distributed tastefully throughout.[54]

Within sight of the Horton House, just a little to the west on the same street, a new courthouse was erected in 1872.[55] A large two-story structure with a classical Greek portico, the first floor contained offices for the clerks and marshals. The upper floor housed a spacious courtroom. It was an easy stroll from the Horton House, where persons connected with the trial took up their headquarters. In these pleasant surroundings, the attorneys, parties, and more respectable witnesses began to take rooms during the second week of January 1873.

Judge Horace C. Rolfe presided over the case. He was the sole judge for the Eighteenth Judicial District which included both San Diego and San Bernardino counties. It was one of the first cases he handled as a judge, having been appointed to the office late in 1872. Born in the state of Maine in 1839, it appears that his family took him to the Mormon

---

[54]Pourade, *Glory Years*, 75-77.
[55]Ibid., 95.

San Diego's Horton
House in 1875.
The participants in the
trial of *Forster v. Pico*
stayed in this hotel.
The courthouse is to
the west in the far
background.
*Courtesy, the Huntington
Library.*

colony at San Bernardino at an early age. During the Indian uprising led by Chief Antonio Garra in 1851, the Mormons built a fort in San Bernardino on which young Rolfe had labored. Later he served as an orderly sergeant in a volunteer company sent out to punish Indians in the San Gorgonio Pass. While a youth, he worked as an ox-driver, carpenter, miner, and whatever else was necessary in the harsh frontier setting of early San Bernardino. At age twenty-four, he began to study law under an attorney named William Pickett. Like many other lawyers of the day, he did not attend law school. He was admitted to the bar in 1860 and elected district attorney of San Bernardino County in 1861, leaving office in 1865. He practiced law in the city of San Bernardino until his appointment to the bench in 1872. Nearly his entire adult life was spent in San Bernardino where he was a well-known and very popular figure.[56]

[56]The sources for this brief treatment of Rolfe's career are: John Brown Jr. and James Boyd, *History of San Bernardino and Riverside Counties*, 1: 122-24 and 2: 678-79; George William Beattie and Helen Pruitt Beattie, *Heritage of the Valley*, 185-86, 233, 304; *Ingersoll's Century Annals of San Bernardino County*, 298, 305; E. P. R. Croft, *Pioneer Days in the San Bernardino Valley*, 97-98.

Rolfe was the product of a remote Southern California backwater. It must have been a challenge for him to confront the array of prestigious lawyers in Forster's lawsuit. Prior to his judicial appointment, he had no professional or social standing equal to theirs. Looking across the court, Rolfe, a former lowly enlisted orderly sergeant, could see Major General Howard, Colonel Gatewood, and Major Ganahl on the Forster side. Opposing them was Colonel Smith, and as a witness, Brigadier General Andrés Pico. These stellar members of Southern California's elite must have been intimidating to some degree. Most were well-educated university graduates and highly experienced, sophisticated men accustomed to positions of rank and power that Rolfe had never known.

In an age of easy admission to the bar, Rolfe's education was a haphazard, homemade affair which was reflected in some of his rulings from the bench. His law practice had been a hard-scrabble, rustic one. Only one year before Rolfe's appointment as a judge, he represented Abel Stearns in the eviction of some squatters from the Rancho Jurupa in San Bernardino County. The special referee who heard the case was none other than Forster's attorney, Volney E. Howard. To his probable chagrin, Rolfe lost the case.[57] Howard's decision would have been particularly galling since Rolfe repeatedly led Stearns to believe he would win the case and accordingly lost little opportunity to exhort him for more fees from time to time.[58]

---

[57]Rolfe wrote to Stearns, "I have great confidence he [Volney E. Howard] will give us judgment." Horace C. Rolfe to Abel Stearns, April 18, 1871, Stearns Collection. Less than two months later he was forced to report, "Howard is making his decision against us . . . I think we can beat them on appeal." Rolfe to Stearns, June 8, 1871. Ibid.

[58]Rolfe took advantage of his infrequent trips to Los Angeles to collect fees. Prior to one such visit he wrote to Stearns, "I shall be in Los Angeles in two or three days . . . I hope you will have some of the '*con que*' for me." Both men knew that by using the Spanish expression "con que," Rolfe was referring to "wherewithal" —i. e., money. Horace C. Rolfe to Abel Stearns, July 18, 1870. Ibid.

CHAPTER EIGHT

The Case for the Picos

The first court session in Forster's case was held on Monday, January 13, 1873. Pío's lead attorney, Andrew Glassell, surprised George H. Smith by assigning him to conduct the trial. Smith did the best he could under extreme pressure to proceed, but he had no time to properly analyze the case and arrive at a theory of why Pío should prevail. He was aware that he was not ready and made every effort to get additional time to prepare. He requested a continuance, which was denied. Next, he demanded a severance of Pío's cause from that of Magdalena Pico and asked that Pío's separate trial be heard by a jury. Arguments went back and forth for several hours without a ruling. Forster's lawyer, Volney E. Howard, opposed the continuance and argued that a jury trial had been waived for failure to demand it in a timely fashion.

The hearing was put over to Wednesday, January 15. Smith filed a written motion for a continuance on that day. The document shows that he was desperately seeking a postponement, scrambling to stall the trial. He gave several unimpressive reasons for delay. The lead attorney, Glassell, he said, had to go to Sacramento on other cases. Pío wanted to add another attorney to his present counsel who would need time to become acquainted with the case. Then, surprisingly, Smith demanded a later trial in order to have time to find the notary public, Ozias Morgan, because "Defendant has been unable to get any information as to his whereabouts, but he believes he can now do so."[1] Smith added unnecessarily that "said O. Morgan is a most material witness." The motion was denied and trial was set for Monday, January 20, at 10:00 A.M.

The reason for Smith's desperation to put off the trial is easy to understand: Pío's lawyers were simply not ready. The grounds asserted for delay in their motion were a mixture of truth and pretext. It is true that Glassell had to go to Sacramento, but it was not true that they had recently found any better information on the whereabouts of Morgan. Most trial attorneys will confess to feeling the anguish Smith probably had for lack of preparation.

But there was also anguish on the other side. On Thursday, January 16, Forster wrote in Spanish to his wife, Isidora, that Pío's attorneys had issued a subpoena for her to testify in San Diego. Part of the letter says:

> My first reaction was that you should not come at the cost of any sacrifice, but my lawyers tell me that if you don't come it might be a ground for them to ask for a continuance or delay of the case. With such delays we will be in the same situation all our lives without being able to see the end. They have done everything they can to get the Judge to give them a postponement. It is better that you make the sacrifice once and for all to bring the matter to a conclusion and thereby end these infamous proceedings forever . . . What they allege is the right to divide the Santa Margarita so that Don Pío gets one-half, Doña Magdalena gets one-quarter, and that which remains to me is only one-quarter. Consider what kind of conscience these vultures have . . .[2]

As it turned out, Isidora was excused from testifying. This rare letter shows Don Juan's deep animosity toward the Picos, even to the point of expressing it to his wife, their sister.

---

[1] Affidavits in support of motion for continuance signed by Pío Pico and filed on Jan. 15, 1873. *Forster v. Pico.*

[2] John Forster to Isidora Forster, Jan. 16, 1873, Forster Collection.

The San Diego courthouse
in 1875. The trial was
held on the second floor.
Courtesy, the Huntington Library.

With what excitement the day of the trial arrived, we cannot know. The *San Diego Union* laconically announced under the heading, "Law Intelligence," the simple statement, "Forster v. Pico. On trial."[3] During the morning of Monday, January 20, 1873, the proceedings began by Judge Rolfe announcing that he had granted the motion of Pío's lawyers to sever their case from that of Magdalena Pico. From that point forward her cause was referred to as the "Piquitos branch" of the case because her husband, being diminutive, had the nickname of "Piquitos" –Little Pico. Throughout the court records the American reporters misspelled the word as "Picitos." Rolfe also ordered that he would hear the Piquitos branch first because no jury had been requested by either side. When the Piquitos branch had concluded, Pío's case would be put on with a jury as he had requested.

The court trial of the Piquitos branch was conducted by Magdalena's attorney, Anson Brunson, from Monday, Janu-

---

[3] *San Diego Union,* Jan. 21, 1873.

ary 20 to Saturday, January 25. Although Brunson began by assisting the lead attorney, Charles B. Taggart, he was forced to take over the case when Taggart became ill and left the country on a trip to Central America for his health. The *San Diego Union* carried short daily reports giving the names of those who testified. Since the courtroom was new, on January 24 the newspaper reported, "The acoustics are exceedingly defective, every sound made in the room vibrating throughout it. Something will be done to remove or at least lessen the defect."

The case of Magdalena Pico and her children was prejudiced from the beginning because the document she claimed was a deed from Pío to her husband did not look like any commonly used instrument of transfer under Mexican or American law. Although a copy of the original writing was recorded with the county clerk in San Diego on August 18, 1853, Pío recorded a declaration on August 14, 1856, stating that the earlier document was a will, a "testamentary disposition," which was "revoked and null and without validity." Brunson correctly argued that a true deed is irrevocable so that the later recording of a "revocation" was without effect. He pointed out that two witnesses were required for a valid will under Mexican and American law, but that the document had none, just like a deed. Forster's lawyers replied that under Mexican military law, witnesses to a soldier's will were not required. Since Pío had been commander-in-chief of the Mexican armed forces in California when he made the document, he therefore had military status. Much evidence was given on this point, including a long, fascinating deposition of Pedro C. Carrillo.

Pío himself gave contradictory testimony which frustrated both Forster and the Piquitos claimants. On the one hand, he admitted that before his flight to Mexico, his brother had promised him to remain on the Santa Margarita during his absence, but only on the condition that Pío would "give him some security that he would not be moved away." Pío said, "I not only told him that I would give him security but that I would make him interested with me in the property. I gave him the document."[4] However, Pío also testified that years after his return, José Antonio requested a grant of part of the Santa Margarita which was refused. Apparently, the brothers failed to recognize the earlier purported one-quarter transfer of the ranch to José Antonio. Pío said that after his return from Mexico, members of the Piquitos branch lived on the ranch only with his permission and without any other right whatever.

The bickering between Forster and the Piquitos branch, together with the incomprehensible evidence, must have been extremely trying for Judge Rolfe. He declined to render a decision on the Piquitos branch until Pío's jury trial was ended. The court's severance ruling had given Pío's attorneys an extra week to prepare. On Monday morning, January 27, Pío's jury trial was ready to commence. The whole day was taken up with jury selection, which was completed by the next day.

Most of the jurors were townsmen and fairly recent American arrivals to San Diego. Their average length of residence in the city was about three years. No Mexicans were among its members, although a potential Mexican juror, José Estudillo, was excluded by Smith. This respected Californio was elected California's state treasurer the next year, a fact which makes Smith's rejection of him more puzzling.

The rapid expansion of downtown San Diego through the efforts of Alonso Horton attracted the kind of men who composed the jury. James M. Pierce was the most influential

---

[4]Stephenson, "Forster vs. Pico," 53.

of them. After the trial he was elected assemblyman to the state legislature.[5] For several years he was a director of the Bank of San Diego and its most powerful stockholder. In 1886, together with Ephraim W. Morse, he erected the Pierce-Morse Building, a pioneering five-story structure with elevators, the first in San Diego.[6]

Several other jury members were prominent in the commercial and civic life of the city. Charles Hubbell was cashier of the Bank of San Diego and a fruit grower. Arthur H. Julian owned a hardware and plumbing business, serving several terms as city councilman. John W. Wescott operated a carriage manufactory and blacksmith shop. He sat on various city commissions throughout his life.[7]

The balance of the jurors, George Geddes, William S. Clendenin, J. H. Pittman, Jerome L. Ward, J. L. Cosper, E. F. Stafford, and William B. Burns, left less of an imprint on the chronicles of the city. At least one, Jerome L. Ward, soon left San Diego. In 1882 he became sheriff in Tombstone, Arizona. Generally, these men were well regarded by their contemporaries. Despite complaints by Forster to Cave Couts, for the time and place, no better men could be assembled.

Forster, waiting for court to resume on the morning of Wednesday, January 29, sent a letter to Couts, who was a prospective witness. Forster had a poor opinion of Smith. Among other things, he wrote:

> I think you need not be in any hurry to come down until I call you. We have now only completed the impanelling of the jury, and Smith's persistent efforts to dodge the question and his having challenged and excused the best men in the community had already to a great extent prejudiced his cause in the minds of the court, jury, and spectators.

[5]Bancroft, *History of California*, 7: 368.
[6]T. S. Van Dyke, *City and County of San Diego*, 90.
[7]*Illustrated History of Southern California*, 214, 325, 358.

Continuing the letter, Forster writes some revealing lines about himself and Pío:

> Don Pío is again beginning to be very shaky. He has urged Ocampus to use his influence with me for a compromise. But I stand accused of false representations and fraud, and am determined to fight it out on the line we are now upon without the slightest doubt as to the result which cannot be otherwise than favorable.

Finally, Forster made an excellent prophecy:

> I believe that Jenkins and Don Andrés go on the stage today to be present at the examining of Don Blas and others at San Juan tomorrow where they will find that they are all pee-ing in the wrong pot.[8]

The Jenkins referred to by Forster was William Jenkins, who later testified on behalf of the Picos. A violent and generally obnoxious character, Jenkins was well known to Couts and Forster. Andrés used him as an interpreter. Jenkins, for all his faults, spoke Spanish well. The subject of the examination referred to was Don Blas Aguilar, the old mayordomo of Forster on the Santa Margarita. Pío's lawyers, of course, wanted Don Blas to state facts showing ownership of the Santa Margarita in Pío, such as giving rodeos and claiming orejanos. His testimony and that of others taken outside of court by stipulation was crucial.

When the trial resumed on Wednesday, January 29, with only the selection of the jury having been completed, Judge Rolfe stated that in his opinion the only real question of fact in the case was whether Forster had duped Pío when a deed was signed for the whole ranch, not just the half of it. This issue was raised solely by Pío's cross-complaint for fraud, and his side had the burden of proof. Therefore, he ruled that Pío would go forward as if he were the plaintiff. Forster, although the actual plaintiff in the underlying quiet title suit, was more

---

[8]John Forster to Cave Couts, Jan. 27, 1873, Couts Collection.

like a defendant since a successful defense to the cross-complaint would establish his right to quiet title. With the burden shifted to him, Smith called Pío as his first witness.

Pío must have been a fairly exotic figure for the American jury. Elegantly dressed, with a certain aristocratic bearing, Pío was a relic of the old ranchero elite. At age seventy-two, he was dark, short, and had a full beard white from his years. He customarily wore an excessive amount of conspicuous jewelry along with medals and decorations awarded to him by the Mexican government.[9] Pío often carried a cane whose handle was an ivory female leg protruding upward, bent at the knee like a can-can dancer. His eyes had a strange, penetrating quality. People sensed a disquieting aura about the Pico brothers. Hubert Howe Bancroft, who met them in Los Angeles during 1874, tried to convey the kind of unsettling impression they created by saying that they were "shrewd" and seemed "remarkably knowing."[10] Pío's testimony was given in Spanish through an interpreter, which partly accounts for the inordinate time he was on the stand, considering how little he actually said.

Smith's questions on direct examination did not follow any particular plan, showing his general lack of preparation. Forster's lawyers raised objections to nearly every question. Following the procedure of the time, each evidentiary ruling was followed by an "exception" from the adversely affected attorney. The trial transcript was written in longhand as fast as the participants spoke. The reporter wrote hundreds of pages of testimony and evidentiary objections in a hasty scrawl with an old-fashioned ink pen. Every few words begin with a stroke darker than the rest where he quickly dipped the pen in ink.

Pío explained that prior to 1862 he and Andrés had each

[9]Newmark, *Sixty Years*, 98.
[10]Bancroft, *Literary Industries*, 490.

owned one-half of the Santa Margarita. In that year Andrés transfered his half to Pío in trust. Thereafter, Pío held one-half as his own property and the other half as a trustee for Andrés. Pío gave no reasons for this transaction, but we know that Andrés made the transfer to thwart his creditors. In 1864, the House of Píoche and Bayerque in San Francisco was about to foreclose on the Santa Margarita. Rather than allow this to happen, Pío and Andrés determined to offer Forster a one-half interest in the Santa Margarita if he would take over the mortgage and prevent a foreclosure. The one-half interest Forster would receive was the part that Pío held in trust for Andrés. After the transfer, Forster and Pío would each be half owners of the Santa Margarita. Andrés would own nothing of it. In addition to giving Forster one-half of the Santa Margarita, Pío would also give him 1,500 head of cattle and 150 horses.

Pío made it clear that he was not involved in making the arrangement with Forster. The whole transaction was handled by Andrés. He said that a short while after he and Andrés had discussed offering one-half the ranch to Forster, he was told by Andrés that Forster had accepted. The next day Forster dropped by the Ranchito with a deed in English, which Pío could not read. Pío signed it and also signed a bill of sale to Forster, giving him ownership of 1,500 head of cattle and 150 horses on the Santa Margarita, part of the livestock owned by Pío and Andrés.

Forster left immediately for San Juan Capistrano by buggy. The two men had been alone during their brief meeting. Pío did not know that the deed was for more than one-half of the ranch and would not have signed it if he had known. Further, Pío never had anyone prepare the deed. Andrés told him that Forster volunteered to get one drawn up.

After executing the deed and bill of sale for the livestock,

Pío kept his nephew José María Pico on the ranch as his mayordomo. He sold thousands of cattle from the Santa Margarita
to brokers for the San Francisco market like Robert Ashcroft.
In 1866 he sold Ashcroft about two thousand head of cattle off
the Santa Margarita for the impressive amount of $43,000. He
gave rodeos and generally operated his interest on the land
without objection by Forster. When he discovered that Forster
claimed ownership of the whole ranch, he sent various people
to adjust the matter with Forster, without success.

When asked about the value of the Santa Margarita, Pío
said, "I would not have sold it for $100,000—only for necessi-
ty.[11] He said that in July 1864, he was in San Francisco and
that as five months had then passed since he gave his deed to
Forster, he went to Píoche and Bayerque to see if Forster had
assumed the mortgage as agreed. Pío claimed he was told
that Forster had not yet done so, but an offer had been
received to buy the Santa Margarita for $75,000. Pío said
John Rains had offered $40,000 for one-half the Santa Mar-
garita in 1861. These offers were known to Forster according
to Pío. Forster had asked him not to sell to Rains since
Forster wanted to buy it himself at that price.

Pío's claims of value for the Santa Margarita were not cor-
roborated in any way. His attorneys did not verify the alleged
offer of $75,000 through Píoche and Bayerque or the pro-
posal of Rains. Francois Píoche was not available to testify
for Pío concerning the claimed offer of $75,000. During the
morning of May 2, 1872, he had blown his brains out with a
heavy Navy pistol at his luxurious San Francisco home at 806
Stockton Street.[12] The probable cause of this unfortunate act

---

[11]WPA, 1: 32. As was explained in note 1 to Chapter 6, this citation refers to the typewritten transcript of the testimony in the case of *Forster v. Pico* prepared by the Works
Progress Administration in 1936.

[12]David G. Dalin and Charles A. Fracchia, "Forgotten Financier: Francois L. A.
Pioche," 1. The building which housed the offices of Pioche and Bayerque at the corner of
Montgomery and Jackson streets survived until the early 1970s when it was torn down for
construction of the Playboy Club.

was his depression over severe financial losses in France. As early as September 9, 1870, Forster had written a letter to Cave Couts from San Francisco in which he referred to Píoche, saying: "... the poor old gentleman appears totally thrown in a heap with the disasters of La Bella Francia."[13] Píoche's partner, Jules Bartholomew Bayerque, had died much earlier, during February 1865.[14]

For reasons which are not clear, Pío's lawyers took depositions and sworn statements of Obediah Livermore and two former employees of Píoche and Bayerque on July 3, 1872, in San Francisco, but did not inquire about the purported $75,000 offer. The proposal of John Rains would be much harder to confirm. He was ambushed and killed on November 17, 1862, near Mud Springs in present-day San Dimas.[15] If Pío could have shown that the mortgage Forster was to pay was only a fraction of the land's real value, then he would have had overwhelming evidence of fraud. But there was no evidence given on the point and Pío's attorneys did not press the issue.

One reads the transcript of Pío's testimony with complete astonishment. Each time he was asked about his agreement with Forster, the old man said he knew nothing about it, that Andrés had made the contract with Forster. There were only two times when Pío came close to describing what the contract might have been. The first time was when he said:

> ... Andrés and I agreed that he should make a proposition to Don Juan Forster that he should take under his care to cancel the mortgage of the Santa Margarita Ranch, offering him

---

[13]John Forster to Cave Couts, Sept. 9, 1870, Couts Collection.

[14]*San Francisco Chronicle*, Dec. 3, 1872.

[15]Esther Boulton Black, *Rancho Cucamonga and Doña Merced*, 69. The assassins of John Rains have never been identified with certainty. The mystery is a favorite subject of speculation among local historians. Rains built one of the first brick residences in San Bernardino County. It is a beautiful one-story structure built around a patio in the Mexican style, but the facade has the appearance of a southern plantation manor house The residence still stands as a museum on Vineyard Avenue, a few blocks north of Foothill Boulevard in the city of Rancho Cucamonga.

the undivided interest of Don Andrés—to him Forster—and that I should give to Mr. Forster 1,500 head of cattle and 150 horses–animals to give him security for the part I was to pay.[16]

The second time Pío nearly described the contract was when he told about a conversation he had with Forster in Los Angeles during December 1870, after a conflict had arisen between them. Pío testified:

> I said to him, "tell me, Godson, this 1,500 cattle and 150 horses you have received—for what were those cattle and horses?" "It is true," he said to me that "It was to pay for half of the ranch." I said, "I am going to call Andrés to settle it." I did not see Don Juan Forster again. I know by my sister that Don Juan has been to the house.[17]

There were no other times during the entire testimony of Pío in which he attempted to explain the nature of the contract he had with John Forster.

Pío's limited testimony on the contract suggests he understood that the amount owing on the mortgage was somewhat greater than the value of one-half the ranch. To retain a 50-percent interest, Pío would be required to make a payment to Forster for the difference between half the value of the land and the slightly greater amount owed to Pioche and Bayerque. Such an "equalizing payment" by Pío would assure that he became a one-half owner with Forster. Apparently, Pío thought the transfer of 1,500 head of cattle and 150 horses was supposed to be the equalizing payment. That is why Pío referred to the livestock as "animals to give him security

---

[16]WPA, 1: 48.

[17]Ibid., 57-58. The conversation referred to by Pío would have taken place during Forster's visit at the Ranchito during December 1870. This was the last meeting of Forster and Pío. It ended when Forster departed without taking his leave, disappointed that Pío had not invited him for a reconciliation, but rather to continue pressing his claim to the Santa Margarita. See Chapter 6, *ante*.

for the part I was to pay." For the same reason Pío claimed that Forster admitted in reference to the transfer of the livestock, "It was to pay for half the ranch."

Three years prior to giving his testimony, Pío had collaborated with his brother Andrés on a letter sent to Forster dated January 31, 1870. In it, they expressed surprise at certain claims Forster made to Pablo de la Guerra, who had been sent to mediate the Rancho Santa Margarita dispute. As we have seen, in that letter the Pico brothers chided Forster, asking him to explain why he told De la Guerra, "That you never received any cattle or horses of ours in payment of the part of the mortgage which corresponded to one-half of said rancho."

To successfully contend that the cattle and horses were an equalizing payment, Pío needed to prove the balance owed on the mortgage and the lesser value of one-half the ranch. Credible evidence of these amounts, together with proof that the livestock was worth the difference between them, would establish that the probable bargain with Forster was for only half the ranch. However, Pío did not testify to what the parties believed the ranch was worth or what was owed on the mortgage when Forster assumed it. He gave no clear testimony of the value assigned to the livestock or why he gave them to Forster. At best, all the jury could understand was that Pío contended he had bargained to transfer one-half of the Santa Margarita and that he planned to pay a portion of the mortgage himself by giving Forster 1,500 head of cattle and 150 horses. Pío suggested a general theory of what the contract might have been, but he utterly failed to set forth hard facts and details to support it. The jury must have been baffled by Pío's explanation of his agreement with Forster.

Additional important issues which would have been involved in the contract were omitted in Pío's testimony. For example, if both men were to be half owners, something should have been said regarding the sharing of expenses such as property taxes. Pío was silent on this point. These costs would logically be borne equally by joint owners, but San Diego tax records show payment of such expenses solely by Forster.[18]

There was an attempt to put the correspondence of Pío's brother-in-law Joaquin Ortega into evidence showing Pío's attempts, after giving an interest to Forster, to deal with living arrangements in the house at the Santa Margarita and the management of the gardens and orchards there. This would show Pío's belief that he was still a one-half owner of the land, but the letters were rejected as evidence and Pío gave no independent testimony on the subject.

Pío's turn on the witness stand was a disaster. He was the first witness and his attorneys presumably regarded him as one of the strongest. However, Pío said nothing of substance to help his case. All he did was confound the jury. The blame must fall on his lawyers for not preparing him to testify reasonably well. His direct examination was improvised, not planned. The questions were asked in a random, thoughtless manner. Pío no doubt tried to respond adequately, but it is clear that he did not know how to tell his story. There was probably a great sense of relief in Forster's camp after Pío's testimony. He had done so little damage to Forster that there was practically no cross-examination.

On Monday, February 3, Forster sent a letter to Cave Couts, which showed a happy, confident frame of mind. He sensed, and his lawyers no doubt confirmed, that he was ahead of the opposition. His letter was full of news and contained a crude joke which Forster explained with a word in parenthesis:

---

[18]At trial, Forster presented certified copies of the tax rolls from 1864 to 1872 to prove he had paid all the taxes assessed on the Rancho Santa Margarita. The original documents are now in the San Diego Historical Society Archives.

The opposite party made a very poor result of their examination of Don Blas in San Juan and they hardly know what to do. We have considerable fun occasionally during the examination of Pío. For instance, owing to the fact of witnesses requesting permission to retire from the courtroom very frequently, Ganahl got off an original on him. Ganahl said that he now knew why the old man was named Pee-o (piss).[19]

The deposition of Blas Aguilar in San Juan Capistrano further damaged Pío's case. Aguilar had been the confidante and mayordomo of Forster over twenty-five years. He would say nothing to injure his compadre, Don Juan. Aguilar denied that Pío gave rodeos, took orejanos, or behaved like an owner at any time on the Santa Margarita after its transfer to Forster. If Pío's lawyers had closely communicated with their client, they would have discovered that Pío had a deep distrust of Blas Aguilar. Three years before, on January 31, 1870, Pío wrote to José María Pico asking him to collect documents to use against Forster in case of a lawsuit, much as Andrés had done earlier in 1869. Pío told José María not to speak of his activities to Blas Aguilar because "Everything you tell him will go right back to Don Juan."[20] Forster knew Don Blas was fiercely loyal to him. It was for this reason that he had written to Couts that when the opposition examined Blas Aguilar, "they will find that they are all peeing in the wrong pot."[21]

During the afternoon of February 3, Andrés Pico took the stand. If the testimony of his brother Pío was a fiasco because he did not know the details of the arrangement with Forster, then Andrés, according to Pío, did. The case might yet be saved. Now was the time to give evidence on every detail of the contract and demonstrate how Forster had committed fraud. Near the beginning of his testimony, Andrés was allowed to make a narrative statement explaining the trans-

[19]John Forster to Cave Couts, Feb. 3, 1873, Couts Collection.
[20]Pío Pico to José María Pico, Jan. 31, 1870, in the private collection of Albert Pico.
[21]See John Forster to Cave Couts, Jan. 29, 1873, *infra*, this chapter

action with Forster. Judge Rolfe deferred ruling on objections until Andrés had entirely completed his version of the contract respecting the Santa Margarita in 1864. Andrés was asked what took place between him and Forster concerning the Rancho Santa Margarita in 1864, and he answered:

> My brother and I were speaking of this subject and I proposed to him that I would go and speak to Mr. Forster. I went to Forster and proposed to give him the interest I had in the Santa Margarita ranch if he would take up the mortgage, arranging with him in this manner: that they should stop the interest, and give him 1,500 head of cattle and 150 horses, and a half of the ranch of Santa Margarita that was my portion. Mr. Forster agreed to this and then I said to him, "You make a document." Then I came to Don Pío and gave him notice that I had made the arrangement with Mr. Forster. Don Pío Pico went to his ranch and I remained in Los Angeles. Then Mr. Forster came to me and said, "Here are the documents already made out." I said to him, "Very well, sign it." "No," he said to me, "it is necessary for my God-father, Don Pío Pico, to sign it because your interest is in Don Pío's name." "Very well," I said to him, "we will go to Don Pío."
>
> The next day we went to the Ranchito, Mr. Forster and I—he in his buggy, and I on horseback. I arrived before him at the Ranchito. There I met Pío, my brother. I said, "There comes Mr. Forster with the document, you will sign it; and besides that you will give him an order for 1,500 head of cattle and 150 horses to pay for the necessary portion due above that, in order to give him a security." He signed it then, but I did not see him. I went to run after some animals. That is what has passed between Forster and me.[22]

The Spanish interpreter, a Captain Rufus K. Porter, did not render the remarks of Andrés in English as well as could be. Even Judge Rolfe intervened from time to time to politely inquire if the testimony might not be translated a different way. Rolfe, an old California hand, understood enough

---

[22]WPA, 1: 75-76.

Spanish to recognize errors and ambiguities coming out of Porter's translation. The odd quality of the words purportedly used by Andrés was no doubt caused by an unartful conversion of languages.

The testimony set out above is nearly everything Andrés said about the understanding with Forster. No detailed exploration of the agreement was elicited by Smith. Immediately after Andrés's narrative, Smith switched to a number of questions wholly unrelated to the contract, such as how many cattle were on the Santa Margarita in 1864, who lived there, and the like. Smith never returned to the subject of the agreement. The few further bits and pieces given by Andrés about the transaction came in response to questions far afield of the understanding with Forster. As a consequence, the jury had no means of understanding the exact nature of the agreement, much less how Forster might have violated it.

In this manner, the best witness Smith had was thrown away. If we allow that Pío's attorneys, Glassell, Chapman and Smith deserved the high reputation they enjoyed in Los Angeles, then their performance in the debacle of Pío's case is truly enigmatic. Although we may acknowledge the more "sporting" nature of trials in those days, as well as the deficiencies in translation and the difficulties that certain eccentricities of Pío and Andrés may have presented, nothing fully excuses the wretched performance of this law firm.

The narrative of Andrés contains one sentence which out of all his testimony gives the only glimpse of what the deal between the parties undoubtedly was. Andrés said he advised Pío of the arrival of Forster at the Ranchito as follows:

> There comes Mr. Forster with the document, you will sign; and besides that you will give him an order for 1,500 head of cattle and 150 horses to pay him the necessary portion due above that in order to give him a security.[23]

---
[23]Ibid.

Like Pío, Andrés recognized that the mortgage owed to
Pioche and Bayerque was greater than the value of one-half
of the Santa Margarita. In order to equalize the interests of
Pío and Forster, it would be necessary for Pío to pay Forster
the difference between one-half the value of the land and the
mortgage balance. That was Andrés's meaning when he
described the purpose of the bill of sale for the livestock as
being "to pay him the necessary portion due above that in
order to give him a security." The cattle and horses would
have been payment by the Picos of the difference to Forster.
Andrés believed the livestock was enough to compensate
Forster completely for the difference between the value of
half the Santa Margarita and the greater mortgage balance.
When Forster met Andrés at the Lafayette Hotel and denied
having received the livestock, it was cause for outrage. To
Andrés, this meant that Forster had reneged on their contract. Shortly afterward, Andrés wrote to José María Pico
about Forster's claim of not having received the cattle and
horses saying, "If he denies this, he will deny everything."[24]

From the foregoing, a vague outline of the case to be made
by the Picos can be perceived, but no testimony was given to
set out the details of the transaction with Forster. Instead,
Smith elicited Andrés's testimony about past experiences
that tended to show Andrés's belief that his brother Pío
retained a one-half interest in the Santa Margarita.

Andrés recalled that during 1866, Cave Couts wanted to
enter the Rancho Santa Margarita to drive some cattle back
to his property, the nearby Rancho Guajome, for a rodeo.
Andrés was visiting the Santa Margarita and refused to let
Couts's vaqueros enter the Santa Margarita for that purpose.
That afternoon, Andrés rode over to attend the rodeo on the
Rancho Guajome. After the rodeo, Andrés met Couts at the

---

[24]Andrés Pico to José María Pico, Sept. 7, 1869, Pico Family File, San Diego Historical
Society Archives.

home of his brother, Blount Couts. The two men sat together on a veranda discussing the rodeo. Couts complained about Andrés's refusal to let his men enter the Santa Margarita to collect his cattle. Andrés described the incident as follows:

> Being seated in one chair, and I in another, we commenced talking about my having given orders to have no rodeo in the Corral de Tierra. There he said to me, "You have nothing in the Santa Margarita." I replied I had nothing, but I came here as representing my brother. Then he rose up and when I saw him I got up and took hold of him very quick. I said, "Don't you do something. It is a custom of yours to insult every poor Spaniard and every poor man that passes along here." Then the women shouted to me, "He is going to kill you, let him loose." I said nothing, but let him go to quiet the women and then we commenced laughing to make out that it was sport as not to frighten the women.[25]

Smith apparently wanted to use this incident to illustrate an assertion of authority by Andrés over the Santa Margarita in the belief that Pío retained an ownership interest. There could have been a less proprietary reason for what happened as well. Later in the trial, Marcos Forster, the son of Don Juan, testified that he attended the same rodeo and had seen Andrés and Couts break out of the herd and come together occasionally "to drink out of a demi-John of whiskey."[26] This apparently went on all afternoon.

Andrés testified that on the same day as the altercation with Couts, he had supper with the Forster family and others at the Santa Margarita. He said:

> While we were eating supper at the house, the wife of Don Juan Forster was there at the table. Francisco Forster was there, Blas Aguilar was there, José María Pico, José Antonio Serrano and I. Don Juan Forster was lying upon a bedstead or

---

[25]WPA, 3: 74.
[26]WPA, 2: 184.

lounge close by. We at the table. When we finished, Forster said to me, "What a bad job you have done with Couts in stopping the cattle I am moving around." "Yes," I said to him, "I ordered them stopped on account of a conversation I had with him in Los Angeles." I gave him to understand that I came representing the interest of Pío in Santa Margarita. Then I said to him, "If I am under this roof, I am here on account of my brother. That garden in front, belongs to my brother, although you have put it in order, and half of the ranch belongs to Pío. I have not an inch on the land for all my interests are yours." Don Forster then said, "I don't say anything to you because he is my God-father."[27]

This testimony of Andrés was offered to show that Forster had admitted that Pío still owned a one-half interest in the ranch. Of course, because of the poor Spanish translation, the admission sounds equivocal in English. Much of the testimony offered by Forster later was in rebuttal to Andrés's claim that Forster had made such an admission on that particular occasion.

Andrés testified that after he had learned of the true content of the deed, he had "hard words" with Forster at the Lafayette Hotel during the summer of 1869. Following that unpleasant confrontation, Andrés said that he and Forster reconciled at a late night meeting at living quarters Forster still owned at the Mission San Juan Capistrano following a dinner at the residence of Juan Avila. Andrés testified:

> . . . I went to the room of Mr. Forster and rapped on the door. He says, "Who is it?" I said, "It is me." Then he opened the door. He said to me, (surprised), "I am writing a letter to my Godfather, Don Pío."
>
> "Sir," I said to him, "I have come to settle the subject of Santa Margarita. Let us make peace as members of the same family."
>
> Then he answered me, "Andrés, I have always believed you to be a generous man of a noble heart."

---

[27]Ibid., 83.

I told him there that so far as anything of a personal nature between us was concerned, here is my hand, and we spoke and looked at one another with tears in our eyes. "Now," said I to him, "recollect the contract you have made respecting Santa Margarita? Do you recollect?"

He said, "Yes." I said, "Did I not tell you I gave up the half of the ranch and 1,500 head of cattle and 150 horses to take away the mortgage?. . . Now let us settle definitely." Then he said to me, "Don Andrés, as it is a very important subject, I have got to go to San Francisco. I am going to set out early in the morning for the old Mission, and from there I am going to catch the steamer and go to San Francisco, and I give you my word that when I return, I will speak of the subject in Los Angeles."[28]

Andrés then described the frustration he felt in attempting to pin down Forster on a settlement concerning the Santa Margarita. He testified that after Forster returned from San Francisco, he eluded Andrés another time. Andrés told the court:

He returned from San Francisco. I was in San Fernando and they sent me word that he had arrived. I went to Los Angeles and met Mr. Forster in the corridor of the house of Abel Stearns. I said to him, "We will settle now." When we were talking, his son, John, came out. When he came out, he [Forster] said, "Excuse me, I am going inside and will return." I remained there a little while, and then I said to his son, "I am going to bring some cigarettes," and I went to the Bella Union. I was occupied a little time and when I returned, Don Juan Forster had taken his carriage and gone.[29]

This was basically Andrés's whole testimony. Although it must have been interesting for the jury to hear intimate details about the lives of the famous parties to the lawsuit, little was proven on the issue of the alleged fraud by Forster.

---

[28] Ibid., 81-82.
[29] Ibid., 82.

The incidents related by Andrés, especially Forster's purported admission of Pío's interest at the Santa Margarita after Couts's rodeo in May 1866, was the subject of much rebuttal. More time was spent by Forster's attorneys refuting Andrés's testimony about these incidents than they deserved. The jury needed concrete facts concerning the agreement of the parties and their conduct respecting it. Andrés did not give this to them. His testimony was not much better than the fatal performance of his brother.

José María Pico was the next to testify. His appearance as a witness did not favor his uncle Pío. Perhaps José María was not inclined to be cooperative because he felt betrayed over some earlier testimony given by Pío during the first five days when the Piquitos branch of the case was heard without a jury. At that time Pío testified that his brother, José Antonio, had not received a grant of an interest to the Santa Margarita in 1846 and only lived there with Pío's consent. This testimony was extremely prejudicial to the cause of the Piquitos branch. No doubt the lack of support by his uncle offended José María. It even surprised Forster who wrote to Couts about Pío's testimony saying:

> . . . without any effort on my part, but purely voluntarily, Pío stated that José Antonio went upon the ranch with his (Pío's) permission only as a tenant-at-will, and never held adversely up to the time of his death.[30]

The pique of José María during his testimony was evident. At one point, Smith put this question to him: "Do you recollect my asking you to come around to my room to talk about this case?"[31] José María acknowledged that he had been asked to do so, but had refused. He said his reaction to Smith's request had been: "I told you I would not go to your

---

[30]John Forster to Cave Couts, Feb. 3, 1873, Couts Collection.
[31]WPA, 1: 112.

room; that what I had to say I would say in court."[32] José María even resisted giving Pío's letters back to him for use as evidence in the trial. During his cross-examination, José María said that Pío had asked him for the letters on the eve of trial in the saloon of the Horton House. José María at first refused, but finally supplied copies of them.

All this, of course, means more than that José María had taken an antagonistic posture regarding his uncle. The fact that Smith had asked José María "to come around to my room to talk about this case"—which room could be none other than one at the Horton House—means that this key witness was ignored until the last minute by Pío's lawyers. Yet, José María was indispensable in proving Pío's belief that he had only conveyed one-half the ranch.

During the five years between the agreement with Forster in 1864 and the confirmation in 1869 that the deed recorded in San Diego conveyed the whole ranch, Pío had sent written communications to José María which evinced a continuing belief that he remained a half owner. Obviously, evidence of a fixed conviction that he remained an owner cast doubt on Forster's claim that Pío intended to give away the whole ranch. It was even remotely possible that standing alone, the testimony of José María and the letters he received from Pío could win the case. José María had strong evidence of Pío's state of mind which inferred a belief by Pío that he had not conveyed the whole ranch.

José María was thirty-six or thirty-seven years old at the time of the trial. He could not state his exact age, a reflection of the primitive conditions in which he had lived as a child. As we have seen, José María was not eager to help Pío. Smith's questions were answered by curt replies. When asked about the nature of his employment by Pío, he simply stated,

----
[32]Ibid.

"In charge of his interest."[33] As he was queried further about the kind of interests he had charge of, he merely replied, "Cattle and horses."[34] Smith did not force him to elaborate. Instead, Smith abruptly told him, "Produce all your letters from Pico to you relating to your charge as mayordomo of Pío Pico on the Santa Margarita rancho."[35] José María handed over nineteen letters which were marked as Pío Pico's exhibits 34 through 53. Smith then added twenty other letters from José María to Pío and moved the court to admit all thirty-nine pieces of correspondence into evidence.

There was no attempt to examine José María on the content of the letters. Smith simply put the mass of correspondence on the clerk's desk and moved for their admission. Forster's lawyer, Volney E. Howard, immediately objected to them because they were hearsay. Smith explained that "The object for which these letters is offered is for the purpose of proving that José María Pico was there as mayordomo during the time named and acting as such for Pío Pico."[36]

Judge Rolfe refused to admit the letters in the wholesale manner proposed by Smith. Strangely, it appears that Rolfe thought the letters were irrelevant to the question of whether fraud had been committed by Forster on the date when the deed was signed. Rolfe seemed unable to understand that Pío's behavior after he gave Forster the deed was the best guide to what Pío believed the deed contained when he signed it. Still, the way the letters were presented by Smith almost guaranteed their rejection. He attempted to get José María to testify independently as to the subject matter of some of the letters, but each question was objected to as being irrelevant, and every objection was sustained by Rolfe. On Tuesday, February 5, José María was excused as a witness without having helped Pío's case.

---

[33]Ibid., 86.   [34]Ibid., 87.
[35]Ibid., 93.   [36]Ibid., 95.

After the testimony of Pío, Andrés, and José María, there was little else for Smith to present. By the end of José María's turn on the witness stand, the general collapse of Pío's case was apparent. If Smith was a man of ordinary sensibility, the last few days of his presentation in court must have been depressing. One wonders how he felt trudging back to the Horton House at the end of each day. Perhaps he found succor with Andrés Pico, a noted drinker, in the convivial atmosphere of the Horton House saloon.[37]

Smith gamely finished up his case with a few minor witnesses. He called José Antonio Serrano, the mayordomo of Pío's Ranchito. Serrano said he had been present at the Santa Margarita in 1866 when Forster allegedly admitted to Andrés that Pío was still an owner. The story Serrano told was identical in every detail to the version Andrés gave in his testimony. Forster's attorneys had rare sport with Serrano on cross-examination.

Incredibly, Serrano could not say whether 1866 had been twenty, fifteen, or ten years prior to the time of trial. He could not recall one single event occurring in his life from 1866 to 1873 even though each year was ticked off separately in a series of questions by Ganahl, obviously relishing the debacle. Serrano did not even know the year in which the trial was taking place. The jury must have had no trouble in dismissing the testimony of the unfortunate Serrano.[38]

Smith then called José Rubio, who briefly testified that he met Forster in San Francisco during 1864 while walking

---

[37]Andrés Pico began to exhibit rather severe symptoms of alcoholism in the last decade of his life. His distress became apparent to his neighbors in the San Fernando Valley. A member of one neighboring family wrote of Andrés's drinking as follows: "They used to say of the General that by about four o'clock in the afternoon he was pretty tight because he drank wine all day, but the old General would say, 'it makes no difference what I am, I is [sic] always a gentleman.' They used to tell about that." See Catherine Dace, "Early San Fernando: Memoirs of Mrs. Catherine Dace," 238.

[38]Serrano was the father-in-law of Benjamin I. Hayes. After the death of his first wife, Hayes married Adeleida Serrano.

down Montgomery Street. According to his testimony, Forster told him that he was there arranging the mortgage on the Santa Margarita because he had bought one-half the ranch from Andrés Pico. When cross-examined, Rubio could not name any street in San Francisco other than Montgomery Street. He could not identify the hotel where he stayed or give its location. He could not say how long he was in the city in 1864 or who he saw besides Forster.

William Jenkins was called to the stand to testify that he saw Forster arrive at the Ranchito some time in February 1864, with Andrés Pico. He saw Forster go into the house with Pío while Andrés, mounted on a black horse, galloped away. This testimony was offered to support the Picos' version of how and where the deed to the Santa Margarita was executed. It was a mistake to use Jenkins for this purpose, however. He had a reputation as a bad man, and like many outlaw types of the Southwest, he had crossed over the law at different times. In 1856 he was a deputy U.S. marshal in Los Angeles. In that position, he unjustifiably shot and killed a Mexican named Antonio Ruiz over a trivial incident. The American authorities refused to punish Jenkins for the crime which provoked an armed riot among the Mexican population. The matter was aggravated by a surly attitude Jenkins adopted toward the Mexican discontents.[39]

Forster sent Couts a letter in 1860 to warn him that Jenkins was passing through their neighborhood on his way to Baja California. He wrote that there were vague reports of "Jenkins being involved in robberies" and that "he was at the head of several outlaws . . ."[40] The reputation of Jenkins was

---

[39] The anger of Los Angeles's Mexican population over this incident is reflected in a series of illuminating and sensitive articles in the Spanish language newspaper, *El Clamor Público*, in every edition from July 26, 1856, to August 23, 1856. The *Los Angeles Star* gave the matter attention in its editions of the same dates. A good treatment of the "Ruiz-Jenkins affair" and an explanation of its significance in early Los Angeles race relations is in Pitt, *Decline of the Californios*, 162–66.

[40] John Forster to Cave Couts, Jan. 2, 1860, Couts Collection.

not helped by press reports of his having shot a Mexican to death during a poker game in San Bernardino County in July 1861.[41]

Jenkins's vague claim in trial that Forster was on the Ranchito about the time the deed was signed had little value compared to the extremely negative effect his presence probably had on the jury. During cross-examination, Jenkins confessed he had once taken "a cut" with a knife at John Forster and had pulled a gun on his son, Marcos Forster. Jenkins excused himself for these incidents saying that both times "I was too drunk to remember much . . . It was all under the influence of the moment."[42]

Worse, Jenkins identified himself as an associate of the Picos. He stated that he was working as an interpreter and making service of subpoenas for them. As a result, they were paying his expenses in San Diego and something else besides. When asked what he normally did for a living he said he was a butcher and a "vegetarian."[43] He explained to the puzzled court that the latter occupation meant that "I have on my place China women raising vegetables to sell on the market."[44] The jury may have been amused, but could not have been favorably impressed by this dangerous man. His identification with the Picos was unfortunate.

Smith's last gambit was to offer in evidence depositions from some of the most distinguished citizens of Los Angeles attesting to Pío's honesty and veracity. Some of them also gave sworn statements regarding Ozias Morgan's reputation for dishonesty. One inference to be drawn from the depositions was that Pío could be believed and was telling the truth about his having intended to transfer only one-half the ranch. Another was that for a price, Ozias Morgan could be

---

[41]*Los Angeles Star*, Aug. 3, 1861.
[42]WPA, 3: 77.
[43]Ibid., 86.
[44]Ibid.

induced to conspire with Forster in a fraud. Judge Rolfe properly refused to admit the depositions in evidence.

During the morning of Friday, February 5, Forster wrote to Cave Couts:

> My case progressed very favorably yesterday, the other party bringing in many depositions damaging to the charac-ter of Morgan and promising Pico is a perfect saint as to truth, honesty, and integrity. But every matter was ruled out and their Los Angeles endeavors are gone up [in smoke]. . . They cannot delay much longer with their proceedings as under the present ruling of the court, they have nothing to offer . . . I think the Judge will keep them to business so as to get through with the case.[45]

Forster correctly sensed that Judge Rolfe was becoming impatient. After one adjournment about this time, he made an aside to the jury on his way to chambers saying, "We put in the time [even] if we don't make much progress." This com-ment infuriated Smith, who later assigned it as a ground of appeal, but Pío's floundering case soon ended.[46] The trial now shifted to the Forster camp for defense.

---

[45]John Forster to Cave Couts, Feb. 5, 1873, Couts Collection.

[46]This ground of appeal and many others are found in an exceedingly rare, and probably unique, bound volume of 305 printed pages entitled "Transcript On Appeal" which is owned by Tony Forster of San Juan Capistrano. Except for some light water stains, it is in excellent condition. On the last page is handwritten in ink, "Hayes & Gatewood, Attys. at Law, San Diego, Cal.," since these men formed an evanescent partnership or association between the trial and Hayes' permanent departure for Los Angeles. There is some margina-lia in red ink and pencil, probably written by Hayes.

The official transcripts, briefs, points and authorities, and other documents filed on appeal to the California Supreme Court are in the State Archives, Sacramento, Case No. 3953.

CHAPTER NINE

The Defense of Forster

Such was the poverty of Pío's case that if the jury could have made their decision without hearing any further evidence, they would almost certainly have ruled against him then and there. But with the ownership of a principality at stake, Volney E. Howard was bound to put on a defense. Predictably, he called Forster himself as the first witness.

Shortly before noon on Thursday, February 6, Forster took the witness stand. It was the first time the jurors would hear the testimony of a major witness without the distracting repetition of a Spanish interpreter. With his faint British accent, dressed in his customary conservative dark suit, Forster was a dignified figure of great authority. He was one of the greatest landowners in Southern California. Like Pío and Andrés Pico, he was famous, a man whose name every juror had heard frequently. Even the most recent newcomers to San Diego on the jury would not fail to recognize the imposing figure of Don Juan Forster.

His attorneys made a thoughtful analysis of what they wanted to present during his testimony before the jury. They began by eliciting the history of Forster's dealings with the Picos regarding the Rancho Santa Margarita over several years. Then they had Forster describe the culmination of these events by explaining, in part, the circumstances surrounding the delivery of the deed of February 25, 1864.

The testimony ended by showing how, as a full owner, Forster had exercised dominion over the property, paid all the taxes, and invested a fortune in the development of the ranch.

Forster began his testimony by stating that as early as the winter of 1859, Pío had called him to his house in Los Angeles to explain that "His notes were scattered out all over Los Angeles, in the city particularly, and he had no means immediately at his disposal to meet the liabilities . . ."[1] Pío proposed to convey one-half the Rancho Santa Margarita to Forster in exchange for the liquidation of his debts up to $20,000. Forster agreed and paid off creditors of Pío "even beyond the amount of $20,000."[2] However, not long afterwards, Forster was riding with Andrés Pico on a ranch owned by the Pico family near Lompoc. Andrés told him that Pío had decided not to transfer Forster a half interest in the Rancho Santa Margarita after all, but that Forster would be repaid by Pío "if he should have to go without a shirt to do it . . ."[3]

Forster produced several little books which contained an accounting of the amounts paid at Pío's request. They were written by Forster himself in an odd melange of English and Spanish. Interestingly, his books of account and personal diaries show that he lived among the Mexicans in California so long that his mind worked in both languages interchangeably.[4] The accounting he presented purported to prove that by 1860 he had discharged over $24,000 in debts for Pío. Forster testified:

> He never did pay me nor pass that deed, but remained indebted to me in the amount of nearly $25,000 which has never up to this date been complied with. He has never paid back fully those amounts.[5]

---

[1]WPA, 2: 5.   [2]Ibid.
[3]Ibid., 6.
[4]The surviving diaries are now in the Forster Collection.   [5]WPA, 2: 6.

Despite Pío's refusal to perform his bargain, he turned to Forster again for relief within a year or two. The House of Pioche and Bayerque in San Francisco had commenced serious threats of foreclosure on the Rancho Santa Margarita during 1861. As a result, Forster said, "I had a conversation on the subject with Don Pío, in which he stated that he was over-flooded with heavy indebtedness, and frequent applications for settlement, and he did not know what to do."[6]

The San Francisco money lenders were well acquainted with Forster. They even communicated directly with him concerning his brothers-in-law. According to Forster, "They applied to me as a kind of mediator, knowing that I took an interest in the Picos' business matters."[7] The concern of Pioche and Bayerque over the Picos' failure to pay their mortgage on the Rancho Santa Margarita began to take on a more strident tone. Forster described the correspondence he was receiving from them:

> Pioche and Bayerque occasionally applied to me to know what they [the Picos] really intended doing, and to find out what really could be done toward the liquidation of the indebtedness. That it was very distressing to them. That they had many previous arrangements with the Picos and they had never paid them.[8]

Forster discussed the demands of Pioche and Bayerque with the Picos on numerous occasions. Their response was to ask Forster "to intercede for a delay of proceedings to allow them an opportunity of paying."[9] But beyond that, Forster claimed, the Picos wanted him "to help them out of it, but my means at the time did not allow me to take upon myself such a heavy burden."[10]

At this time, the court permitted the deposition of a Los

[6]Ibid., 11.   [7]Ibid.
[8]Ibid.   [9]Ibid., 14.
[10]Ibid.

Angeles merchant named Adolph Portugal to be read to the jury, supposedly as a basis to ask Forster questions about his dealings with Portugal. In his deposition, Portugal said that he was hired by Pío to persuade Forster to assume the debt owed to Pioche and Bayerque in exchange for the Rancho Santa Margarita. Forster then testified that Portugal had indeed approached him many times on behalf of Pío. Their conversations were inconclusive. Forster described his talks with Portugal:

> They were between 1861 and 1864 and continued over the whole series of that time, he always manifesting to me that Pío wished me to negotiate this matter, and I continually refusing to do so, because my circumstance was not such at that time that I could take upon myself such a heavy obligation.[11]

For something in excess of two years, from late 1861 to the first part of 1864, Forster stood off the propositions of the Picos and their agents to undertake the mortgage on the Rancho Santa Margarita in consideration of ownership of the property.

After taking Forster this far in his testimony, his attorney, Volney E. Howard, handed him the deed to the Rancho Santa Margarita he had received from Pío. "State all the circumstances connected with the execution of that deed as near as you can remember them," he demanded.[12] Forster, who had just testified that he consistently refused all offers over a period of more than two years to take the Rancho Santa Margarita in exchange for paying the mortgage, told a strange story in response.

On the morning of February 25, 1864, Forster was in Los Angeles during one of his constant business trips. While walking north on Main Street near the Bella Union Hotel he met Andrés Pico. Forster casually stopped to exchange com-

---

[11]Ibid., 16.   [12]Ibid., 17.

pliments of the morning with his brother-in-law but found him in a desperate state of mind. Andrés told him that he had just offered to give the whole Rancho Santa Margarita to Pioche and Bayerque together with all the cattle on it if they would cancel the mortgage. The firm had refused the offer. It was in need of money and demanded an immediate pay-off in cash. Andrés said he intended to renew his offer but he would also throw in valuable real estate in San Jose and Santa Clara as a final, last-ditch attempt to liquidate the debt. His proposed last offer was disastrous for the Pico family, but nothing else could be done. Of course, there was one other further possibility, which was that perhaps Forster would take it upon himself to settle the matter.

In light of his previous conduct, Forster's reaction to this information was amazing. He testified:

> I asked him where was Pío. He said, "He is at his house." We went together to see Pío. We came to the arrangement that I would, as an act of desperation, take upon myself the liquidation. To take the property and settle the debt.[13]

Forster's version of his meeting with the Picos that morning is unequivocal. All three men agreed that Forster would pay off the mortgage to Pioche and Bayerque and take the Rancho Santa Margarita in return.

After only a brief discussion, Andrés went out in search of Ozias Morgan, a notary public, who was personally known to all concerned. Andrés soon returned with Morgan, who wrote out some notes reflecting the transaction. Morgan left for his office to prepare a deed which would be signed that same afternoon. At the time appointed, about three o'clock, Morgan returned to Pío's home with the deed. Although the deed was written in English, a language of which Pío was perfectly ignorant, Forster claimed that the contents of the deed were known to Pío and the document was regularly executed:

---

[13]Ibid., 18.

The deed was read and translated every word (I cannot say every word for every word might not have been translated) but the substance of the deed was translated and then Don Pío affixed his signature and acknowledged it for Morgan, and we all were satisfied as to the results, and the business was concluded.[14]

When asked if Morgan spoke Spanish, Forster answered, "Very well, as well as I speak it." His lawyer persisted: "Do you speak the Spanish language well?" Forster, who recorded his private diaries in Spanish and spoke the language every day of his life, dryly replied, "Tolerably well."[15]

Forster had an explanation of the transaction that was very simple: "The bargain was that I should go to San Francisco and assume their indebtedness, and take in consideration the ranch of Santa Margarita."[16] He did not tell the jury why, with uncharacteristic, almost impetuous haste, he plunged into the transaction and completed it on the same day, within hours of meeting Andrés on the street. The testimony of Forster did not disclose the amount of money the parties believed would have to be paid to release the mortgage. In fact, according to Forster, the deed showed a "nominal consideration" of only $14,000, "because we did not know the actual amount of the indebtedness to the House of Pioche and Bayerque."[17] This assertion was astonishing since both Forster and the Picos had received numerous written demands for payment in which the balance owed was stated.

Forster failed to say whether any value was assigned to the Rancho Santa Margarita during his brief discussion with the Picos. Obviously, if the value of the ranch exceeded the mortgage balance, Forster would get a windfall to that extent. His attorney asked him what the Rancho Santa Margarita was worth at the time he took the deed. Forster said:

---

[14]Ibid.   [15]Ibid.
[16]Ibid.   [17]Ibid.

Well, I don't know what was really the value of it. I know I paid a very high price for it. It was only through a desperate effort of mine that I bought it at that price. Nobody else would have done it but me.[18]

Forster's maintaining that he did not know the value of the Rancho Santa Margarita is remarkable. If anyone knew the approximate value of real estate in San Diego County during the drought, he did.

Forster had sold the Rancho de la Nacion to Pioche and Bayerque previously.[19] He acted as their agent in paying taxes on the land afterward.[20] He was unusually well informed on the ebb and flow of commercial activities in California, going back to the days of the early hide trade. During his constant business trips he sought out information on everything: land prices, interest rates, cattle prices, taxes, and more. This information was relayed to Cave Couts by an almost daily correspondence. Forster's letters show a farsighted, questing mind which was preoccupied with business affairs and the increase of his wealth. Moreover, he had maintained a close relationship with Pioche and Bayerque for many years.

The general manager of the firm, Obediah Livermore, had long been an intimate friend and companion of Forster. This fact was known to the Picos and was probably the reason they initially requested Forster to intercede with Pioche and Bayerque. Because of his close connections and constant contacts with Pioche and Bayerque, Forster was at all times familiar with the most minute details concerning the Picos' relations with the firm and the status of their loan. It takes little imagination to picture Forster with Livermore, dining

---

[18]Ibid., 52.

[19]James M. Jensen, "John Forster—a California Ranchero," 41.

[20]Forster, acting as an agent, signed tax declarations on real property owned by Pioche and Bayerque up to the time of trial. See Lists of Property, Real and Personal, Subject to Taxation in the County of San Diego, 1864 to 1872. San Diego Historical Society Archives.

in San Francisco, leisurely discussing the Rancho Santa Margarita well before Forster's fateful meeting with Andrés Pico on Main Street in Los Angeles.

The minimal testimony given by Forster of his meeting with the Picos and the bargain they consummated on the same day implies a rushed, "desperate" transaction of the kind stated in his testimony, but Forster had waited years before committing himself, resisting all efforts to persuade him to take the ranch. His testimony did not reveal, and even obscured, the calculations of his facile mind.

Since Forster failed to give testimony about the balance owed on the mortgage or the value of the Rancho Santa Margarita, it was impossible to determine if he had received a windfall. As we have seen, the Picos implied, but did not prove, that the Rancho Santa Margarita was worth more than the balance owed on the mortgage. They said that Forster was given 1,500 head of cattle and 150 horses "as security" for that part of the mortgage Pío was to pay. This inferred that the mortgage exceeded one-half of the property's value but the livestock was compensation to Forster for the difference. Accordingly, when Pío executed the deed he intended that Forster take only one-half of the ranch.

Forster's lawyers argued that the cattle, which were nearly worthless because of the drought, had been given to Forster as a gesture toward payment of Pío's old indebtedness to him. In effect, the cattle were not part of the bargain other than a further inducement to take the ranch. They had little value in 1864. Forster stated that cattle were dying in such great numbers at the time that they were only worth the value of their hides, a paltry two and a half dollars. Even then, it cost about a quarter to take the hide so that the net value per head was even less.[21] The issue of the cattle as an element of the bargain was thereby reduced to a trifling matter.

---

[21]WPA, 2: 27.

Having disposed of the bargain with the Picos, the testimony of Forster shifted to his operation of the ranch, particularly with respect to the sacrifice and investment he had made in reliance on the deed giving him full ownership. He said that he moved to the Rancho Santa Margarita from San Juan Capistrano almost immediately after taking the deed on February 25, 1864. Between February and July 1864, Forster struggled to save his livestock from the drought. He drove cattle into the mountains around Santa Ysabel and Julian where some of the grass had not yet died and where an occasional creek contained a little water.

The loss of cattle was staggering. Despite his best efforts, about half his livestock perished from thirst and hunger in 1864. Curiously, he admitted that none of the cattle given to him by Pío died. It was not until July 1864 that Forster was able to travel to San Francisco to arrange the matter of the mortgage. As the Picos probably suspected, Forster did not have to pay off the mortgage in cash. Instead, he was able to obtain a series of new notes and a favorable payment schedule with the general manager, his good friend, Obediah Livermore. This is not to say that the new payment schedule was not onerous. During the trial Forster was shown the notes and asked if he recognized them. He answered in a way that must have deeply impressed the jury: "I should, it cost me many a sweat to pay them."[22]

In the ensuing years, he testified, he was the only person who gave rodeos or claimed orejanos. This was crucial, since as we have seen, only the owner could order rodeos or claim orejanos. Pío never gave a rodeo or claimed an orejano, according to Forster. Further, he truthfully asserted that Pío had never paid any property taxes on the Rancho Santa Margarita during the entire time Forster was in possession. Forster also testified that he invested over $30,000 in

---

[22]Ibid., 28.

improvements on the property which included a complete remodeling of the main ranch house, the installation of over eighteen miles of fencing, and the construction of a road system. All this was done at his expense, he said, because he regarded himself as the owner of the entire property.[23]

An important incident repudiating Forster's claim to full ownership was the sale by Pío of 2,000 head of cattle to Robert Ashcroft in 1867. Pío had testified to this transaction as proof that he retained an ownership interest in the Rancho Santa Margarita. Forster attributed the sale to his own generosity:

> Don Pío had all his property mortgaged . . . The San Fernando, and the Ranchito and whatever other lands he had all were mortgaged and he could not get out of it, and so I allowed him to make use of the cattle to help him out of the difficulty. It was not the first time I had helped him out of his difficulties.[24]

Forster said he helped Pío by giving rodeos and gathering cattle. The whole process took eight days. He even said that "I allowed him the use of a portion of my cattle to make up his complement, because he was in a very tight place . . ."[25] However, Pío gave no rodeos nor acted like an owner, according to Forster. In discussing the roundups of cattle so Pío could sell them, Forster described what Pío was doing at the time:

> He was going around like any other neighbor coming to the ranch. He lived then like every other neighbor during the rodeos. Camped out like a party of Gypsies. His wagon there moving about, and his provisions and cook and the paraphernalia of a camp, just as I used to see the Gypsies do when I was very young.[26]

Pío sold about two thousand head of cattle to Robert

---

[23]Ibid., 39-40.   [24]Ibid., 37.
[25]Ibid.   [26]Ibid., 37-38.

Ashcroft as a result of all these efforts. The amount he received was about $43,000. Forster alleged that he fully cooperated in the sale and even allowed some large, but undetermined number of his own cattle to be sold by Pío. All this sacrifice on behalf of Pío was "to help him out of the difficulty."[27]

The question of José María Pico's status on the Rancho Santa Margarita after Forster's occupation was brushed by briefly. Forster said that José María had lived on the Rancho Monserrate in his own house. He denied that José María had his own room at the main ranch house on the Santa Margarita. Deliberately, no doubt, Forster was never squarely asked by his attorney how he accounted for José María's activities on the ranch unless he was Pío's mayordomo. The issue was later neglected by Pío's attorney in his cross examination of Forster and was never addressed by either side again. It was good tactics by Forster's camp not to do so. On Pío's side, it was inexplicable negligence.

Before concluding his turn on the witness stand, it was deemed necessary that Forster make some response to Andrés's testimony. Not surprisingly, he alleged that nothing Andrés had said was true. Forster was read Andrés's earlier testimony about the incident while having dinner at the Santa Margarita ranch house in 1866. According to Andrés, following a rodeo of Cave Couts, he told Forster that Pío still had a half interest in the ranch, and Forster supposedly agreed. Forster responded by saying that during the time in question he was in San Francisco.

Forster testified that the story Andrés told of their late night meeting at the Mission San Juan Capistrano was completely wrong as well. There was such a meeting, averred Forster, but nothing was discussed about the Rancho Santa Margarita. He denied that there were tears in their eyes, as

---

[27]Ibid.

Andrés had stated. Forster claimed that he had tried to apol-
ogize to Andrés for the "hard words" in 1869 at the Lafayette
Hotel, but it had not worked. Forster refused further contact
with Andrés because "He never was willing to accept my
apology and so I never wanted any more talk with him."[28]

In this manner, the well-planned direct examination of
Forster ended. His eloquence, as revealed through the old
trial transcripts, must have been forceful and sometimes even
magisterial. Pío's lawyer, George H. Smith, began his cross
examination with a series of questions to discredit Forster's
testimony that he was in San Francisco at the time Andrés
claimed he had admitted Pío's half interest during dinner at
the Rancho Santa Margarita in 1866. Nothing resulted from
these questions except an extremely interesting narrative
about the boarding houses and hotels of old San Francisco
where Forster used to stay, including the addresses, names,
and personal characteristics of their proprietors.

Smith moved to a review of the claims Andrés Pico had
made against Forster. There was a surprising degree of animosity shown by Forster to Andrés when answering these
questions, especially considering that Andrés was present
and the trial was heavily attended by the public. Smith asked
Forster if he had received a letter from Andrés requesting
him to explain his deed to the whole Rancho Santa Margarita. Forster answered:

> Very likely about that time I did. I recollect receiving one
> letter from him in which he proposed to claim some interest
> or other but I did not recognize any such claim, and I did not
> consider his letter as worth any kind of attention.[29]

This same letter was thrown away by Forster because, "I am
not in the custom of retaining letters of a frivolous nature."[30]

Smith was permitted to read aloud the letter Andrés sent

---

[28]Ibid., 49.   [29]Ibid., 60.   [30]Ibid.

to Forster on January 31, 1870, following the unsuccessful attempt of Pablo de la Guerra to negotiate a settlement of the Santa Margarita question. This letter asked Forster to explain his pretention to full ownership of the Rancho Santa Margarita. Forster made an incredible response to the reading of the letter. He struck out wildly against Andrés, saying:

> Don Andrés has been in the habit of mixing himself up and troubling me very often with his unfounded claims. I have hardly had the patience to keep my temper when I received his proposition.[31]

Smith did not insist on asking anything further about the letter, one which called for a response and was a keystone in the case for the Picos.

There were some questions about the heated confrontation between Andrés and Forster at the Lafayette Hotel in 1869 in Los Angeles. Forster dismissed that episode by stating that Andrés had not made any claims for his brother Pío, but had asserted that he himself had a half interest in the Rancho Santa Margarita. Forster went on to say that he had not paid any attention to Andrés because: "His conversation is generally so very frivolous in its nature that I do not retain it in my mind."[32]

Andrés was not the only subject of Forster's contempt. Smith inquired into the unpaid account of Pío that Forster testified was owed him in 1864. He was asked if any credit was given to Pío for some purchase money received from the Rancho Jamul, which Forster had sold years before as an agent for Pío. Forster said that after he had innocently taken a down payment from some purchasers of the ranch, he discovered that Pío had previously sold it to someone else. Indignantly, Forster accused Pío of fraud, saying: "He had sold it already when he employed me to come down here and

---

[31]Ibid., 72.   [32]Ibid., 74.

swindle somebody else."[33] According to Forster, when he advised Pío that he needed a deed to pass title to the ranch, Pío sat down and wrote out a spurious document in Spanish showing a grant from "Pío Pico, Governor, to Pío Pico, Citizen," which was falsely antedated to the Mexican regime.[34] Forster assured the court that he had withdrawn from the transaction when he saw Pío's fraudulent behavior, but after that, he said, Pío himself sold the land "to the Widow Burton." Thereby, Forster claimed, Pío had "sold the land three times over."[35]

Smith unwittingly opened the door for Forster's accusations of fraud by Pío. It was not cleared up in further cross examination. The negative effect it had on the jury may have been substantial. This testimony shows the depth of Forster's bitterness, and perhaps even hatred, toward Pío. Forster, who for decades had addressed Pío in his correspondence as "Godfather, Brother, and Compadre," was prepared at trial to publicly call him a criminal.

Out of the random, scattered questions of Smith came a few significant admissions by Forster. One was that despite his earlier testimony, he was aware when he took the deed from Pío to the Rancho Santa Margarita that the balance owed on the mortgage was "approximately" $40,000. When he went to San Francisco to settle up in July 1864, Forster found that the actual balance owing was $43,972, about what he expected. Indeed, he had received more than twenty letters from Pioche and Bayerque concerning the debt on the Rancho Santa Margarita prior to taking the mortgage and had likewise himself written to them frequently about the matter "up to the time of the settlement of this mortgage."[36]

Not much else came out of Smith's cross-examination of Forster even though it was two and a half times longer than

---

[33]Ibid., 94.   [34]Ibid.
[35]Ibid.   [36]Ibid., 104.

Forster's examination by his own attorneys. Generally, the questioning of Forster by both sides was a ringing affirmation of his position; a magnificent, even if somewhat spiteful performance. Among the Forster camp, there must have been great cheer in the Horton House. Don Juan was emerging victorious.

Robert Ashcroft was next called as a witness. He had been one of Forster's closest friends since 1855. Although Forster was considerably older, the two men had much in common, particularly the fact that they were both from England and had ended up in the cattle business in California. Ashcroft acted as a broker for large cattle companies such as Miller and Lux, buying herds directly from ranches and arranging their shipment to market in San Francisco. Since much of his business was conducted with California Mexicans, he spoke Spanish as effortlessly as Forster. Ashcroft had a wife and children in Oakland, but his business forced him to stay for extended periods in Southern California. Whenever possible, Ashcroft put up as a guest with Forster on the Rancho Santa Margarita, sometimes for months.

Ashcroft testified that he met Pío on Montgomery Street in San Francisco during July 1864. They stopped to speak because they were acquainted with each other and had done cattle transactions together previously. Pío supposedly told him that he had sold the entire Rancho Santa Margarita to Forster. Ashcroft acknowledged that he had bought two thousand head of cattle from Pío, which were moved off the Rancho Santa Margarita in 1867, but said that he had first received permission from Don Juan Forster, as owner. It is perhaps, strange that the written contract he had with Pío at the time made no mention of permission being required from anyone to conduct the sale. However, Pío's lawyers missed this point and asked no questions about it. Ashcroft testified that he was familiar with the Rancho Santa Margarita and the surrounding area. He said that when Forster told him what he paid for the ranch, he had responded: "I told him he was crazy, that it was a wild trade."[37]

Cave Couts briefly gave some testimony in which he said that, in his opinion, the Rancho Santa Margarita was only worth about $30,000 in 1864. In other respects he bolstered Forster's claims concerning the giving of rodeos, claiming orejanos, and other acts of dominion over the land. Couts was treated gently and hardly even cross-examined. The deference shown to Couts by Pío's lawyers is strange. Of course, Forster and Couts were known to be almost like brothers, so fast was their friendship. Couts was a stone wall who could never be induced to say a single thing not entirely favorable to his beloved compadre, Don Juan. Perhaps Pío's lawyers did not want to bother with him, knowing he would never help their case.

There is a possible explanation about the attitude of Pío's lawyers toward Couts which is more sinister. It is interesting to note that two of Pío's lawyers, A. B. Chapman and George H. Smith, had dealings with Couts before and after the trial that very likely constituted a conflict of interest with Pío. For example, in 1870 Couts shot and critically wounded a young man named Waldemar Muller on his Rancho Guajome. Sheriff James McCoy of San Diego arrested Couts in a violent manner and beat him up severely.[38] Glassell, Chapman and Smith had a hand in representing Couts in this affair. On May 27, 1870, Chapman wrote to Couts: "I fear your excitability from drink —as a friend let me ask you to keep sober. It is the only way to get even with the miserable judge and afterwards the Irish Sheriff."[39]

The case against Couts for shooting Muller ended with a

---

[37]Ibid., 167.   [38]Sullivan, "James McCoy," 46-47.
[39]A. B. Chapman to Cave Couts, May 27, 1870, Couts Collection. The "miserable judge" was Murray Morrison and the "Irish Sheriff" was James McCoy.

questionable dismissal. Over the years, there were a series of conflicts and criminal charges in which Couts was embroiled, more than can be recounted here. It is perhaps understandable, given the less rigid ethical climate of the bar in those days, that Couts was not roughly treated by Pío's lawyers during the trial with Forster. Couts was, after all, one of their clients. And not only that, Couts was one of the best kinds of clients. He was wealthy, alcoholic, and had a prodigious ability to get himself in trouble.

After Couts stepped down, Juan Avila was called to give testimony. He was a fixture in the village of San Juan Capistrano, where for years, as the wealthiest Mexican around, he was known as *El Rico*. One of his daughters had married John Forster's son Marcos. Avila confirmed Andrés Pico's story about having seized Cave Couts by the collar for challenging his right to give orders concerning the Rancho Santa Margarita in 1866. Avila was an eyewitness to the event. However, everything else he said favored his daughter's father-in-law. He was at supper at the Rancho Santa Margarita in 1866 when Andrés Pico said Forster admitted that Pío had a half interest in the ranch. According to Avila, however, Forster was not home that day.

Avila said that only Forster gave rodeos, took orejanos, and operated the Rancho Santa Margarita like an owner. His testimony showed a desire not to offend any of the parties. He obviously had great affection for them all and had been drawn into the contest against his will. He constantly referred to his old friends in his testimony as "my Compadre Don Andrés" or "my Compadre Don Juan" or "my Compadre Don Pío." But, sadly for him, his testimony had to favor one party or the other, and like many witnesses, he probably left the court with a vague feeling that he had betrayed someone, not knowing exactly who.

Don Juan's side ended up with the testimony of all the

Forster boys: Chico, Juan, and Marcos. These young men, half-Mexican and half-English, preferred to speak Spanish among themselves. They ran the crews of vaqueros and did the hard work on the Rancho Santa Margarita. When separated over the vast expanse of the ranch, they frequently communicated between themselves by sending vaqueros flying on horseback with notes written in Spanish. Their letters to others, especially their parents, were usually in Spanish as well.

These young men testified that their father had always had full and exclusive control of the Rancho Santa Margarita. Only Don Juan gave rodeos or claimed orejanos. Juan and Marcos testified that their father was not on the Rancho Santa Margarita when their uncle Andrés claimed that Forster had conceded that Pío still had a half interest there. Chico said that his father was in San Francisco at the time, a fact which he knew for certain because he was with him.

The Forster side of the case concluded, more or less, with the end of his sons' testimony. Closing arguments began on February 19, 1873. The *San Diego Union* reported: "Argument opened by Col. Geo. H. Smith, who occupied the entire day in reviewing the voluminous testimony elicited during the trial for fraud."[40] The next day, Volney E. Howard completed his argument, but not too soon for Don Juan. At this time Forster was in a hurry to end the case because he learned that Max Strobel, his agent in Europe for the subdivision of the Rancho Santa Margarita and the sale of Santa Catalina Island, had died.

---

[40] *San Diego Union*, Feb. 20, 1873.

CHAPTER TEN

The Verdict and its Aftermath

It became extremely urgent for Forster to depart for Europe in order to continue the delicate arrangements begun by the deceased Strobel. If Forster's European enterprise was neglected, his British and Dutch investors might evaporate, taking their fortunes into other ventures. Just days before his death in London, Strobel sent Forster a copy of a letter he had written to a London investment broker, George Underwood. Strobel's letter referred to a sum of 600,000 British pounds sterling that was apparently then being offered for Santa Catalina Island. It also implied that there was an interest by Holland's Rotterdam Bank in Forster's projected land sales on the Rancho Santa Margarita. The letter sent to Underwood was dated January 17, 1873. By the time a copy of it travelled to San Diego, weeks had passed.[1]

Soon after Forster received word of the progress made by Strobel before his death, he wrote a report to Cave Couts on February 20, 1873, from the Horton House:

> Last night the arguments were concluded at 5:00 p.m. We thought that the case would be submitted but the judge proposed to the jury to act upon it or choose to have it submitted this morning, which of course they adopted, so we may have a decision before you receive this . . . I am in quite a hurry for the decision as it is imperative upon me to go to London without loss of time to complete the arrangements made by

---

[1] Max Strobel to George Underwood, Jan. 17, 1873, Forster Collection.

poor Strobel—it appears that he died from abscess of the lungs.[2]

On the morning this letter was written, the court instructed the jury to answer the following three questions:

First, did Pío Pico in 1864 sell to Juan Forster the whole or only a half of the ranch?
Second, was Pío Pico induced to sign the deed by fraud?
Third, did Forster know that only one-half was intended to be conveyed?

Only twenty minutes after retiring to deliberate, the jury was back with a verdict.[3] The jury's answer to the first question was that Pío had sold Forster the whole ranch. The other two questions were answered in the negative. They determined that Pío was not induced to sign the deed by fraud and Forster did not know that only one-half of the ranch was intended to be conveyed.

The speed of the verdict was a complete repudiation of the Picos and their attorneys. It was as if the jury wanted to convey a sense of disdain for the Pico cause. We cannot know what the parties said or did when the verdict was read, but we know that the Picos never spoke to Forster again. The harsh words and insults of Forster at trial had irreparably damaged relations between the Forster and Pico families for the lifetimes of those involved. Faint echoes of the bitterness between Forster and his brothers-in-law can still be heard among the distant cousins who are their descendants, even today, as we shall see.

After the jury verdict, Judge Rolfe gave the decision he had reserved on the Piquitos branch of the case. Rolfe ruled that the copy of the alleged deed presented in court lacked authenticity since it was not precisely the same as the original. Pío had testified that the copy was only similar to the

---

[2]John Forster to Cave Couts, Feb. 20, 1873, Couts Collection.
[3]*San Diego Union*, Feb. 23, 1873.

document he had signed. Further, although all sides agreed that the document was executed in 1846, the copy erroneously gave the year as 1845. Because of the obvious error of the date, together with the equivocal testimony of Pío, Rolfe rejected the document. He found it could not support the claim of Magdalena Pico and her children to one-quarter of the Rancho Santa Margarita.

The ruling on the Piquitos branch of the case is understandable. Judge Rolfe was asked to construe an instrument with no obvious validity under either Mexican or American law. By rejecting the copy presented in court because it was not an exact duplicate of the original, Rolfe avoided having to put a meaning on the puzzling document. Whether justice was actually served in denying the claims of those in the Piquitos branch is uncertain, but, given the circumstances, Rolfe's decision was not unreasonable.

Based on the evidence presented to the jury, their verdict against Pío was inevitable. The testimony of the Pico brothers provided elliptical explanations of the transaction not likely to illuminate the jury. Their statements that Forster received 1,500 head of cattle and 150 horses "for the part" Pío was to pay might have been understood by the more perceptive jury members to mean that the livestock was a kind of equalizing payment to Forster in dividing the land, but this possibility was not clearly set forth in detail. Without more facts, the jury was required to speculate about what happened between the men. They would not strip Forster of half his greatest asset and destroy his personal honor by upholding the allegations of fraud, based on the incomplete, ephemeral testimony of the Picos. It was their duty not to do so.

The trivial incidents related by the Pico side which were offered as Forster's "admissions" to Pio's ownership were not persuasive. The jury would not tamper with ownership of a ranching empire because of Forster's casual responses to the persistent and possibly harassing demands of the Picos. Andrés' testimony about Forster's attempts to avoid confronting him may not have been regarded as evidence of Forster's guilty knowledge, but rather efforts to avoid an unreasonably hostile person. The evidence of Pío selling cattle off the land and his employment of José María Pico as a mayordomo may have given the jury pause, but taken alone, was not conclusive.

In an age of racism, the jury does not seem to have been overtly influenced by prejudice against the Picos or undue sympathy toward Forster. Pio's case collapsed because no satisfactory evidence of his true intent at the time of the transfer to Forster was presented. Without clear and convincing proof of Pío's belief that he had conveyed only half the Rancho Santa Margarita, and Forster's knowledge of it, no jury, whatever its composition, would say that Pío had been defrauded.

Nevertheless, Pío's lawyers had access to powerful, even overwhelming, proof that Forster knew their client intended to give him only half the ranch. This crucial evidence was not presented to the jury because Pío's counsel failed to recognize it. They were not assisted by Pío or Andrés in understanding the case because neither of the Pico brothers had a firm grasp on the details of their contract with Forster. Each gave vague testimony that suggested they believed Forster was to get half the ranch and that a transfer of livestock somehow balanced out his interest with Pío's, but they offered no hard facts to support these assertions. Their nebulous testimony must have severely strained the ability of the jury to take their case seriously.

However, the jury received a false impression of what happened between Forster and the Picos. From our perspective, well more than a century after the trial, we can see that the Picos were right. Pío never intended to give Forster more than half the ranch, and it was nearly impossible for Forster not to know this. Ironically, the document which leads to this conclusion was introduced in evidence by Forster's own lawyers. It is the bill of sale for the livestock which Forster received from Pío at the same time the deed was given to him.

The bill of sale states on its face that it transferred 1,500 head of cattle and 150 horses to Forster for a total price of $4,920.[4] Without understanding its significance, George H. Smith asked Forster on cross-examination how the value of the livestock was determined. Forster said that both the cattle and horses were agreed to be worth only three dollars a head because of the drought. According to Forster, they were given to him as a gesture toward repayment of Pío's alleged longstanding indebtedness to him. They had nothing to do with the sale of the Rancho Santa Margarita.

During a course of random questions, Smith got around to asking Forster how the exact number of livestock shown on the bill of sale was chosen. Forster replied that the number was a matter of coincidence; it simply represented the quantity of animals Pío had on the ranch at the time. Smith did not accept this answer and reminded Forster of earlier testimony that Pío could have had as many as five thousand head of cattle on the Santa Margarita in 1864. Forster admitted that Pío probably had more cattle on the ranch than was given to him. José María Pico had earlier guessed that Pío usually ran between three thousand to five thousand head on the Santa Margarita.

Since Pío had abundant cattle on the ranch, Smith could have pressed Forster to explain the reason why the bill of sale transferred the exact number of livestock that it did and not some greater or lesser amount. But instead, Smith drifted into further aimless questioning. Forster must have been

---

[4]Plaintiff's exhibit 3.

relieved by Smith's failure to persist in asking him about the bill of sale. Pío's bumbling attorney had come dangerously close to the crux of the true contract. When placed in its proper context, the bill of sale is the key to understanding the transaction between Forster and the Picos.

Although their testimony on the point was not free of ambiguity, it appears that both Pico brothers believed that the Santa Margarita was worth about $75,000 when they treated with Forster in 1864. Pío said that he received an offer of that amount for the ranch through Pioche and Bayerque just after his transaction with Forster. He implied that this offer validated his opinion of the land's value when he dealt with Forster. Andrés shared Pío's belief. As we have seen, he wrote a letter to Forster on January 31, 1870, demanding answers to several questions. The very first question put to Forster in the letter was, "Before you redeemed the mortgage of Santa Margarita did you not know that they offered my brother Pío for that Rancho, the sum of $75,000?"[5]

Of course, Forster's lawyers correctly pointed out that the drought conditions prevailing when the transaction took place had drastically reduced land values. Forster said, "Nobody would have bought it but me at that price." Robert Ashcroft described his reaction to what Forster paid for the ranch by saying, "I told him that it was crazy, that it was a wild trade." Couts testified that the land was barely worth $30,000 in 1864. Pío's own lawyers passively assumed that the property would never have been worth $75,000 during the drought. The idea was so absurd that the claims of the Picos were not even investigated.

Let us assume that the essence of what the Pico brothers said in trial was true. Suppose it was agreed that the whole Rancho Santa Margarita would sell for $75,000 and that

---

[5]Andrés Pico to John Forster, Jan. 31, 1870, defendant's exhibit PP 55. *Forster v. Pico.*

Forster bargained to acquire one-half of it by taking over the mortgage. Naturally, Forster would pay no more than $37,500 for his half of the land. To preserve his corresponding half interest, Pío would pay Forster the difference between $37,500 and any greater amount owed on the mortgage. Such an equalizing payment would balance each man's half ownership. By subtracting $37,500 from the debt owed on the mortgage, the amount of the equalizing payment could be determined. This calculation would probably be made as of February 25, 1864, when the deed and bill of sale for the livestock were delivered to Forster. If what the Picos said was true, on that day, we would expect the balance owed on the mortgage in excess of $37,500 to be about $4,920, the value assigned to the livestock in the bill of sale. In fact, this is what actually happened. The records of Pioche and Bayerque show that the amount owed on the mortgage beyond $37,500 on the day Forster took the deed was right at $4,795.90.[6]

Unfortunately, no statement of account exists to show what Pioche and Bayerque claimed was owed just prior to February 25, 1864. Their demands on the Picos have not been preserved so we cannot see how precisely they communicated the amount due. However, John Forster received a detailed statement 145 days later on July 18, 1864, when he went to San Francisco to assume the mortgage. At that time, the balance owing was $43,972.30. Appendix A shows the statement received by Forster on July 18, 1864.

A close examination of the statement in Appendix A reveals that Pioche and Bayerque were charging 12 percent

---

[6]Defendant's exhibit PP 29 shows the statement of account from Pioche and Bayerque given to Forster on July 18, 1864. *Forster v. Pico.* The amounts of interest on the principal and for various expenses was calculated by interest at 12 percent per annum based on 360 days per year. By reducing the accrued interest by 145 days, the balance on February 25, 1864 was reached. See Appendix A and Appendix B for an illustration.

annual interest on a daily basis. To do this, they multiplied each item of principal as well as cash advances by 12 percent, then they divided the result by 360, the number of days most banks use for a year. Each daily increment of interest thus obtained was multiplied by the number of days accrued since the debt was placed on the books. The total principal and interest, less some credits, was the balance owed of $43,972.30 on July 18, 1864.

By running the daily interest rate backward for the 145-day period from July 18, 1864, to February 25, 1864, we can closely approximate the loan balance when the transaction between Forster and the Picos occurred. In such manner, Appendix B shows a hypothetical statement of account from Pioche and Bayerque on February 25, 1864. It appears that the amount actually owed by the Picos on February 25, 1864, would have been $42,295.90. Someone attempting to calculate an equalizing payment would find that the excess of the loan balance over $37,500.00 was $4,795.90. This amount is only $124.10 less than the price of $4,920.00 fixed on the bill of sale for the cattle.

The error of $124.10 is quite understandable, given the circumstances. It is highly doubtful that someone in Los Angeles attempting to figure out an equalizing payment on or about February 25, 1864, had the benefit of an abstract of the books and records of Pioche and Bayerque. The calculations made at the time Forster received the deed and bill of sale for cattle would have been based on a series of demand letters from Pioche and Bayerque which stated progressively greater amounts owed without an exhaustive accounting. Even so, the difference between a hypothetical equalizing payment of $4,795.90 and the $4,920.00 placed on the bill of sale is only 2.5 percent, not a bad calculation for someone with incomplete records acting in great haste. Moreover, to such a person, the total loan balance would appear to be $37,500.00 plus $4,920.00, i.e., $42,420.00. We know from reworking the records of Pioche and Bayerque, as shown in Appendix B, that the true balance owed on February 25, 1864, was $42,295.90. The difference between these two numbers is tiny, a trifling amount of less than .03 percent. In light of this, it seems reasonable to conclude that the transfer of livestock to Forster was intended as an equalizing payment, just as the Picos said.

The notary public Ozias Morgan wrote out the bill of sale for Pío's signature. We do not know whether Morgan made the necessary calculations himself or whether the amount of money representing the value of the cattle was simply given to him. Pío denied any direct participation in formulating the contract. He claimed that Andrés made the contract and all the arrangements with Forster. Pío said he only signed what was placed in front of him in reliance on what Andrés and Forster told him.

As for Andrés, he acknowledged that he arranged the terms of the contract with Forster verbally, but he had no part in preparing the written documents. He testified that after striking the bargain with Forster to transfer one-half the ranch, he told him, "You make the document." The lack of concern by Andrés about the deed and bill of sale is shown by his testimony that he did not even accompany Forster into Pío's office at the Ranchito when they were signed. Andrés said: "He signed it then, but I did not see him. I went to run after some animals."[7]

This casual, even negligent attitude toward written documents was unfortunate. Apparently, the Picos did not retain copies of the deed and bill of sale that were signed. Otherwise, Andrés would not have had to go to San Diego in 1869 to see

---

[7]WPA, 1: 76.

the deed at the recorder's office. The bill of sale surfaced at the trial as one of Forster's exhibits. Pío never had a copy of the original. It is likely that Smith did not see the bill of sale until after he had rested his case and Forster's attorneys produced it in rebuttal evidence. By then, even if Smith had grasped its great significance, it would have been too late to use it properly.

One of the most important consequences of the Picos' failure to participate in the preparation of the documents with Forster and to retain copies of them was that the Picos were unaware of important details they contained. The Picos did not have the benefit of being able to go over relevant papers before giving their version of the story to the jury. Both men had to rely entirely on memories of events which occurred nine years before the trial. This problem was compounded by their lawyers, who did not prepare them to testify.

Forster attempted to dissociate himself from the deed and bill of sale. Apart from a meeting he attended with the Picos and Ozias Morgan, he denied any role in making them. Yet Forster was the only one of the men who had continuous possession of the documents, and it is difficult to imagine how he could not have controlled their preparation. The proof that he did was the complete inability of the Picos to explain their contract with Forster during the trial, when they had every motive to do so.

Forster's greatest ally was his silence. His refusal to enlighten the Picos about the rationale for their transaction won the case for him. The jury never heard the insurmountable evidence showing that the livestock transfer was well calculated as an equalizing payment. A division of the ranch was at the heart of the transaction. This was communicated to Pío who blindly signed the deed and bill of sale he could not read, relying on what he heard from Forster and Andrés. The jury verdict, founded on incomplete and deceptive evidence, was wrong.

We now know why Pío regarded himself as a one-half owner. The true nature of the contract and Pio's actual intent can be demonstrated with near mathematical certainty. Pio's conduct after the transaction with Forster makes perfect sense. Some of the evidence never seen by the jury, such as Pío's correspondence with his mayordomo, José María Pico, contained orders concerning the use of the land. Pío gave rodeos, sold cattle, and kept a staff of employees on the ranch at considerable expense. All this was because Pío genuinely thought he was a half owner. The pursuit of Forster after the Picos learned of his perfidy was intensely emotional because they were simply astonished by their brother-in-law's behavior. Andrés was particularly enraged since he had personally made the agreement with him.

Forster's conduct toward the Picos was misleading. He did not challenge Pio's use of the Rancho Santa Margarita until he actually filed the suit to quiet title in 1872. Before and during the trial, he never explained anything about the transaction, such as the price he agreed to pay, the reason for the exact number of livestock he received from the Picos, or his actual opinion of the value of the land. His refusal to divulge any details was because he might inadvertently provide a clue to the Picos or their bungling attorneys that would allow them to deduce what had really happened. He had no burden of producing evidence at trial. His attorneys gave a masterful illusion of providing an explanation of the transaction, but they actually revealed nothing.

The acquisition of the Rancho Santa Margarita, together with nearby land he already owned, made Forster one of the greatest landowners in California. As such, he most assuredly did not care to have Pío as a joint owner of the ranch. Throughout the years prior to 1864, Pío constantly complained of his delicate financial condition. He frequently sought money and advice from Forster when attempting to raise oppressive mortgages from his property. As soon as Pío was restored to relative solvency, he immediately involved himself in other financial disasters. From Forster's perspective, it seemed that Pío could not possibly avoid bankruptcy for very long after 1864. Pio's economic demise would drastically affect Forster's interest in the Rancho Santa Margarita since creditors would seize Pio's half of the ranch and liquidate it at a distress sale. Forster's investment would be badly affected, a risk he was not prepared to accept.

Forster's concern about the financial viability of Pío was well founded. Less than a year after the trial in San Diego, Pío was trying to sell the last two thousand acres he owned on the Rancho San Fernando. This land, known as the "Pico Reserve," had been retained around the mission where Andrés lived following the sale of the Rancho San Fernando lands to Isaac Lankershim in 1869. It was intended to guarantee a homestead to Andrés, but Pío was doing his best to sell it anyway, even if Andrés was dispossessed as a result.

Forster would not have agreed with one writer who stated that Pío had an "entire lack of malice or ill-will towards any human being."[8] In fact, as Forster knew, there was a considerable feeling of hostility toward Pío in Los Angeles and elsewhere because he was capable of willfully damaging the interests of other people. On one occasion, several prominent persons in Los Angeles signed sworn affidavits on behalf of Pío to support his request that a trial in which he was involved be moved to another city. These affidavits stated that there was "a violent prejudice against Pío Pico in Los Angeles."[9] Clearly, there was no universal sentiment in support of Pío during his lifetime. He habitually borrowed money from those whose sympathy he captured, but went to great lengths to avoid repayment. This characteristic did not

[8]Barrows, "Pío Pico," 64.
[9]Affidavits of George H. Smith, James G. Howard, and A. J. King in *Pío Pico v. Rómulo Pico*, Case No. 3292, filed Nov. 25, 1878, Los Angeles Superior Court Archives.

endear him to those creditors who were his erstwhile friends. Many of them were particularly outraged to see Pío freely spending large sums of money without attempting to settle their long-overdue debts.

Ignacio del Valle was one critic of Pío who recorded his thoughts in a letter he wrote to the *San Francisco Examiner* in defense of the verdict in favor of Forster. It does not appear that this letter was published, and it has no date other than "June, 1873." Perhaps Del Valle was prejudiced against Pío because he was related by marriage to John Forster. His daughter Josefa was the wife of Juan Fernando Forster. Still, even allowing for any bias of Del Valle, his comments doubtlessly reflect a considerable body of opinion concerning Pío in Los Angeles. Del Valle wrote:

> His friendship is the bane of all his acquaintances and would bankrupt a Rothschild or a Vanderbilt. See what it has done for his more noble and generous brother Don Andrés. He has dissipated a colossal fortune, which had Don Andrés not been coerced and disspoiled of, would make him one of the richest capitalists in California, in place of which he is now reduced to a small reservation on San Fernando. But even that last resort to Don Andrés for a home, he Don Pío, although he has mortgaged it for its full value is now hawking on the streets of San Francisco for sale. But then, in recompense for all Andrés's generous conduct, he promises forsooth to make him inheritor of whatever property he may leave at his death, when poor Don Andrés, broken down in spirit and health, is more likely to precede him. Magnanimous man! Good friend! Kind brother! [He] who after gulping the oyster whilst living promises to bequest the shell to his generous hearted brother in return for having kept him in a state of utter ruin during a long series of years.[10]

Pío finally compromised with Andrés and only sold one thousand acres of the Pico Reserve. He then deeded the

---

[10]Ignacio Del Valle to editor of the *San Francisco Examiner,* June 1873, Del Valle Collection.

other one thousand acres to his brother. In turn, Andrés gave one hundred acres of what remained to his common-law wife, Catalina Moreno, so that he ended up with nine hundred acres, which he clung to until his death.[11] Forster could see how Pío was getting rid of the last traces of the once-magnificent Rancho San Fernando, even at the expense of his brother. He knew that Pío would be quite capable of doing the same to him on the Rancho Santa Margarita.

From Forster's point of view, his difficulties in the Santa Margarita affair largely arose from certain of Pío Pico's personal characteristics. Pío had a strong, dominating personality and little patience with details. He carried out business in an imperious manner, sending his brother Andrés or agents like Albert Johnson, Adolph Portugal, and a host of others to arrange transactions with only vague, general instructions. Throughout his life he exhibited behavior modern psychologists attribute to a "bulldozer" personality. He plunged ahead with little reflection, conduct which led to frequent disasters. It was possible to deceive Pío, but exceedingly difficult to engage him in a lengthy, reasoned discussion. These qualities were unattractive to a cautious man like Forster.

Over the years that the Pico brothers urged Forster to pay off the Santa Margarita mortgage, they offered him only one-half the ranch in exchange. Accustomed to living on the brink of collapse, and being of a stubborn nature, Pío refused to consider any other proposition. Forster understood the high price demanded for one-half the land and the enormous risk in having Pío as a joint owner. He therefore refused to accept. No one knew Pío better than Forster, though his personal knowledge of Pío had unhappy results. Despite close family connections and formal protests of esteem and affection in correspondence, Forster did not like Pío or Andrés.

---

[11]This transaction is mentioned in the cross-complaint in *Pío Pico v. Rómulo Pico*, Case No. 3292, filed Nov. 25, 1878, Los Angeles Superior Court Archives.

Obviously, he had little respect for their business judgment. The contempt he expressed toward them during the trial did not develop overnight.

When Forster met Andrés in the street on February 25, 1864, he learned of Pío's increasingly desperate financial situation. Although there seemed to be no chance of recovery, Forster knew Pío would tenaciously, even recklessly, adhere to the original offer of one-half the ranch. Rather than sacrifice the Santa Margarita because of what he regarded as Pío's foolish obstinacy, Forster resolved to take the land in his own name without telling the Picos. He therefore negotiated for one-half the land as if it had a value of $75,000 as shown by the equalizing payment in the livestock bill of sale, but he had no intention of carrying out the agreement. It was clear to him that Pío was destined to lose the Rancho Santa Margarita no matter what he did. The whole ranch would either be taken by Forster or creditors would seize it.

From the standpoint of Forster, his deception of the Pico brothers would cause no harm. After the inevitable bankruptcy of Pío and the loss of all the land the Picos had acquired, there would be no recriminations against Forster for having saved the Rancho Santa Margarita from an army of Pío's creditors. In the meantime, he would allow Pío the use of the Rancho Santa Margarita. This arrangement would only last until Pío's downfall.

Unfortunately for Forster, the final collapse of Pío took years longer than he expected. When his deed to the whole ranch was accidentally discovered, the wrath of the Pico brothers turned on him since he refused to confess what he had done. He would not return half the land which had vastly increased in value, nor give away his capital investment, hard work, and dreams of subdividing the ranch. The rage of the Picos was regrettable but had to be endured. Their friendship was not worth having in any event. It was both expensive and dangerous to befriend them, something Forster learned after many years of forced family intimacy.

The trial took place because Forster miscalculated the length of time Pío would remain solvent. Once legal action was imposed on him, he was well prepared to deal with it. As the most knowledgeable and active party to the contract, Forster had more than an inkling of what the Pico brothers could prove. He was aware of how little the intractable Pío and the careless Andrés knew about the details of their arrangement. Based on long experience, he was confident that his brothers-in-law would never make convincing witnesses in a court of law. Besides, they had no documents. By limiting the evidence, Forster knew he could probably defeat them, just as he did.

After the trial, Forster had little time to celebrate his victory. The lawsuit had largely been about securing his title to the Rancho Santa Margarita so he could subdivide it and make a great fortune. With the death of Max Strobel, there was extreme urgency in getting to London. Just thirty-two days after the trial, Forster was in New York waiting for the departure of the German line steamer, *The City of New York* for Europe. He had one of his attorneys, Frank Ganahl, as an advisor and travelling companion. Forster sent a letter to Cave Couts from New York dated March 25, 1873, in which he complained about already having waited five days for his ship to depart, an indication of the haste with which he left California.[12]

On his arrival in Liverpool, England, during the first part of April 1873, Forster sent a letter to his son, Chico. Since Forster knew that Chico was scheduled to arrive in San Francisco with several droves of cattle, he sent the letter in care of Obediah Livermore, his trusted confidante. On April 29, 1873, Chico replied to his father from the Occidental Hotel

---

[12]John Forster to Cave Couts, March 25, 1873, Couts Collection.

in San Francisco. The letter in Spanish was addressed to Morley's Hotel, Telegraph Square, London, and contained some startling news:

> Today Mr. O. Livermore gave me your letter from Liverpool. I am pleased that you had a good trip. I have just received a letter from Mr. Egan in San Juan Capistrano saying that Pío Pico went to the Santa Margarita to remove all the cattle of the Guiterreno and Corazon brands and was arrested and taken to San Diego. According to my information, his attempt to take the cattle was not successful. It seems that he was waiting for me to leave for San Francisco before he entered. I suspected something like this might happen so I left Marcos and Juan prepared for his arrival in case he came. I am waiting for a letter from Marcos with further details.[13]

Chico's remark to his father that he suspected Pío might enter the ranch to take away cattle suggests that there might have been some threatening outburst from Pío after the verdict. For whatever reason, Chico had been on guard against a raid on the Rancho Santa Margarita by Pío since the trial.

A full report of Pío's activities was sent to Forster's hotel in London on May 22, 1873, by Robert Ashcroft. He wrote that Pío entered the Rancho Santa Margarita on April 23, 1873, when none of the Forster sons were present to protect the place. Chico was in San Francisco, Marcos was in Los Angeles on business, and Juan was lying immobile from the effects of poison oak at Mission San Luis Rey. Ashcroft implied that Pío knew his nephews would not be there. Hugh Forster, a brother of Don Juan, raced to San Diego to see Jeff Gatewood, the same attorney who was active in the trial. Gatewood gave Hugh Forster a notice to quit for delivery to Pío. When it was given to Pío, he refused to leave, "stating that he had as much right there as you and would remain there until put off by law."[14]

---

[13]Francisco P. Forster to John Forster, April 29, 1873, Forster Collection.
[14]Robert Ashcroft to John Forster, May 22, 1873, Forster Collection.

Forster's son Juan, known affectionately in the Forster family as *Juanón*—Big John—and so referred to by Ashcroft in his letter, gave word from his sick bed at the mission to send some vaqueros out to run off his uncle Pío. Several of Forster's men, led by a vaquero nicknamed "El Chapo," meaning "a short, stout person," confronted Pío and his men. El Chapo ordered that some livestock which had already been rounded up by Pío's men be turned loose. At that point, according to Ashcroft:

> Don Pío . . . attempted to shoot El Chapo who prevented him from doing so by seizing the barrel of the gun. Don Pío pulled the trigger and the gun fortunately misfired or you would most likely have been minus a horse.[15]

El Chapo effected a citizen's arrest of Pío and took him before a local justice of the peace, where an impromptu farce of a trial was held. The magistrate said that Pío was justified in what he did and ordered him released. Ashcroft wrote:

> Everyone seemed to sympathize with Don Pio. Free whiskey was bountifully served out, and the welkin rang with cheers for the ex-Governor.[16]

But this affair was not over yet. Hugh Forster had meantime gone again to San Diego. He returned with the San Diego sheriff who had a warrant for Pio's arrest. This time Pío was escorted to a proper jail in San Diego and locked up. The arrest and confinement of Pío "created quite a sensation among the paisanos who came forward and bailed him out."[17] By that time Juanón Forster had risen from his sick bed. He took charge of the vaqueros and made certain that all of Pío's men were removed from the ranch. Volney E. Howard and Jeff Gatewood obtained an injunction from Judge Rolfe against further trespass by Pío. There was a grand jury investigation in San Diego of the matter, but Pío was not indicted.[18]

---

[15]Ibid.   [16]Ibid.
[17]Ibid.   [18]*San Diego Union*, May 7, 1873.

A view of San Diego toward the west in 1880.
The courthouse is profiled against the bay in the center of the
picture. Point Loma extends across the horizon beyond.
Courtesy, Security Pacific Collection, Los Angeles Public Library.

Pío was not resigned to his loss in San Diego. He instructed Glassell, Chapman and Smith to appeal the case. At the
same time that Pío lost his lawsuit with Forster at San Diego,
he was involved in other lawsuits in Los Angeles. During the
course of the trial in San Diego, Andrew Glassell had
returned to Los Angeles to postpone at least two trials pending in that city.[19] One of them was a lawsuit between Pío and
Antonio Cuyas over a partnership agreement for the operation of the Pico House Hotel.[20] Another was a suit brought
by some purchasers of a small parcel adjacent to the Ranchito
in which the deed accidentally described the land conveyed
as the whole Ranchito, not merely a few acres.[21] This trans-

---

[19]*Los Angeles Star,* Jan. 28, 1873, Feb. 5, 1873.
[20]*Pío Pico v. Cuyas,* 47 California Reports 174 (Oct. 1873).
[21]*Pío Pico v. Coleman,* 47 California Reports 65 (Oct. 1873).

action was one of a series which redounded in great loss and even tragedy for Pío, because he almost never troubled to make sure he understood the documents he was asked to sign. The plaintiffs in the Ranchito case unconscionably sought to take advantage of Pío's mistake.

Pío lost both his cases in Los Angeles and took them on appeal to the California Supreme Court. These cases, as well as his appeal from the Forster trial, were heard by the supreme court during November and December 1873. Forster was present in Sacramento to attend the oral arguments on the appeal of the Santa Margarita case. He returned from Europe in August 1873 without successfully concluding his schemes to sell Santa Catalina Island and subdivide the Santa Margarita. Forster had written to his wife from the Netherlands that the English investors were *fanfarrónes*—braggards—incapable of meeting their promises.[22] On December 2, 1873, Forster was in San Francisco having just returned from Sacramento and wrote to Couts about the appeals before the supreme court:

> ... The Pico party are in very bad odor, not only in court, but amongst the whole profession. Today the Ranchito case will be argued and I am almost sorry with the strongest conviction that they will lose, this causing them utter ruin because they will not only lose the property but they'll have to indemnify purchasers which cannot be effected with less than 150,000 dollars. The old gentleman [Pío Pico] ... is about town hunting money for the 2,000 acres of land reserved in their sale of San Fernando. He has not been up to Sacramento, probably it is better for him to remain away as his presence might prejudice his cause. Smith and Glassell are in attendance on the court.[23]

Pío did not lose the Ranchito case. Even if he had lost, the effect would not have been as great a catastrophe as Forster

---

[22]John Forster to Isidora Forster, May 8, 1873, Forster Collection.
[23]John Forster to Cave Couts, Dec. 2, 1873, Couts Collection.

imagined. The case against Antonio Cuyas was sent back to Los Angeles for a new trial. The supreme court quickly disposed of the Santa Margarita appeal. The judgment was affirmed without much comment.[24] The ranch was irremediably lost to Pío.

After winning the struggle for the Rancho Santa Margarita, Forster continued in the cattle business. He was resigned to the fact that his European adventures had come to nothing. During his stay in the Netherlands, Forster attempted to recruit Dutch settlers for the Santa Margarita by promising each man 160 acres of free land, five cows, two horses, and a supply of seed and grain for planting. In exchange, he wanted them to pay rent after the second or third year of farming. The government of Holland refused to accept without a prior inspection to determine the land's suitability for colonization. Several Dutch officials accompanied Forster and Ganahl back to the United States for this purpose. The party arrived in San Diego on August 18, 1873, during the hottest part of the year.[25] The arid soil and wide vistas of a harsh country overrun by brown, lifeless chaparral, did not favorably impress the agriculturalists from the Netherlands. They declined Forster's offer and presumably returned to their green homeland.

Undaunted, throughout the period of a little more than eight years in which Forster was able to enjoy undisputed title to the ranch before his own death, he ceaselessly strove to develop the property. In 1878 he established a townsite which he called "Forster City" on the northern coast of the Rancho Santa Margarita, just below the present-day city of San Clemente. It extended from the San Mateo Valley southward to San Onofre, where a nuclear power plant is now located. Forster invested considerable sums of money on

[24]*Forster v. Pico*, 1 California Unreported Cases 841 (1874).

[25]Michael Edward Thurman, "A History of Rancho Santa Margarita y Las Flores to 1882" (Master's Thesis), 90-93.

the project. The site was professionally surveyed and platted. One plat, still in existence, shows the names of streets Forster chose for his city. Couts Street and Livermore Avenue were among the principal thoroughfares.[26]

At Forster's expense, redwood was shipped in for private and commercial construction. The nascent community eventually grew to about two hundred men, women, and children. In April 1879, San Diego County made it an official voting precinct. Until 1882 about thirty-five of the eligible male voters regularly cast their ballots in general elections. By 1881 wheat was harvested and shipped by schooner to San Francisco. Pablo Soto built a general store and was soon joined by other entrepreneurs who installed a stage depot, blacksmith shop, livery stable, and a hotel. Even a one-room school and a post office were established.[27]

But the tiny colony did not exist because of the compelling economic, social, or geographic reasons that give rise to cities. Forster set it up to attract settlers who would increase the value of his land. In a sense, it was an unnatural community. It required constant infusions of money, time, and effort to persist. Forster could not give it his full attention because he never lived on the site. He preferred the comforts of his distant Mexican adobe ranch house. Moreover, he was fully engaged trying to make a profit out of the uncertainties of cattle ranching and to promote other aspects of his vast estate such as the production of grapes, citrus, and olives. Beyond demands the land made on his time, Forster was busy promoting a railroad to San Diego, fighting taxes, and stumping for Republican political candidates. Consequently, most of the direct supervision of Forster City was delegated to his son Marcos.

Forster City was too dependent on the support of its founder to survive his death. After the passing of Don Juan in

---

[26]This document is in the possession of Thomas Anthony "Tony" Forster of San Juan Capistrano.

[27]Thurman, "History of Rancho Santa Margarita," 93-98.

1882, the little group of colonists disbanded. Some of the houses erected with materials supplied by Forster were dismantled and hauled to San Juan Capistrano. A few of them are standing today, such as the house of Lupe Combs on Verdugo Street.[28] Others are found on Rios Street west of the train depot, just across the railroad tracks. The houses are made entirely of wood and have an old, ramshackle appearance. They can be easily recognized because they are extremely small, almost like doll houses. Except for these picturesque remnants, Forster City has utterly disappeared.

The bitter struggle waged by Forster to attain his prize, the great Rancho Santa Margarita y Las Flores, did not result in the prosperity he desired. The operation of the ranch proved to be exceedingly expensive. His attempts to subdivide did not approximate the success of the Robinson Trust in Los Angeles County, and the cattle market was too volatile to create reliable profits. Over the course of the short period he had left to live after the trial, he was forced to borrow great sums of money. Although his huge land holdings gave him an appearance of wealth, by the time of his death, Forster was quite unstable financially. On September 4, 1875, Forster borrowed $29,157.73 from the Farmers and Merchants Bank, secured by mortgages on property in Los Angeles County. His old nemesis, Andrew Glassell, was the bank's attorney and promptly foreclosed on the properties when Forster defaulted.[29] Chico Forster had borrowed $19,563.29 from the same bank on September 7, 1875. When Chico could not raise money to pay off his loan, his father was unable to rescue him. Chico was forced to file a petition for insolvency, the equivalent of a modern bankruptcy, and was discharged from his debts in disgrace on March 10, 1880.[30]

---

[28]Hallan-Gibson, *Two Hundred Years*, 79.

[29]Notice of Action recorded Nov. 12, 1879, in *Farmers and Merchants Bank v. John Forster, et al.*, Forster Collection.

[30]Decree of Final Discharge in *F. P. Forster v. His Creditors*, filed on March 10, 1880.

Apparently, at least part of John Forster's land in Los Angeles County was lost to foreclosure at about the same time.

Forster soon made a last effort to revive himself economically. He borrowed the enormous sum of $207,000 from Charles Crocker, the San Francisco railroad magnate, on February 9, 1881.[31] The whole ranch was deeded to Crocker, but it was supposed to be returned to Forster if he repaid the loan within four years. The desperate gamble made by Forster was that he could sell off enough of the Santa Margarita to repay Crocker without losing the whole ranch. His dream of subdividing was put to a final test, but he did not survive long enough to carry it out. Forster was dead one year later.

Aside from his economic problems, life sometimes unfolded in the most tragic and unexpected ways for Forster in his later years. Just eight months after the California Supreme Court affirmed the verdict in Forster's favor, his compadre, Cave Couts, died at the Horton House in San Diego on June 10, 1874.[32] Couts suffered from an aneurysm of the aorta, probably exacerbated by his alcoholism. He was only fifty-three years old. His death was a devastating blow to Forster, who lost the greatest friend he had in life.

On February 12, 1876, Robert Ashcroft committed suicide by taking strychnine poison. At the time, he was living at Rancho Boca de la Playa near San Juan Capistrano. He was forty-five years old. This shocking event was barely mentioned in the local press. The *Anaheim Gazette* gave the following opinion on his suicide: "it is believed it was caused by depression, caused by excessive drinking."[33] An undated letter from a relative of Forster in England expressed sorrow on

---

[31]Copy of Memorandum of Agreement between John Forster and Charles Crocker dated Feb. 9, 1881. Ibid.

[32]*San Diego Union*, June 11, 1874; Death Certificate of Cave Couts, San Diego Historical Society Archives.

[33]*Anaheim Gazette*, Feb. 14, 1876; *Los Angeles Daily Star*, Feb. 15, 1876. Strangely, although Ashcroft had a wife and children in Oakland, where he had lived for years, no paper in that city or anywhere else in the Bay Area referred to his death.

hearing of "the death of Mr. and Mrs. Ashcroft."[34] Perhaps his wife predeceased him and his grief over that event was the true cause of his suicide. We only know that he died a solitary death.

Two days after Ashcroft's suicide, on February 14, 1876, Andrés Pico died in his home at 212 North Main Street, Los Angeles. He had been in a coma for several weeks before he expired. His death involved a considerable air of mystery. Although some newspapers attributed it to natural causes, others mentioned traumatic injuries to the head consistent with his coma.[35] Family tradition has it that Andrés was severely beaten and dumped on his doorstep. Some relatives later claimed that Pío spent a small fortune trying to identify the assailants of Andrés.[36]

The probate of his tiny estate was unnecessarily prolonged by a bitter dispute between Pío and Rómulo Pico over who would be the administrator.[37] Pío claimed that Rómulo was not the natural or adopted son of Andrés. However, Rómulo got the best of the argument and could produce his mother, Antonia María Dominguez de Moraga, who offered to testify that Rómulo was the result of an adulterous affair between herself and Andrés.[38] The only asset of Andrés was nine hundred acres of land, the remainder of two thousand acres reserved around his home on the Rancho San Fernando. In 1883, after seven years of senseless litigation stirred up by Pío, his attorney, Andrew Glassell, concluded the probate

[34]Anna Ellen Forster to John Forster, undated, Forster Collection.

[35]*Los Angeles Evening Express*, Feb. 14, 1876; *Los Angeles Daily Star*, Feb. 15, 1876; *San Francisco Chronicle*, Feb. 15, 1876.

[36]The *Los Angeles Times*, Nov. 27, 1895, published a story based on an interview with a member of Pío Pico's family who related this information.

[37]*Estate of Andrés Pico*, Case No. 1159, Los Angeles Superior Court Archives.

[38]José G. Moraga, who was Rómulo Pico's maternal half-brother, wrote a bitter letter in Spanish to him, saying in part, "You have induced our mother, for vile motives, to swear adultery and infidelity before the courts . . . I disown you and I will inform my brothers of what has happened so they will know how far you have lowered yourself." Affidavit of José G. Moraga, filed on May 12, 1876. Ibid.

and took this land as his fee by court order.[39] Only the lawyers benefited from what little Andrés had left.

Benjamin I. Hayes moved back to Los Angeles not long after the trial in San Diego. He briefly practiced law until 1875, when his health began to fail and his activities diminished. About that time he sold his historical scrapbooks to the historian Hubert Howe Bancroft. Hayes had desired to make a gift of his collection but he was too pressed for money not to accept Bancroft's offer to buy it. Hayes told Bancroft: "I would gladly give it to you, did I not need money so badly. It is not pleasing to me to make merchandise of such labors."[40]

His scrapbooks and diaries are now in the Bancroft Library on the Berkeley campus of the University of California. Hayes died on August 4, 1877, at the age of sixty-two.[41] Chauncey Hayes, who frequently appears in the diaries of his father as an endearing young boy, married Felipa Marron of San Diego, by whom he had fourteen children. He lived for many years in Oceanside where he was a lawyer, banker, land promoter, and justice of the peace.[42]

The greatest tragedy for Don Juan was the murder of his forty-year-old son, Francisco "Chico" Forster in Los Angeles on March 15, 1881.[43] Chico was a handsome man who never married. He was known for having a callous attitude toward women. While in Los Angeles he seduced a beautiful half-Basque, half-Mexican eighteen-year-old girl named Lastania Abarta by a promise of marriage. The day after having taken her virginity, Chico reneged on his promise. She shot

---

[39]Return and Account of Sale of Real Estate and Petition for Order Confirming Sale, filed Sept. 17, 1883. Ibid.

[40]Bancroft, *Literary Industries*, 482.

[41]*Los Angeles Star*, Aug. 6, 1877.

[42]Clarence Alan McGraw, *City of San Diego and San Diego County*, 2: 370. See also, Leland G. Stanford, *Tracks on the Trial Trail in San Diego*, 39-41.

[43]*Los Angeles Herald,* March 16, 1881; *The Evening Express,* March 16, 1881.

Francisco "Chico" Forster
Courtesy, Thomas Anthony "Tony"
Forster Private Collection,
San Juan Capistrano.

him on a public street in Los Angeles to avenge her honor in conformity with the social mores of the time. After a jury trial in a courtroom jammed to capacity, she was found not guilty by reason of insanity. The verdict was enthusiastically applauded by those in attendance.[44]

Eleven months after Chico's death, a dispirited Don Juan himself passed away and his body was brought to Los Angeles for burial. His death, on February 20, 1882, was widely publicized throughout the state. The funeral was one of the largest ever held in Southern California.[45] Forster was an extremely popular person known for his unstinting hospitality to all who passed by the Santa Margarita. For years there was a great white cross on a hill overlooking the ranch house which was a beacon to travelers. Don Juan did not die a pauper, but he had been forced to borrow huge sums of money

[44]*Los Angeles Herald*, April 29 and April 30, 1881; *The Evening Express*, April 28 to April 30, 1881.

[45]*Los Angeles Daily Times*, Feb. 21 and Feb. 24, 1882; *Los Angeles Herald*, Feb. 21, 1882.

secured by the Rancho Santa Margarita. His financial condition was precarious when he died, despite a life-long quest for great wealth in which he was largely successful.

Volney E. Howard retired from the practice of law during 1879. On November 1 of that year, he was elected as judge to the newly established Superior Court of Los Angeles. He served in that court until January 5, 1885. This was the last public office he held, having purportedly refused an appointment to the California Supreme Court. For many years he resided in the Las Tunas Adobe, an old Spanish structure a few hundred yards southeast of the Mission San Gabriel.[46] This building, now remodeled, still stands as a private residence, barely recognizable as an ancient adobe. Sadly, it is shut off from sight of the mission by modest apartment buildings and houses. Long ago, when it was in open country surrounded by gardens and tuna cactus, with the mission and the towering San Gabriel Mountains in the background, it was a quaintly beautiful place to live and a social center for the Los Angeles elite. On May 14, 1889, Howard died in Santa Monica, where he had been taken a month before.[47] His death received extensive coverage in the press. Howard County in west Texas is named in his honor today as a remembrance of his career in that state. He was a truly notable figure.

The associate of Volney E. Howard, the genial Frank Ganahl, left Los Angeles after the death of his friend. He established a prosperous law practice in Idaho where he probably died shortly after the turn of the century.[48] This flamboyant man never attained great success in Southern California outside the shadow of Howard.

On September 11, 1894, Pío Pico, age ninety-three years, died in Los Angeles.[49] He lived for over twenty-one years after his lawsuit with Forster and remained solvent for much

[46]Kreider, "Volney Erskine Howard," 126, 128 (photo).
[47]*Los Angeles Times*, May 15 and May 17, 1889.
[48]Graves, *Seventy Years*, 14.   [49]*Los Angeles Times*, Sept. 12, 1894.

longer than anyone expected. This strange man, a mixture of guile, innocence, cunning, and ignorance, finally lost his fortune to a moneylender named Bernard Cohn for reasons partly based on his old habit of not understanding, or caring, about documents that he signed. Pío gave Cohn a deed to the Ranchito with an agreement that it would be treated as a mortgage. When Pío attempted to pay off the "mortgage," Cohn refused the money saying that he owned the property just as the deed said. A trial was held to determine whether the transaction was for a deed or a mortgage. One of Pío's cronies was bribed by Cohn to falsely swear that Pío intended to give a deed. On his deathbed the false witness recanted his testimony, but the California Supreme Court refused to reverse a judgment in favor of Cohn.[50]

Pío was ejected from the Ranchito by Cohn's heirs and spent his last few remaining years living off the charity of friends in Los Angeles. He had a more or less derelict existence, a pathetic figure well known to those in the city who saw him riding in a carriage about the streets and loitering in the Plaza where he had once owned a townhouse, the Pico House Hotel, and several other properties besides. Pío died possessed of some personal effects and nothing else.[51] His landlady claimed he owed her for two years' rent at the time of his death. He left his three known surviving illegitimate children, Griselda, Joaquina, and Alfredo, with nothing.

Following the trial in San Diego, Andrew Glassell amassed a fortune from the practice of law, in part from his representation of Pío Pico over the years. On December 3, 1878, he was elected the first president of the Los Angeles Bar Association.[52] He became the attorney for the Farmers and Merchants Bank and the Southern Pacific Railroad

---

[50]*Pico v. Cohn*, 91 California Reports 129 (1891). An interesting article about the case as well as an interview with Pío and a description of the Ranchito is found in the *Los Angeles Times*, Feb. 12, 1891.

[51]*Estate of Pío Pico*, Probate Case No. 1010, Los Angeles Superior Court Archives.

[52]Robinson, *Lawyers*, 6.

Company as well as a large shareholder in both corporations. Together with his partner, A. B. Chapman, he was active in the formation and subdivision of the city of Orange during the 1870s and 1880s, which accounts for the existence of Glassell Street and Chapman Avenue in that part of Orange County today. His real estate holdings were so extensive that he retired from the full-time practice of law around 1880 to administer them. Glassell died on January 28, 1901, a well-regarded figure in Los Angeles.[53]

Judge Horace C. Rolfe was not elected to another term after the lawsuit between Forster and the Picos in San Diego. As might be expected, he returned to the practice of law in San Bernardino. In 1878 he joined Volney E. Howard as a delegate to the state constitutional convention in Sacramento where the present system of municipal and superior courts was established.[54] In 1879 he was appointed to the superior court bench, probably as a reward for his participation in the convention. After serving one term, Rolfe retired once again to private practice. He was a preeminent figure in the San Bernardino bar who was noted for assisting young attorneys in making their careers. In later years he wrote a good deal about local history and politics. His efforts are preserved in a special collection at the San Bernardino Public Library.[55] He was not successful economically despite his great prestige. This dignified man died in San Bernardino in 1906 leaving his surviving wife a little land but absolutely no money.[56] Forced to sell the family homestead, she spent her declining years after his death as a resident of a local boarding house.

---

[53]*Los Angeles Times*, Jan. 29, 1901. See also, McGroarty, *From the Mountains to the Sea*, 3: 730-33.

[54]Bancroft, *History of California*, 7: 402, n.46.

[55]For example, Rolfe wrote, "A Political History of Early San Bernardino County" and "Pen Sketches of the Early San Bernardino Bar." Both are essays in the History Room of the Main Public Library, San Bernardino.

[56]*Estate of H. C. Rolfe*, Probate Case No. 2771, Probate Clerk's Office, Central San Bernardino Superior Court.

George H. Smith continued to practice law in Los Angeles after his disastrous role as trial counsel for Pío Pico in San Diego. He served as a state senator from Los Angeles during 1876 and again in 1880. His marriage to Andrew Glassell's sister ended in tragedy. She died of breast cancer in November 1883, when only forty-eight years old. Thereafter, Smith served as a commissioner of the California Supreme Court and reporter of decisions. From 1905 to 1907, he was a justice of the District Court of Appeals. During his later life, Smith wrote a number of books on logic and jurisprudence which achieved fair success. His most famous work, *Theory of the State*, won a prestigious prize from the American Philosophical Society of Philadelphia. Several of his books are still on library shelves today.[57] For many years he maintained an avid correspondence with those who shared his interests, including the British philosopher Herbert Spencer. The poor showing he made at the trial in San Diego can best be attributed to his being thrust into the role of trial counsel by Andrew Glassell without adequate notice or preparation. Smith had a good mind and a courageous spirit which might have prevailed in San Diego if he had more time to analyze the case. He passed away while working quietly at his desk on February 6, 1915, at age eight-one.[58]

Marcos and Juan Forster were forced to dispose of the Rancho Santa Margarita shortly after their father's death in order to pay Charles Crocker and other creditors. During October 1882 they sold the Rancho Santa Margarita to Richard O'Neill of San Francisco, who was backed by the financier James Flood. The total price was $450,000. An immediate payment of $250,000 was advanced to liquidate all of Forster's debts. The balance was paid when the probate court declared that the claims of all creditors were sat-

---

[57]The Los Angeles County Law Library has six books by Smith.
[58]*Los Angeles Times*, Feb. 7, 1915.

Juan Fernando Forster
Courtesy, Thomas Anthony "Tony"
Forster Private Collection, San
Juan Capistrano.

isfied.[59] Despite paying off the loans of their father, Marcos and Juan were able to realize enough money from the sale to begin new and prosperous lives.

Marcos settled in his father's old haunt, the beautiful little town of San Juan Capistrano. His descendants live there today and have traditionally played prominent roles in the social and political life of the place. One such descendant is Thomas Anthony "Tony" Forster, a West Point graduate and successful businessman. A congenial man and a great story-teller, he has an encyclopedic knowledge of the lore and legend of San Juan Capistrano and the Forster family.

Albert Pico, who lives in very comfortable circumstances in Riverside, is a distant cousin of Tony Forster. He is descended from José Antonio Pico, the brother of Pío and Andrés. An intelligent, distinguished man in his seventies,

---

[59] Draft of Memorandum of Agreement between Marcos A. Forster, John F. Forster, and Richard O'Neill, dated only October 1882, Forster Collection.

Marcos Forster and his family. After his father's death, he settled in San Juan Capistrano where most of his descendants still reside today.
Courtesy, Security Pacific Collection, Los Angeles Public Library.

he is a university graduate and retired from ranching and business. He owns various original letters of Pío, which he graciously permitted to be copied. Albert Pico can remember his old aunts telling him about the astonishment of Andrés Pico, that Forster refused to recognize that he had only been given a one-half interest in the Rancho Santa Margarita. The story still has currency in the family after all these years. When Albert Pico was asked if he thought his ancestors had been defrauded by Forster, a little smile appeared and he said, "Yes, I believe they were."

Once a year, during December, the Marine Corps opens the old adobe ranch house to a few invited guests, particularly descendants of the original owners. Recently, on one such occasion, Tony Forster was introduced to an elderly stranger whose first name he cannot remember, but whose last name was Pico. As they began to shake hands, the unknown Pico heard the person introducing them say that Tony's last name was Forster. He instantly dropped his hand, spun around, and angrily stalked away. This unpleasant incident occurred in the very same room where, according to his testimony, Andrés had confronted John Forster with the claims of Pío in 1866. After more than a century, there was an unexpected echo of the bitterness that divided their families several lifetimes ago. There are men still living for whom the trial is not forgotten. The rage of the Picos was so deeply felt that it has been transmitted to succeeding generations. There could be no better measure of the emotions aroused in the old San Diego courthouse.

Forster's Statement of Account

	PRINCIPAL.	DEBTOR.	DAYS.	INTEREST.
1861.				
June 29,	$32,863.00.	To balance as per ac't....	1,115	$12,547.78
1863.				
May 15,	27.54.	" cash telegram to Washington.....	431	3.95
" 31,	250.00.	" cash to Gitchell	415	34.58
June 15,	250.00.	" " " "		
" "	12.00.	" for a box..........		
" "	40.00.	" cash Att'y of Mont'y	399	40.16
Aug. 7,	50.00.	" sundry documents.....		
" 7,	250.00.	" T. Perry, abstract of title............	346	34.60
Sept. 10,	52.00.	" Wells, Fargo & Co...	312	5.74
1864.				
July 18,	12,052.02.	"Interest..........		
	$45,847.55.			$12,666.81
	$43,972.30.	To new account.		

	PRINCIPAL.	CREDIT.	DAYS.	INTEREST.
1859				
Oct. 25,	$ 475.25.	By cash....	1,362	$215.79
1862.				
Mch. 16,	1,400.00.	" " from Forbes.....	855	399.00
July 18,		" Balance of interest		12,052.02
" "	43,972.30.	" Balance		
	$45,847.55.			$12,666.81

E. E. San Francisco, 18 July 1864.

Hypothetical Statement of Account

	PRINCIPAL.	DEBTOR.	DAYS.	INTEREST
1861.				
June 29,	$32,863.00.	To balance as per ac't....	970	$10,916.53
1863.				
May 15,	27.54.	" cash telegram to Washington.....	286	2.62
" 31,	250.00.	" cash to Gitchell	270	22.49
June 15,	250.00.	" " " "		
" "	12.00.	" for a box..........		
" "	40.00.	" cash Att'y of Mont'y	255	25.66
Aug. 7,	50.00.	" sundry documents.....		
" 7,	250.00.	" T. Perry, abstract of title............	202	20.20
Sept. 10,	52.00.	" Wells, Fargo & Co...	168	2.91
1864.				
Feb. 25,	10,375.62.	"Interest..........		
	$44,171.15.			$10,990.41
	$42,295.90.	To new account.		

	PRINCIPAL.	CREDIT.	DAYS.	INTEREST.
1859				
Oct. 25,	$ 475.25.	By cash....	1,362	$215.79
1862.				
Mch. 16,	1,400.00.	" " from Forbes.....	855	399.00
Feb. 25,		" Balance of interest		10,375.62
" "	42,295.90.	" Balance.......		
	$44,171.15.			$10,990.41

E. E. San Francisco, 25 February 1864.

Bibliography

MANUSCRIPTS

Albert Pico, Private Collection, Riverside, CA: Pío Pico Letters.

California State Archives, Sacramento, CA: Forster v. Pico, No. 3953. Transcripts on Appeal, Briefs, Points and Authorities on Appeal.

Huntington Library, San Marino, CA: Brent, Joseph Lancaster. Brent Collection. California Historical Documents Collection. Couts, Cave. Couts Collection. De la Guerra Collection (also known as the Guerra Collection). Forster, John. Forster Collection. Stearns, Abel. Stearns Collection. Wilson, Benjamin Davis. Wilson Collection.

Los Angeles County Museum of Natural History, Los Angeles, CA: Del Valle, Ignacio. Del Valle Collection.

National Archives, Laguna Niguel, CA: Dorsey, Hilliard P. Letters. Records Group 49. Bureau of Land Management Records. Los Angeles Office, Records of the Register; U.S. Land Commission, Case No. 388, "Rancho Santa Margarita," Spanish-Mexican Private Land Grants Records - California.

San Bernardino Public Library, CA: Rolfe, Horace C. Rolfe Collection.

San Diego Historical Society, San Diego, CA: Forster v. Pico, Case No. 898A. Pleadings, Motions, Depositions, Exhibits, Transcripts of Testimony and Objections, Jury Instructions, Verdict, and Exceptions; Pico Family File. Papers and Letters.

Santa Ana Public Library, CA: Forster v. Pico, Works Progress Administration, Orange County Historical Project #3105, 4 vols. Typescript.

Thomas Anthony "Tony" Forster, Private Collection, San Juan Capistrano, CA; John Forster Letters, Papers, Diaries and Books of Account.

UNPUBLISHED LEGAL CASES

Andrés Pico v. Arnot Durant, Case No. 985 (1863). Los Angeles Superior Court Archives.

Estate of Andrés Pico, Case No. 1159 (1876). Los Angeles Superior Court Archives.

Estate of Pío Pico, Case No. 1010 (1894). Los Angeles Superior Court Archives.

Estate of H. C. Rolfe, Case No. 2771 (1906). Office of the Probate Clerk, San Bernardino Superior Court (Central).

Pío Pico v. Rómulo Pico, Case No. 3292 (1878). Los Angeles Superior Court Archives.

PUBLISHED LEGAL CASES

Forster v. Pico, 1 California Unreported Cases 841 (1874).

Henry Hancock v. Pío Pico, 40 California Reports 153 (1870).

McFarland v. Pico, 8 California Reports 626 (1857).

Pico v. Cohn, 91 California Reports 129 (1891).

Pico v. Coleman, 47 California Reports 65 (1873)

Pico v. Colimas, 32 California Reports 578 (1867).

Pico v. Cuyas, 47 California Reports 174 (1873).

U.S. v. Pico, 72 U.S. Supreme Court Reports 695 (1866).

GOVERNMENT DOCUMENTS

Lists of Property, Real and Personal, Subject to Taxation in the County of San Diego, 1864 to 1872, San Diego Historical Society Archives.

Los Angeles County Bureau of Vital Statistics. Death Certificates of Alfredo Pico and Griselda Pico.

United States Census of 1860, Schedule 1, San Juan Township, Los Angeles County. Federal Archives, Laguna Niguel.

United States Census of 1870, Vol. 1, Population and Social Statistics, Population by State and Counties, 1790-1870, Tables I and II. (Published by the Department of the Interior).

NEWSPAPERS

Alta California (San Francisco), 1851-1861.

Anaheim Gazette, 1876.

California Star (San Francisco), 1847.

El Clamor Público (Los Angeles), 1855-59.

Los Angeles Evening Express, 1876.

Los Angeles Herald, 1881.

Los Angeles Daily Star, 1876.

Los Angeles Star, 1852-62.

Los Angeles Times, 1882-1925.

San Diego Union, 1873-74.

San Francisco Chronicle, 1876-97.

San Francisco Herald, 1851-52.

San Francisco National, 1859.

Semi-Weekly Southern News (Los Angeles), 1862.

Southern Vineyard (Los Angeles), 1859.

ARTICLES

Barrows, Henry D. "Pío Pico." *Annual Publication* Historical Society of Southern California 3 (1894): 55-65.

Bishko, Charles Julian. "The Peninsular Background of Latin American Cattle Ranching." *Hispanic American Hist. Rev.* 32 (Nov. 1952): 491-515.

Brand, Donald D. "The Early History of the Range Cattle Industry in Northern Mexico." *Agricultural History* 35 (Jan. 1961): 132-39.

Dalin, David G. and Charles A. Fracchia, "'Forgotten Financier: Francois L. A. Pioche." *California Hist. Quar.* 53 (Spring 1974): 17-24.

Dixon, Elizabeth I. "Early San Fernando: Memoirs of Mrs. Catherine Dace." *Southern California Quar.* 44 (Spring 1962): 219-267.

Engstrand, Iris Wilson and Thomas L. Sharf. "Rancho Guajome: A California Legacy Preserved." *Journal of San Diego History* 20 (Winter 1974): 1-14.

Forbes, Jack D. "Black Pioneers: The Spanish-Speaking Afroamericans of the Southwest." *Phylon* 27 (1966): 233-46.

Forbes, Jack D. "Hispano-Mexican Pioneers of the San Francisco Bay Region: An Analysis of Racial Origins." *Aztlan* 14 (Spring 1983): 175-89.

Griswold del Castillo, Richard. "The del Valle Family and the Fantasy Heritage." *California History* 59 (Spring 1980): 2-15.

Guillow, Lawrence E. "Pandemonium in the Plaza: The First Los Angeles Riot, July 22, 1856." *Southern Calif. Quar.* 77 (Fall 1995): 183-97.

Guinn, J. M. "The Passing of the Cattle Barons of California." *Annual Publication* Hist. Soc. of Southern Calif. 8 (1909): 51-60.

Hollingsworth, John McHenry. "Journal of John McHenry Hollingsworth." *Calif. Hist. Soc. Quar.* I (January 1923): 207-70.

Imboden, John D. "The Battle of New Market, Va., May 15th, 1864," in *Battles and Leaders of the Civil War.* (Secaucus, NJ: Book Sellers, Inc., reprints from *Century Magazine,* 1884–87), 4: 480-86.

Jensen, James M. "John Forster—A California Ranchero." *Calif. Hist. Soc. Quarterly* 48 (1969): 37-44.

Kreider, Samuel Lanner. "Volney Erskine Howard: California Pioneer." *Hist. Soc. of Southern Calif. Quar.* 31 (March and June 1949): 119-34.

Mason, William. "The Garrisons of San Diego Presidio, 1770-1794." *Jour. of San Diego Hist.* 24 (Fall 1978): 399-424.

McCusker, John J. "How Much Is That in Real Money? A Historical Price Index for Use as a Deflator of Money Values in the Economy of the United States." *Proceedings of the American Antiquarian Soc.* 101 (Oct. 1991): 297-373.

McKain, Walter C., Jr. and Sara Miles. "Santa Barbara County Between Two Social Orders." *Calif. Hist. Soc. Quar.* 25 (1946): 311-18.

Miranda, Gloria. "Racial and Cultural Dimensions of *Gente de Razon* Status in Spanish and Mexican California." *Southern Calif. Quar.* 70 (Fall 1988): 265-78.

Morrisey, Richard J. "The Northward Expansion of Cattle Ranching in New Spain, 1550 1600." *Agricultural Hist.* 25 (July 1951): 115-21.

Ogden, Adele. "Boston Hide Droghers Along California Shores." *Calif. Hist. Soc. Quar.* 8 (Dec. 1929): 289-305.

Parks, Marion. "In Pursuit of Vanished Days, Visits to the Extant Historic Houses of Los Angeles County." *Annual Publication* Hist. Soc. of Southern Calif. 14 (1929): 135-207.

Pleasants, J. E. "A Visit to Santiago Canyon." *Orange County History Series* 1 (1931): 141-46.

Robinson, W. W. "The Rancho Story of San Fernando Valley," *Hist. Soc. of Southern Calif. Quar.* 38 (1956): 225-34.

Servín, Manuel P. "The Secularization of the California Missions: A Reappraisal." " *Southern Calif. Quar.* (June 1965): 133-49.

Splitter, Henry Winfred. "Los Angeles Recreation, 1846–1900," *Hist. Soc. of Southern Calif. Quar.* 43 (1961): 35-68.

Stephenson, Terry E. "Forster vs. Pico, a Forgotten California Cause Celebre." *Hist. Soc. of Southern Calif. Quar.* 18 (June 1936): 50-68.

Sullivan, Susan. "James McCoy: Lawman and Legislator." *Jour. of San Diego Hist.* 23 (Fall 1977): 43-57.

Tanner, John D. Jr. and Gloria R. Lothrop. "Don Juan Forster, Southern California Ranchero." *Southern Calif. Quar.* 52 (1970): 195-230.

Tanner, John Douglas, Jr. "Campaign for Los Angeles." *Calif. Hist. Soc. Quar.* 48 (1969): 219-41.

Tays, George."Pío Pico's Correspondence with the Mexican Government, 1846-1848." *Calif. Hist. Quar.* 13 (June 1934): 99-149.

Tyler, Helen. "The Family of Pico." *Hist. Soc. of Southern Calif. Quar.* 35 (Sept. 1953): 221-38.

Van Nostrand, Jeanne Skinner. "The American Occupations of Rancho Santa Margarita y Las Flores." *Calif. Hist. Soc. Quar.* 22 (June 1943): 175-77.

Woodward, Arthur. "Lances at San Pasqual." *Calif. Hist. Soc. Quar.* 26 (1947): 21-62.

BOOKS

Armstrong, Richard L. *25th Virginia Infantry and 9th Battalion Virginia Infantry.* Lynchburg, VA: H. E. Howard, Inc., 1990.

Bakken, Gorden Morris. *The Development of Law in Frontier California.* Westport, Conn.: Greenwood Press, 1985.

Bancroft, Hubert Howe. *History of California.* 7 vols. San Francisco: History Co., 1885-88; reprint by Wallace Hebberd, Santa Barbara, 1966.

_____. *Literary Industries.* San Francisco: History Co., 1898.

Beattie, George William and Helen Pruitt Beattie. *Heritage of the Valley.* Pasadena, Calif.: San Pasqual Press, 1939.

Bell, Horace. *On the Old West Coast.* N. Y.: William Morrow & Co., 1930.

Beltran, Gonzalo Aguirre. *La Población Negra de México.* Mexico, DF: Fondo de Cultura Económica, 1972.

Black, Esther Boulton. *Rancho Cucamonga and Doña Merced.* Redlands, CA.: San Bernardino County Museum Assn., 1975.

Bolton, Herbert Eugene. *Anza's California Expeditions.* 3 vols. Berkeley: Univ. of Calif. Press, 1930.

Brent, Joseph Lancaster. *The Lugo Case A Personal Experience.* New Orleans: Searcy & Pfaff, Ltd., 1926.

Brown, John, Jr. and James Boyd. *History of San Bernardino and Riverside Counties.* 2 vols. Chicago: Western Hist. Assn., 1922.

Caughey, John Walton. *California.* New York: Prentice-Hall, Inc.

Chapman, Charles E. *A History of California: The Spanish Period.* New York: Macmillan Co., 1925.

Clary, William W. *History of the Law Firm of O'Melveny and Myers.* Los Angeles: Privately printed, 1966.

Cleland, Robert Glass. *Cattle On a Thousand Hills.* 2d ed. San Marino, CA: Huntington Library, 1975; reprint of 1951 edition.

Coronel, Antonio. *Tales of Mexican California.* Ed. by Doyce B. Nunis, Jr. Santa Barbara: Bellerophon Books, 1994.

Couts, Cave. *Hepah, California.* Tucson: Arizona Pioneers' Hist. Soc., 1961.

Croft, E. P. R. *Pioneer Days in the San Bernardino Valley.* Self-published, 1906.

Dakin, Susanna Bryant. *A Scotch Paisano in Old Los Angeles.* Berkeley: Univ. of Calif. Press, 1939; reprint 1978.

_____. *The Lives of William Hartnell.* Stanford Univ. Press, 1949.

Dana, Richard Henry. *The Journal of Richard Henry Dana.* Ed. by Robert F. Lucid. 3 vols. Cambridge: Belknap Press of Harvard Univ. Press, 1968.

Delauter, Roger U. *62nd Virginia Infantry.* Lynchburg, VA: H. E. Howard, Inc., 1988.

Dumke, Glenn S. *The Boom of the Eighties.* San Marino, CA: Huntington Library, 1944.

Eldredge, Zoeth Skinner. *The Beginnings of San Francisco.* 2 vols. San Francisco: privately printed, 1912.

Engelhardt, Zephyrin. *San Juan Capistrano Mission.* Los Angeles: privately printed, 1922.

Evans, Clement A., ed. *Confederate Military History.* 15 vols. Atlanta: Confederate Pub. Co., 1899.

First Los Angeles City and County Directory. Los Angeles: The Ward Ritchie Press, 1963.

Gates, Paul W. *California Ranchos and Farms, 1846–1862.* Madison: State Hist. Soc. of Wisc., 1967.

Graves, Jackson A. *My Seventy Years in California.* Los Angeles: Times-Mirror Press, 1928.

Grenier, Judson A. *California Legacy.* Carson, CA: Watson Land Co., 1987.

Hague, Harlan and David J. Langum. *Thomas O. Larkin.* Norman: University of Oklahoma Press, 1990.

Hallan-Gibson, Pamela. *Two Hundred Years in San Juan Capistrano.* Norfolk, VA: Donning Co., 1990.

Hayes, Benjamin. *Pioneer Notes from the Diaries of Judge Benjamin Hayes.* Ed. by Marjorie Tisdale Wolcott. Los Angeles: privately printed, 1929.

Hutchinson, C. Alan. *Frontier Settlement in Mexican California.* New Haven: Yale Univ. Press, 1969.

Illustrated History of Southern California. Chicago: Lewis Pub. Co., 1890.

Ingersoll, L. A. *Ingersoll's Century Annals of San Bernardino County.* 2 vols. Los Angeles: L. A. Ingersoll, 1904.

Jackson, Sheldon G. *A British Ranchero in Old California.* Glendale, CA: The Arthur H. Clark Co., 1977.

Janssens, Agustín. *The Life and Adventures in California of on Agustín Janssens.* Ed. by William H. Ellison and Francis Pierce. San Marino, CA: Huntington Library, 1953.

Keffer, Frank M. *History of San Fernando Valley.* Glendale, CA: Stillman Printing Co., 1934.

MacPhail, Elizabeth C. *The Story of New San Diego and of its Founder Alonzo E. Horton.* San Diego: San Diego Hist. Soc. 1979.

McGraw, Clarence Alan. *City of San Diego and San Diego County.* 3 vols. Chicago and New York: Amer. Hist. Soc., 1922.

McGroarty, John Steven. *Los Angeles From the Mountains to the Sea.* 3 vols. Chicago and New York: Amer. Hist. Soc., 1921.

Miller, Henry. *Account of a Tour of the California Missions & Towns, 1856.* Santa Barbara: Bellerophon Books, 1989.

Monroy, Douglas. *Thrown Among Strangers.* Berkeley: Univ. of Calif. Press, 1990.

Nadeau, Remi. *City-Makers.* Corona del Mar, CA: Trans-Anglo Books, 1977.

Newmark, Harris. *Sixty Years in Southern California.* 4th rev. ed. Los Angeles: Zeitlin & Ver Brugge, 1970; originally published in 1916.

Nichols, Roy Franklin. *The Democratic Machine 1850–1854.* New York: Columbia Univ., 1923.

Northrop, Marie E. *Spanish-Mexican Families of Early California: 1769–1850.* 2 vols. Burbank: Southern Calif. Genealogical Soc., 1984.

Orton, Brig. Gen. Richard H. *Records of California Men in the War of the Rebellion.* Sacramento: Calif. State Printing Office, 1890.

Patton, Robert H. *The Pattons.* New York: Crown Publishers, Inc., 1994.

Pico, Pío. *Historical Narrative.* Ed. by Martin Cole. Glendale, CA: Arthur H. Clark Co., 1973.

Pitt, Leonard. *The Decline of the Californios.* Berkeley: Univ. of Calif. Press, 1966; third printing, paperback, 1970.

Pourade, Richard F. *The Glory Years.* San Diego: Union-Tribune Pub. Co., 1966.

_____. *The Silver Dons.* San Diego: Union-Tribune Pub. Co., 1963.

Robinson, John. *Los Angeles in Civil War Days, 1860–65.* Los Angeles: Dawson's Book Shop, 1977.

Robinson, W. W. *Land in California.* Berkeley: Univ. of Calif. Press, 1948; reprinted in paperback, 1979.

_____. *Lawyers of Los Angeles.* Los Angeles: Los Angeles Bar Assn., 1959.

_____. *Los Angeles From the Days of the Pueblo.* Rev. and ed. by Doyce B. Nunis, Jr. San Francisco: Calif. Hist. Soc., 1981.

_____. *Ranchos Become Cities.* Pasadena, CA: San Pasqual Press, 1939.

_____. *The Story of the San Fernando Valley.* Los Angeles: Title Insurance and Trust Co., 1961.

Rolle, Andrew. *California, A History.* 3rd ed. Arlington Heights, IL: Harlan Davidson, Inc., 1978.

Salvator Luwig Louis. *Los Angeles in the Sunny Seventies.* Los Angeles: Jake Zeitlin, 1929; reprint from 1876.

Saunders, Charles Francis and Father St. John O'Sullivan. *Capistrano Nights.* New York: Robert M. McBride & Co., 1930.

Sherwood, Midge. *Days of Vintage, Years of Vision.* 2 vols. San Marino, CA: Orizaba Pubs., 1987.

Smythe, William E. *History of San Diego.* 2 vols. San Diego History Co., 1908.

Stanford, Leland G. *Tracks on the Trial Trail in San Diego.* San Diego: Law Library Justice Foundation, 1963.

Taylor, Bayard. *Eldorado.* Glorieta, NM: Rio Grande Press, Inc., 1967; reprinted from an original 1850 edition.

Truman, Benjamin C. *Semi-Tropical California.* San Francisco: A. L. Bancroft and Co., 1874.

Tyler, Daniel, *The Mormon Battalion in the Mexican American War, 1846–1848.* Glorieta, NM: Rio Grande Press, Inc., 1969; reprinted from 1881.

Van Dyke, T.S. *City and County of San Diego.* San Diego: Leberthon & Taylor, 1888.

Williams, David A. *David C. Broderick: A Political Portrait.* San Marino: Huntington Library, 1969.

Witkin, B. E., *Summary of California Law, Ninth Edition.* 13 vols. San Francisco: Bancroft-Whitney Co., 1987.

Witty, Robert M. *Marines of the Margarita.* San Diego: Fry & Smith Ltd., 1970.

UNPUBLISHED THESES

Tanner, John Douglas, Jr. "Pioneer Data from 1832; The Reminiscences of Don Juan Forster, An Englishman in Mexican California." Master's Thesis, Claremont Graduate School, 1967.

Thurman, Michael Edward. "A History of Rancho Santa Margarita y Las Flores to 1882." Master's Thesis, University of Southern California, 1960.

Index

Printed in the USA
CPSIA information can be obtained
at www.ICGtesting.com
CBHW021712220224
4600CB00007B/504

9 780806 190976

Rivers under Siege

The Troubled Saga of West Tennessee's Wetlands

Jim W. Johnson

Outdoor Tennessee Series • Jim Casada, Series Editor

The University of Tennessee Press / Knoxville

The Outdoor Tennessee Series covers a wide range of topics of interest to the general reader, including titles on the flora and fauna, the varied recreational activities, and the rich history of outdoor Tennessee. With a keen appreciation of the importance of protecting our state's natural resources and beauty, the University of Tennessee Press intends the series to emphasize environmental awareness and conservation.

Library of Congress Cataloging-in-Publication Data

Johnson, Jim W., 1940–
Rivers under siege : the troubled saga of West Tennessee's wetlands / Jim W. Johnson. — 1st ed.
    p. cm. — (Outdoor Tennessee series)
Includes bibliographical references.
ISBN-13: 978-1-57233-490-8 (alk. paper)
ISBN-10: 1-57233-490-8 (alk. paper)
1. Stream restoration—Tennessee, West.
2. Rivers—Tennessee, West.
3. Nature—Effect of human beings on—Tennessee, West.
I. Title.

QH76.5.T2J64 2007
333.91'6215309768—dc22   2006021750